First Gen Transfer

A TRANSFER GUIDE FOR FIRST-GENERATION CALIFORNIA COMMUNITY COLLEGE STUDENTS

BY LEZRA CHENPORTILLO, M.ED

CAREER AND TRANSFER COUNSELOR, SAN JOSÉ CITY COLLEGE

SAN JOSÉ CITY COLLEGE
SAN JOSÉ EVERGREEN COMMUNITY COLLEGE DISTRICT
SAN JOSÉ, CALIFORNIA

SAN JOSÉ CITY COLLEGE, SAN JOSÉ, CALIFORNIA 95128

SAN JOSÉ EVERGREEN COMMUNITY COLLEGE DISTRICT, SAN JOSÉ, CALIFORNIA 95128

ISBN: 9798857905326
DOI:

Copyeditor: Vicki Sheri Towne
Graphics Editor: Jazzmin Chizu Gota

This work has been published by San José City College and the San José Evergreen Community College District as part of the student equity initiative for increasing transfer and dual enrollment success measures.

Additional Resources

_____

To download this guide and view additional videos and materials related to this content, please visit: www.firstgentransfer.com

You are also invited to all follow **First Gen Transfer** on social media to view updates, videos, and additional opportunities for CCC transfer students.

  YouTube ·  Facebook  Instagram

@firstgentransfer3473   @firstgentransfer   @firstgentransfer

Disclaimer

This guide is not intended for the purpose of offering individual advice. Instead, this guide is a starting point for students seeking to understand the overall concepts involved in upper-division transfer from a California Community College (CCC). Please speak with your CCC Counselor for individualized counseling and guidance toward transfer.

Accessibility Statement

We checked this document's content for the elements listed below using Microsoft Word's Accessibility Checker Tool.

Organizing Content

- ☐ Contents are organized under headings and subheadings.
- ☐ Headings and subheadings are used sequentially (e.g., Heading 1, heading 2, etc.)

Images

- ☐ Images that convey information include Alternative Text (alt-text) descriptions of the image's content or function.
- ☐ Graphs, Charts, and Maps also include contextual or supporting details in the text surrounding the image.
- ☐ Images do not rely on color to convey information.
- ☐ Images that are purely decorative contain empty alternative text descriptions. (Descriptive text is unnecessary if the image doesn't convey contextual content information).

Tables

- ☐ Tables include row and column headers.
- ☐ Table includes title or caption.
- ☐ Table does not have merged or split cells.
- ☐ Table has adequate cell padding.

Weblinks

- ☐ The weblink is meaningful in context, does not use generic text such as "click here" or "read more."
- ☐ Weblinks do not open new windows or tabs.
- ☐ If weblink must open in a new window, a textual reference is included in the link information.

Font Size

- ☐ Font size is 12 point or higher for body text.
- ☐ Font size is 9 points for footnotes or end notes.
- ☐ Font size can be zoomed to 200%.

 # Dedication

For my students and fellow Counselors.
For our first-generation college students, most especially.
Your questions were once my questions. Your stumbles, I've made them too.
I hope this guide will offer you clarity in the process of transfer
and a friendly whisper of wisdom and encouragement
from someone that is always in your corner.

Acknowledgments

This guide was my sabbatical project for the 2021-2022 academic year within the San Jose Evergreen Community College District. As such, I would like to extend my deep appreciation to our San Jose City College President, Dr. Rowena Tomaneng, to our former Dean of Counseling, Dr. Eliazer Ayala-Austin, and to our San Jose Evergreen Community College District Professional Recognition Committee, which included: Eric Narveson, Colleen Calderon, Zerrin Erkal, Daniel Garza, Rachel Hagan, Manjit Kang, Michael Masuda, Leslie Rice, and Elvira Valderrama. Thanks to you all for believing in this project—from proposal to outline, to early draft, and now the finished product. A special thank you to Rachel, Leslie, and Eric for your encouragement and wonderful enthusiasm for this work!

I would also like to express my gratitude to our former Vice President of Student Affairs, Roland Montemayor. You have left your mark on each of us in Student Affairs at San Jose City College. Your dedication to student equity and supportive leadership pushed us all to tap into our own sense of advocacy and leadership on behalf of our students. I don't think I could have imagined this endeavor without your belief in me and your fundamental approach to finding ways that go the extra mile for our students.

To my colleagues in Student Affairs, and especially our Counselors at San Jose City College, I extend my deep appreciation for all that you do, for all you have taught me, and for your unequivocal dedication to our students. My deep gratitude to our long-standing Career Transfer Center Program Coordinator, Ms. Carol Vasquez, who has dedicated countless years to our transfer students and continues to serve our students with humility and compassion.

To our SJCC instructional faculty, our dedicated staff and leadership, and our entire San Jose City College community, I extend my deep appreciation for everything you do to serve our students day in and day out and make our community whole. The pandemic has tested every kind of community, with none left untouched by the challenges and grief left in its path. And yet, it's our values of equity and social justice that continue to bind us together and light the path forward. We know our students and the neighborhoods we serve in our region were some of the most impacted by the pandemic. And so, it's equally on us to continue to press forward together for them, to give our students the learning experiences they deserve and opportunities to fully express their potential and reach their goals. In short, as we say, let them— Unleash their Brilliance!

On a personal note, I must always share my deep gratitude to my mother, Alicia, who raised me as a single mom and often worked two jobs to make ends meet. She never took a college course and could never write me the map of navigating college systems and cultures. What she did do was pour her love and belief into me so purely and courageously that even to this day, it never fails to give me wings. What can't we do when we are so loved beyond measure? Thank you, mom.

Finally, I share my love and gratitude for my wife. I am blessed to have found you and to share our life together. Thank you for all your expressions of love and care, for all the ways you lift up our family, and especially on this project, for all the times you stepped in with a nudge of support during the long writing days. I could not have completed this project without you, my love. To our children, who, at three and six years old at the time, never ran out of curious questions about Mami's book and students. Asking, "What is this book about, mom?" "What page are you on?" "Are you finished yet?" And finally, saying to me one day, "It's pretty, Mami. I hope your students like it." I hope so too! I love you both so much, and I hope the essence of these pages is one you will always carry with you. Stay golden and go get it, my darlings, because you, too, are loved beyond measure.

Lezra Chenportillo, M.Ed.
Career and Transfer Counselor at San Jose City College

Forward

In my educational journey, I have transferred twice. The first time, I was 21 years old and transferred from De Anza Community College to CSU Long Beach. I was a Sociology major and had rushed through the transfer process straight out of high school. My parents could not guide me on how to sign up for college or what steps to take to choose the right major. Transitioning from high school into community college, I was also an introvert and struggled to study and complete my homework independently. In addition, I lacked self-awareness of how valuable building school relationships with my classmates can be.

There was so much I didn't know when I began college straight out of high school. I didn't take advantage of asking questions and meeting with academic advisors. I didn't seek out a career mentor. I didn't connect with my classmates to form study groups. I was too shy to ask questions in class, introduce myself to others, and start study groups. I lacked the social skills to communicate with my Counselor to obtain the help needed for transfer. I was intimidated by everyone and worried more about working to help my financial situation.

I transferred to CSU Long Beach with a major in Sociology because I wanted to help others like myself who have struggled with social or cultural inequality. But I hadn't taken the time to understand all my options for colleges and majors. It wasn't until the day of my orientation at Long Beach that I realized I was pursuing something I was not truly passionate about. My true passion was to help the environment and to become an Environmental Engineer. So, I decided to withdraw from CSU Long Beach and set my sight on San Jose City College to pursue my real dream.

My educational path hasn't been straightforward. Between working to make rent, buying food, and becoming a student in STEM—the stressors of college were often overwhelming. I began my series in Math and Science at below transfer level. I initially would take breaks from school and withdraw from courses to also take care of my well-being while coping with some difficult times, like losing a dear friend.

It wasn't until I developed a steady income and stable daily life that I could return to school to finally achieve the success in school I had so desired. I leaned on tools I gained from working with a therapist to heal and develop my sense of self-care, which helped me believe in myself and become my own caregiver and cheerleader. I told myself, "If you want change, then you must become that change and step out of your comfort zone. Be comfortable with being uncomfortable."

With dedication, perseverance, care, and effort, I completed courses starting from Pre-algebra into Calculus, Linear Algebra, Differential Equations, and Calculus-based Physics. I began to approach my time at San Jose City College differently. I even went on to become Peer Led

Team Leader (PLTL) tutor in Calculus at SJCC. I broke out of my shell and made friends in class with students from different cultures, backgrounds, and age ranges. Through this new approach at SJCC, I found myself. A classmate who had been in the country for only three years became my very close friend and introduced me to my Counselor, Lezra Chenportillo. Lezra helped me create my transfer plan and encouraged me to join a club on campus, the Society Advancing Chicanos and Native Americans in Science (SACNAS), where I also met Dr. Jose Cabrera, a Chemistry professor and great mentor.

I learned to network with STEM professionals who then shared opportunities for internships and mentorships. Since beginning my journey at San Jose City College, I have visited laboratories at Stanford University, volunteered with Genentech scientists, fundraised to go to the SACNAS Hawaii Conference, applied for and received the 2020 Latinos in Technology Silicon Valley Community Foundation Scholarship, and participated in the JOIDES Resolution summer research expedition abroad—an earth core drilling ship off the Panama Basin.

At the age of 30, I transferred a second time—this time to UC Riverside with a major in Environmental Engineering. I am now entering my senior year at UCR and have continued to grow so much. Being open and letting life take me into new positive environments and my educational path has helped me build my courage to take on any obstacle or adventure the future may hold in engineering and just life. At SJCC, I told myself I would say "yes" and not hesitate to take on a new opportunity or internship or make new friends.

This transfer guide that Lezra has written is something really special. I wish this had been around at the beginning of my journey. It really helps to understand how all the parts come together for transfer. Lezra is also a wonderful counselor and person; I know she put her heart into this because she really cares. I encourage all students beginning their journey to transfer to take time to read this guide, use it as a launching point, and not set limits on themselves but to go for their true dreams. Once I decided to pursue my true passion for Environmental Engineering, even though it was a long path to follow, I told myself there was no Plan B. It took me time to get to that mindset and to fully believe in myself. But once I did, at San Jose City College, with the support of friends, mentors, teachers, and counselors, I found myself, and I wish you all the best adventure to find yourselves.

Sincerely,

Cassandra Vargas
San Jose City College, *Transfer Alumni 2020*

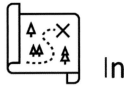

Introduction

This guide is written in five sections and is modeled after my **Guide 10: Transfer Success** course at San Jose City College. I hope to provide a curriculum for teaching and understanding the transfer process for California Community College (CCC) students. I hope this guide will provide CCC students with a starter kit for transfer, a place to learn the language of transfer admissions, and my fellow Counselors with some much-needed visual aids and content to aid during counseling sessions and utilize for instruction in Counseling courses. The five sections in this guide include the following items:

1. a description and explanation for all five elements of the transfer process;
2. a comparison of the different public systems of higher education, namely the California State University (CSU) and the University of California (UC), and transfer information for California private colleges and out-of-state options tailored for CCC students;
3. an overview of the transfer application process primarily to UC and CSU;
4. a review of financial aid, scholarships, and budgeting resources that are available for CCC transfer student use; and
5. a personal inventory that shows not only how to begin but also how to keep your goals and choices aligned when selecting a major, college, or career.

To my knowledge, this guide is the only reference written specifically for CCC students from a Counselor's perspective, tailored for first-generation college students, which brings together information about the transfer process for every transfer option, including the CSU, the UC, California private colleges, and out-of-state options.

Why does a Counselor's perspective matter?

Transferring from a 2-year campus to a 4-year campus is a process of growth and change, goal setting, taking risks, and ultimately betting on your dreams and yourself. The closer you get to applying for transfer and completing the many steps of the process, the more emotional it can get. The anxiety is real, the excitement is incredible, the fear of making a mistake sets in, and ultimately the transformation and sense of accomplishment you reach when you do transfer will stay with you for years to come. But this process doesn't happen alone.

Students do not sit in front of a computer, click on admissions options, then suddenly the wheels spin, and change happens. **Transfer is both a plan and a process**. The plan, in some ways, is technical, and Counselors offer information and guidance on admissions steps, financial aid, major options, career information, college courses, campus resources, and so much more. We provide information and draft a student education plan together with our students. Still, that plan—while a necessary step—is also like plugging in a destination onto your Google maps and assuming that's all you have to do to get there. It's not.

Transfer is innately a process and a very human one. It doesn't happen alone but with the guidance, care, investment, support, and encouragement of the counselors, instructors, and campus professionals of a campus community that exists at each CCC and plays a vital role in humanizing education for our students. Counselors do something that is special and hard to fully define: we walk you, our student, through that process from start to finish—and that process is different for every single student. Counselors serve as your hub, your coach, your cheerleader, your confessional, your go-to person for questions, your advocate throughout the process, and so much more.

Every Counselor, in their own way, is searching for the DNA of their students, the thing that makes them tick, what they're really trying to say but struggling to put into words, the thing that holds them back, the words or resource or experience that might unlock what's getting in their way. Some students don't need as much as others, so a straightforward roadmap might do the trick. **However, the large majority of CCC students are not only new to college but also first-generation college students. They have questions they may not know how to ask, goals that start as only a vague direction, and hovering doubts held inside, which threaten to take them down if given too much weight.** Doubts like: *Can I even do this? I was never very good at school; what's different now? Why am I going back to school at this age? How can I manage school and everything else I have on my plate? This is going to take SO long; how do I even know I can finish? How am I going to pay for college? Is all this sacrifice even worth it?*

So, this guide is written with a Counselor's approach for CCC first-generation college students who are learning things not only inside the classroom but also outside the classroom: how to *be* college students, how to navigate college systems like financial aid, and most especially how to reach their goals and earn that degree. Because it's not *information about the transfer* process that moves the needle but the essential human perspective, care, and trust we share with our students that lets them know *they CAN move the needle. That's* counseling.

How should you use this Guide?

In truth, it's a little impossible to write a book about the transfer process and get everything right. The reason is simple, *policies and practices at the CSU, UC, or within our own CCC system are ALWAYS changing from year to year*. Meaning most anything written in this guide could change in a heartbeat. As I write, there's a proposal to create a singular GE pattern for transfer that would outdate the GE pattern section in this guide ("Submit Input on AB 928"). Transfer admission practices also change ALL THE TIME. It can be exhausting to track and then explain these changes to our students. Yet, for all the changes that will be made year to year, there is an overall arc to the transfer process that continues to hold true. It's from that place I have written this guide, in hopes that our students can gain a kind of fluency around the transfer admissions process itself. Transfer is riddled with so many details and specifics about why something may hold true in one scenario yet may not stay true in another. It can feel nearly impossible to say one universally true thing about transfer. Yet there are universal truths, like the one you'll hear me often say: *protect your GPA, protect your GPA, protect your GPA (more on this later).*

I hope this guide can serve as a starter kit for students trying to unpack and decode what transfer involves and how it works from a bird's eye view. However, I want to be clear that ***this guide is not a substitute*** for working with a CCC Counselor, engaging 4-year university admissions representatives, or turning to a Transfer Center for help. Quite the opposite. **This guide is a supplement to all the good work they do.** First and foremost, ALWAYS:

- Ask your Counselor
- Ask your University Admissions Representative
- Ask your Transfer Center

These are YOUR Transfer experts. These are the folks you need to connect with and make sure that any questions or ideas that this guide might inspire are vetted through them. *They are the experts best suited to provide you with individualized guidance based on your special situation or question.*

Last, why am I writing this guide?

I am a first-generation college student. I did not transfer to a 4-year university. I grew up in East Los Angeles, raised by a single mom, and like everyone around me, "working poor. Although I had been admitted to UC Berkeley and had always dreamed of attending Cal, I decided to attend the University of Southern California (USC), mostly because moving out of Los Angeles was out of the question for my mom. My experience of the four and half years I spent at USC as a first-generation college student—making constant stumbles as I moved forward—has never left me and is what informs me most when I work with my students as a CCC counselor.

When I see my students pause with a blank look, noticeably processing the information I just shared, oh my goodness—*I get it*. I know how foreign a college campus can feel and how it t will surprise and frustrate you over and over again when trying to understand why you do not qualify for financial aid *this* semester, even though you did *last* semester. I understand what it's like when you are sent from one office to the next, each office saying some version of "that's not what we do here" and pointing you across campus for answers no one seems to be ready to share. I get why the process of requesting your official transcripts from every single college you have attended is costly and confusing and can make you want to procrastinate on a process that will cost you your entire transfer application if you are not careful.

During my first semester as an undergraduate at USC, I spent the first eight weeks walking over to the bookstore, camping on the floor of the book stacks for hours to complete my course readings for class. I knew I had financial aid, and I knew it was generous, but I had no clue how that money would end up in my hands so that I could buy my books for class. I had no idea that I could reserve my books for class at the library to save money. This was 1995, long before book rentals and free OER textbooks were even an option. It wasn't until one day, when I heard someone in our dorm talking about the Cashier's office and how their check would arrive late— that I thought, wait— what's a "Cashier's Office"? I then bought a copy of our college catalog at the bookstore, back when they were printed and available for purchase and cost five dollars. And there it was, **the bible to college**, the answers I'd been looking for. I poured over that heavy book, took notes, highlighted courses I wanted to take, and read and *re-read the fine print of our graduation requirements*. I didn't know it then, but I had found a way to teach myself the "social capital"— the social and relational knowledge shared between networks which becomes a form of capital or wealth —I was missing as a first-generation college student. The next week, I found the Cashier's office, got the semester's check for indirect costs that had been built into my financial aid package, and bought my books for class. A few semesters later, I learned about book vouchers and scholarships available for hardship at our Mexican Alumni Association chapter, which I applied for and received as well. Everything helped; I just kept wishing I had learned this earlier.

Nothing about college came forthright. It was always something I somehow stumbled into, and oh my goodness, how I hated that. If I were in a class, even a difficult one, like the senior-level course on Russian Philosophy I mistakenly enrolled myself in during my first year. I could learn the material because it was a class with a curriculum and a teacher. *But where was the curriculum for understanding college? Who was the instructor? Why was there no class that taught all this?*

What tripped me up in college was not so much what was happening *inside* the classroom; it was everything happening *outside* the classroom that was foreign to me. "Foreign" was learning how to understand graduation requirements and missing the **March 2nd financial aid deadline.** I learned the hard way that financial aid packages change from one year to the next and that one error of missing the March 2nd deadline cost me a good portion of aid in grants and scholarships, some of which never came back. "Foreign" was learning not to let the person at the front counter or the major adviser get in the way of me understanding the information I needed when they could sound patronizing while answering my questions and making me feel small for even asking them anything. After all, if I didn't ask them questions and learn what I needed, it would not hurt them one bit, but it would have major consequences for me.

I wrote this guide from *a place that knows all too well how colleges—all colleges—can make first-generation college students feel small, misplaced, culture-shocked, and demoralized.* I have written as much as I know about the transfer process that can be relayed in this format, largely based on what students have told me over time *they* want to understand, and also in a way that aims to be conversational, to tell more of a story about transfer instead of a report— aka, not put you to sleep!

College is hard and demanding in so many ways. I have learned this over time, not only in my own journey but most especially from my students, that the hard parts of college—or life, for that matter—are the parts that stand to transform us the most and that *transformation is essential for growth*, especially for first-generation college students. Nearly every time we dream of becoming something—a doctor, engineer, entrepreneur, nurse, artist—that dream will ask, if not require, that we go outside of ourselves, our world, our comfort zone, and into a completely new world, new culture, new way of being. To get where we—that is, you— want to go, you cannot stay in the same place you started from or even stay the same person. That is scary and hard and jarring. Yet, if you can manage the terrain of getting there, of the transformation itself, it is so very worthwhile.

College *is* an absolute *alchemy*. You can bet on that and believe in it. The transformation from a college first-year student into a college graduate is truly an act of **turning lead into gold**.

Final, final words?

Stay golden, and go get it!

Works Cited

"Submit Input on AB 928." Academic Senate for California Community Colleges, 2022, https://asccc.org/content/submit-input-ab-928. Accessed 03 Jan 2023.

Table of Contents

Part I: Five Steps to Transfer

Getting Started

Where to start? Let's start with the 1960 Master Plan for Higher Education in California—a set of documents and policies—which essentially designed the current three systems of public colleges and universities in California today, including the: University of California (UC) system, the California State University (CSU) system, and the California Community College (CCC) system. UC's Office of the President describes the "California Master Plan for Higher Education" as an initiative aimed at making higher education in California affordable and accessible for all students.

> *"The transfer function is an essential component of the commitment to access. UC and CSU are to establish a lower division to upper division ratio of 40:60 to provide transfer opportunities to the upper division for Community College students, and eligible California Community College transfer students are to be given priority in the admissions process."*
> ("California Master Plan," par. 2)

So, what does this mean for you, our transfer student? It means that **by design, our California Community College (CCC) upper-division transfer students have a place reserved for them at the UC and CSU. So, *by design,* you have a place at the table**. There *is* no imposter syndrome to transfer; those seats are waiting for you, which is important to know as you begin your journey. We have thirty-two public universities in California, distributed across every region of our state, specifically designed for you to transfer into. That means more public university options for transfer exist in California than in any other state in the country. What do you need to do to get there? You need to meet the *eligibility standards for transfer admission*.

We're going to talk about what that means, but first, throughout this guide, we will use the term *Transfer* as a shorthand reference for the **upper division transfer of CCC students** holding priority admission to CSU and UC. *Upper division* refers to a student transferring into Junior level standing or with a **minimum of 60 semester or 90 quarter transferable units**—more on this soon.

Now, let's unpack the *eligibility standards for transfer admission* to UC and CSU. If the process of transferring from a California community college to a 4-year University were summed up in five simple steps, here is the basic overview of what you will **need to complete** to transfer successfully:

1. complete **60 transferable units** with passing grades, as determined by the transfer University you are applying to enter;
2. meet the **GPA eligibility** for *admission into the college* and also *into the major* for which you are applying;
3. complete the transferable **GE pattern** of lower division coursework—the CSU GE pattern or the IGETC GE pattern at your local CCC (recommended, though not required);
4. complete the **major preparation courses** and major prep GPA in those courses, as identified for transfer admissions; and
5. complete each step of the transfer **application**, which includes: completion of your education plan for transfer with your Counselor, submitting complete and correct admissions applications for transfer, following each *next step* after applying to each campus, and completing the *next steps* after accepting your admissions offer.

Let's break it down further into five simple steps one can easily memorize: GE Pattern, Major Prep, GPA, 60 Units, and Application.

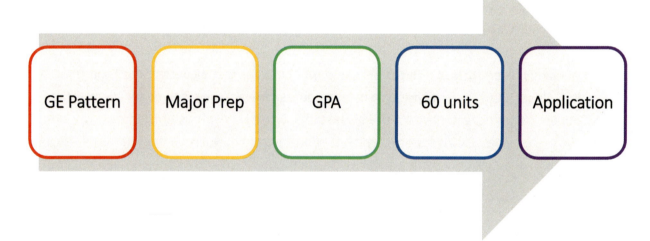

Figure 1Fig.1-1. Five Steps for Transfer - GE Pattern, Major Prep, GPA, 60 Units, Application

Simple right? Easy no? I wish I could tell you it was either simple or easy. In theory, this is how the architecture of the transfer process for CCC students is built. In practice, however, each of the steps entails a whole world of details, with if's—and's—but's that change depending on the student, the goal, the context, and the transfer campus.

Understanding *transfer* is not like knowing the rules of a track race where the lines are clear and simple, and the object is to complete four loops; it is much more like understanding the nature of mountain climbing. (I know, I know—I've reached that point in life where I sometimes make long-winded, boring analogies, but stay with me here!) In mountain climbing, when we stand hundreds of yards away, the lines appear clear and straightforward, and we think, "yeah, I could climb that." Yet, once we get to the mountain's base and start climbing, things look and feel much different. Forks along the path present themselves, and elevations appear that we hadn't anticipated, which can feel scary and sudden; we may realize we packed too much or not enough for the journey and find ourselves either overburdened or underprepared. The process of transfer is A LOT like mountain climbing. Unfortunately, we talk about the transfer process and measure student progress as though we're talking about a track race where everyone starts at the same place, goes in the same direction, and takes the same amount of time to reach the same four loops. It's just not how transfer *actually* happens.

Any student who started their coursework at one college only to have to move to another college and try to register for classes knows how complicated things can get. They suddenly find that the process of reconciling their coursework from College A to College B is not the most elegant. Even more complicated, any student who takes a turn mid-way in their community college journey by changing their major or their target transfer college suddenly finds themselves in a long meeting with their counselor. However, that person is doing their absolute best to make the tally of credits, courses, articulation, and requirements add up in a way that doesn't alter the student's transfer timeline too radically or make them feel like they must go backward instead of forward to make the changes.

The process of transfer can be simple: *if* you never make a single change and pass every class from start to finish, *if* you register perfectly and create the best schedule that suits your life every time, *if* you have enough money each semester or quarter for books and rent and gas and parking, and so much more, *if* you never change your major, and *if* a major event or crisis doesn't interrupt your studies and timeline (like a pandemic). However, the college reality is not that simple for the large majority of our CCC students because they are new to college. They are ***first-generation college students*** who will stumble as they move towards their goals because their learning includes more than what is happening inside a classroom. Their learning includes the rules, the norms, and the culture of college itself. The large majority of our students will register with the help of financial aid. They will often need to take courses part-time in order to manage school and work, family, or all three. And here's the thing—that's perfectly okay.

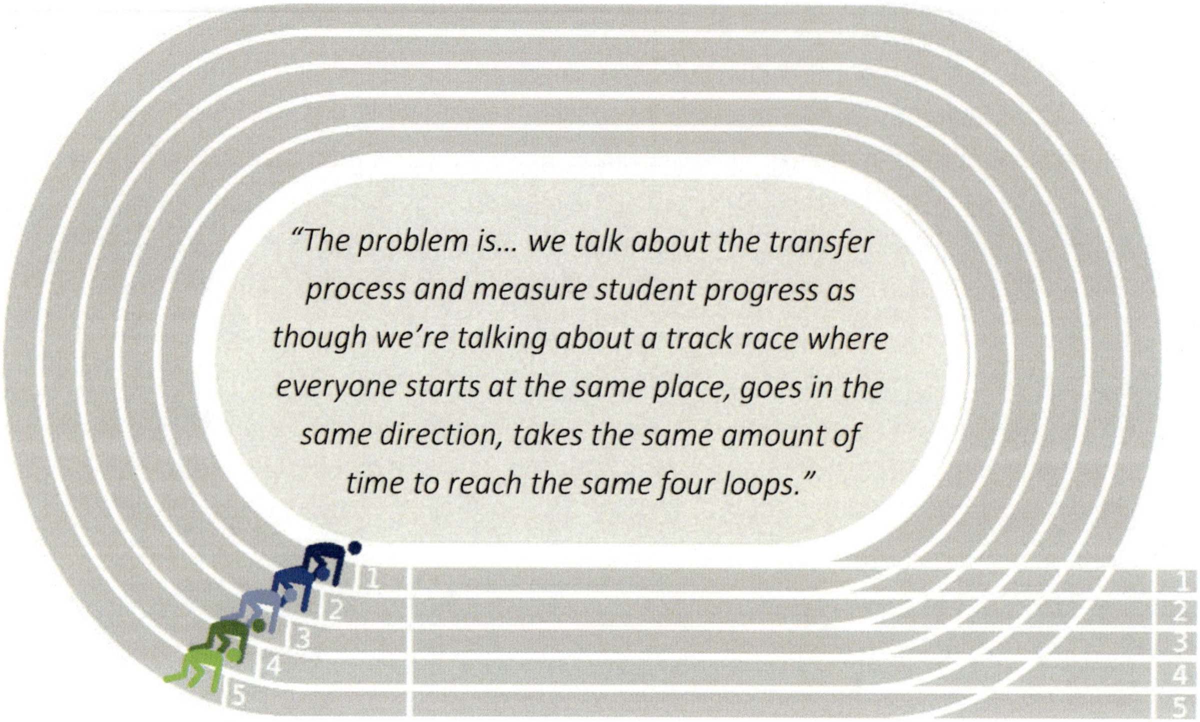

"The problem is... we talk about the transfer process and measure student progress as though we're talking about a track race where everyone starts at the same place, goes in the same direction, takes the same amount of time to reach the same four loops."

Fig. 2-2. Transfer is a process not a race.

Transfer is not a race, and the process of transferring is not at all like being in a track race. When students walk into my office heavy-hearted because they failed a course or had to withdraw due to family obligations or even mental health, the first ping of frustration that runs through me is not with them or their situation but with *the story about transfer that has built up over time.* A story so embedded in my students that they measure and punish themselves by it. We've all heard the story that: **students must finish community college in two years or be considered behind, and people starting college at any age over 23 or 25 years old are somehow** *too old* **to be there because they are behind even as they begin, and a community college is a lesser college experience.** The story we tell ourselves about transfer is broken. Transferring can, in fact, be complicated and confusing. That's especially true for those starting the process unclear about what direction they hope to take or if they're new to college and also learning how to become a college student. If the process includes making some stumbles while moving forward, all of this is okay. They can and will still transfer. Let's just let out that self-induced pressure valve that says to our students there's one way to do this. There isn't. Our students should feel proud and empowered every day that they show up for themselves, for the dreams they are nurturing, and take a chance on something that's innately hard and complex.

To some degree, this mindset begins with the transition from high school to college. What I tend to see in my students—especially those newly out of high school—is something like a high school mentality applied to a college experience. In high school, generally speaking, you move through classes in a block schedule format, in lockstep with peers, by the sound of a bell, and towards the goal of checking off the same boxes towards graduation. It's easy to measure how you're doing in high school by comparing yourself to classmates. However, once you graduate, everyone goes in different directions and follows a new sense of time and achievement that only they can define. College is so very different from high school because, in college, students have a world of choices. Instead of running a race against peers, you are on a journey towards discovering your true self, one that is based on personal goals, personal load, resources, tools, and where you're trying to go.

Personal Load, Major Climb, and College Terrain

I have yet to meet a student that doesn't want to transfer as quickly as possible, if not yesterday. While I'm certainly *for* transferring quickly, there are some common pitfalls students make in trying to get there *faster*. In the name of *faster*, students often seek to pile on classes or register for a difficult schedule that might not work with their day-to-day lives. Some students can power through that approach, but many inevitably get stuck in the back-and-forth movements of college that follow a pattern. Namely, *taking a class, not passing that class, and re-registering for the same class again.* In my experience, being able to move quickly is less about speed and more about **focus and accuracy** while hitting your marks each step of the way. For example, meeting regularly with your Counselor so that you can verify you're taking the best set of courses for each term and truly know what grades you need to earn in each class to meet the GPA requirements of the University. It also means using your community resources like tutoring services, writing centers, and accessibility centers to ensure you have all the academic tools you need to succeed. **Getting there quicker is less about *measuring time* than *measuring progress*.**

In my experience, there are essentially three areas that will define how quickly you can transfer. Staying with the mountain climbing metaphor, let's call these: *Personal Load, Major Climb, and College Terrain.*

 Personal Load

Personal load simply refers to the load you carry as a college student, be it personal challenges, academic struggles, home life pressures, or limitations you must work around. Every student's personal load will vary widely. For a first-generation college student, personal load includes the feeling that everything about college is foreign; you may lack the fluency to know what questions to ask, don't know where to go for help, and end up being more likely to make mistakes as you go. The personal load can also be academic—like those who struggle in math (as most students do) but must pass at least four math courses to pursue a major in Business. Other types of personal loads may include managing your schedule, focus, and energy between school and working full-time or as a parent with young children. Those loads can also be struggling to access tutoring and accessibility resources as a student with a learning or physical disability, just as not speaking English as your native language with the added work of getting through courses that require academic writing and research is a load. The loads we carry may include the added hurdles one must work through as an undocumented student, who is vulnerable to the legal landscape of the moment, and the stressors that add to everyday life. It can be the emotional load carried when we worry about a loved one who is ill or coping with the stressors of life during a pandemic, as everyone experienced with Covid 19. It can be the mental load of managing anxiety or depression, which can rob us of the mindset needed to complete a 5-page essay or to participate in group projects. Finally, the personal load could include the personal crisis that arises from coming out or transitioning during college.

The many kinds of mental, emotional, financial, and physical loads students bring with them as they step onto any campus are very real. As a student, you should know there's great power in acknowledging your personal load, being honest about what you're carrying, and being kind to yourself. It means that when students set off to register for classes and are working with a counselor, it is important to factor in things you may need, like a certain schedule, added learning supports, or working with a therapist available at your campus. The beauty of attending a community college, in my mind, is that it starts with one word and one value: **COMMUNITY**. Community means that YOU matter. You and your well-being come first because to move forward and be successful, then the WHOLE of you matters. One of the best parts of our California Community College (CCC) system is that we go BIG on support services and resources for our students. Our campuses offer food pantries, book vouchers, free bus passes, health centers, and special programs to help our most vulnerable community members, including our undocumented students, parents, students with disabilities, and formerly incarcerated students. We have programs like EOP&S, CalWORKs, Guardian Scholars, Umoja, Puente, METAS, and student accessibility centers, among others, that specialize in helping students find the supports they need to achieve as college students. Still, those programs can only work when students like you check in with us, walk through the door, and let us know what's going on.

It's so important to learn as a student how to ask for help, to find those go-to staff that you can lean on in college when you have questions, and to find the resources you need and also utilize them as you. Once you transfer to a 4-year campus, college only gets busier and more difficult because you'll be completing upper-division coursework. But if you can begin to learn now while attending a community college—which can be smaller and easier to navigate—how to find the supports you need, how to manage and organize your life to meet your school commitments, and how to ask for help, then it's like you're building a very important muscle that only gets stronger with time and will help you make the transition to a 4-year college where coursework and assignments may get harder; the difference is you will have learned how to get stronger and lean on the resources available to you to aid you as you go.

Major Climb

I once had two students, twin brothers, that sought to transfer along the same timeline. One was an Anthropology major, and the other a Biology major. They transferred two years apart, although they took nearly the same general education courses. Reason? **When it's a different major, it's a different climb.**

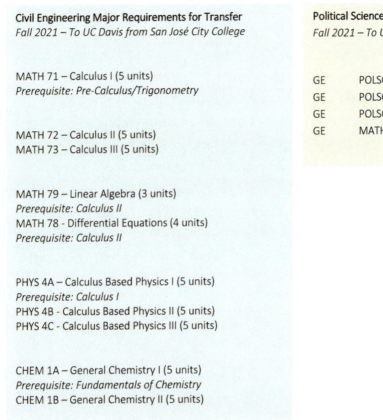

Civil Engineering Major Requirements for Transfer
Fall 2021 – To UC Davis from San José City College

MATH 71 – Calculus I (5 units)
Prerequisite: Pre-Calculus/Trigonometry

MATH 72 – Calculus II (5 units)
MATH 73 – Calculus III (5 units)

MATH 79 – Linear Algebra (3 units)
Prerequisite: Calculus II
MATH 78 - Differential Equations (4 units)
Prerequisite: Calculus II

PHYS 4A – Calculus Based Physics I (5 units)
Prerequisite: Calculus I
PHYS 4B - Calculus Based Physics II (5 units)
PHYS 4C - Calculus Based Physics III (5 units)

CHEM 1A – General Chemistry I (5 units)
Prerequisite: Fundamentals of Chemistry
CHEM 1B – General Chemistry II (5 units)

Political Science Major Requirements for Transfer
Fall 2021 – To UC Davis from San José City College

GE	POLSC 1 – Politics and Government	(3 units)
GE	POLSC 2 – Comparative Politics	(3 units)
GE	POLSC 4 – International Relations	(3 units)
GE	MATH 63 – Elementary Statistics	(3 units)

Fig. 0-1. Comparing Transfer Requirements for Civil Engineering and Political Science.

Here's the old logic you will hear about community college. Folks will say something like, "Just go and knock out your GE courses at a community college for about a year, save some money, and then transfer." While that's sort of true, it is not how transfer really works because if you want to save time, selecting GEs will be based on your major. In fact, taking *that first approach* of just waiting until you're done with your GEs before thinking about a specific major is a great recipe for taking more classes than you need. Here's an example. Compare the following two lists of major prep course requirements for transfer to the same campus—UC Davis—but in two very different majors: Civil Engineering versus Political Science.

Figure 1-3 shows that the Civil Engineering requirements at UC Davis include a long list of rigorous, STEM-based courses that must be taken *sequentially*—meaning you can't pile Calculus 1, 2, and 3 in the same semester because each course builds off of the next. These major preparation courses alone can take a student 2-3 years to complete, especially if they are trying to earn a B grade or higher in each course to qualify for the UC Davis TAG or major requirements. A student pursuing Civil Engineering at UC Davis for Transfer may need to go slower as each course averages five units. That is a very different picture compared to a student pursuing a Political Science major at UC Davis because, in that situation, each of the four major preparation requirements may double count towards the student's IGETC general education requirements. In their situation, the Political Science student will likely fall short of units needed for Transfer and will need to take additional elective units that transfer to the UC.

It's so important that when students measure their progress, it is based on *their* major, *their* coursework, *their* academic strengths and preferences, and *their* preferred college for Transfer instead of comparing themselves to others or what the culture tells us a two-year community college timeline should be. It's important that parents and well-meaning loved ones understand this too. Many of our CCC students often feel a certain kind of pressure to transfer quickly. Yet, perhaps they could benefit more from an extra set of courses that lets them explore which major is best suited to them, earn a workforce certificate, or achieve an Associate degree—like Medical Assistant, Early Childhood Education, or Bookkeeping. These certificates and degrees stand to increase their income and also sustain their ability to remain in school and achieve a Bachelor's degree. The bottom line is when it's a different major, it's a different climb.

 College Terrain

Applying to the University of California (UC), the California State University (CSU) system, or a private college, such as the University of Southern California (USC), all require a separate approach. The *terrain* of each system of higher education is unique and different. For example, the CSU and UC systems have a separate set of general education requirements—the UC includes GE requirements for a foreign language while the CSU will include two different GEs, one in Area E, Lifelong Learning, and one in AREA F, Ethnic Studies. If you are a Psychology major applying to the CSUs, you'll most likely need to complete a course in Statistics to satisfy the GE in Mathematics and Quantitative Reasoning. However, in addition to Statistics, most UCs will also require either Pre-Calculus or Calculus for Psychology majors. Calculus, for most students, is a major **gatekeeper course**—*a course that's required to move forward but has a low rate of students passing the first time*—and this one policy can impact your timeline for transfer if you have to take and re-take the same course. The CSUs and UCs will differ in the GPA requirements for similar majors. Generally speaking, the UCs require a 2.8 and above for non-selective majors, while the CSU will require a 2.0 and above for non-impacted majors. Each system of higher education will evaluate your coursework for credit differently. The CSUs generally allow for more coursework completed at a community college to transfer in. Courses like CIS - Web Design or

Administration of Justice - Juvenile Corrections will likely satisfy the CSU evaluation for transfer credit, though not likely for the UC. The UCs will not accept any courses with a grade of D for transferable credit, while the CSUs will accept D grades for transferable credit—though there are many limitations on how a D grade can be used.

Comparing private colleges adds even greater complexity, only rather than comparing systems of higher education, the rules will change from campus to campus. Some universities, like the University of Southern California (USC) or Santa Clara University (SCA), host comprehensive sites for transfer students and provide useful resources for transfer planning. Out-of-state colleges like Historically Black Colleges and Universities (HBCU) or Arizona State University (ASU) have worked tirelessly to create a seamless pathway for California Community College students to transfer. Campuses like Holy Names University (HNU) offer a unique cohort-based adult completion program at a reduced cost that is a great fit for working adults. Overall, a big benefit of private colleges is that they set the rules for their individual campus, which affords them greater flexibility in their admissions policies and usually benefits transfer students.

College terrain also includes a wide array of policies and practices that can make it easier or harder to apply for transfer. For instance, does the system have rolling admissions deadlines like many out-of-state colleges so that students can apply throughout the year? Do they have Fall and Spring admissions windows like most CSUs so that students do not have to wait an entire year to apply? Does the university actively recruit transfer students? For example, Columbia University is the one Ivy League campus that will actively recruit for transfer admissions, but the Ivy League campus closest to us in California—Stanford University—admits less than [1% of transfer applicants](#) (Dominic). How much financial aid does the transfer college offer? Does the college offer any application fee waivers to enable more students to apply? Does the campus offer specialized majors like Cogswell College or Woodbury University, which offer Animation, Game Design, Software Development, and Fashion? There are so many variables to each college's admissions process, and each one can make all the difference as to whether that campus is a good fit and accessible to our students.

So, what are the main takeaways as we begin?

To start with, California Community College (CCC) students, by design, have a place at the table within the UC and CSU higher education systems. In order to transfer, students need to meet transfer admissions eligibility standards for those systems, which we can break down into five basic steps: Units, General Education, Major Prep, GPA, and Application. Sadly, the culture surrounding how we think and talk about *Transfer* is broken. It's focused on the idea of getting in and out in two years rather than acknowledging how varied and complicated the transfer process can be and how each student's progress will differ. In practice, CCCs were designed as open-door colleges where all students could begin their journey, no matter their starting point.

This journey is not a race but a climb. If you truly want to save time and money and transfer efficiently, then you need to understand how your *Personal Load, Major Climb,* and *College Terrain* will impact your process. Most CCC students are first-generation college students. They will lean on financial aid for help, often enroll part-time, and need support as they go. That's perfectly okay. We just need to stop approaching the community college experience and the goal of transferring as if it's a race when it is actually a journey. It is a powerful journey that will stay with you for years to come, a journey that will likely teach you more about yourself, your desires, resilience, and direction if you will give yourself the time, energy, and focus that all living things need to learn and grow properly.

 That said, let's begin digging into the details of transfer and start our climb together.

Works Cited

California State, Legislature, Senate. SB 1440, Padilla. California Community Colleges: Student

    Transfer. *California Legislative Information*, 29 Sept. 2010,

    leginfo.legislature.ca.gov/faces/billNavClient.xhtml?bill_id=200920100SB1440. Accessed

    23 Jan. 2023. 2009 Legislature, Senate Bill 1440 (enacted).

Dominic. "Stanford University Transfer Acceptance Rate Rankings." *StudentMajor,*

    studentmajor.com/stanford-university-transfer-acceptance-rate/. Accessed 12 Apr. 2022.

Chapter 1: 60 Transferable Units

Suppose you ask any admissions representative from CSU or UC and, in many cases, the private colleges in California what is required to transfer to their college. In that case, you will hear them say *"60 transferable units"* and see that term in their list of admissions requirements for entry. But what exactly does that mean?

First, let's understand the word *units*. Basically, a unit is a form of college credit assigned to a course based on the number of hours the class requires for work – both in class and outside of the classroom such as homework, discussion, and labs.

Next, we need to understand the word *transferable*. A *transferable course* is a CCC course considered **comparable** to a course offered at CSU or UC. Therefore, the units for this course are credited as *transferable units* and counted towards the 60 units of transferable credits required to transfer.

Year 1		Year 2	
Fall Semester	**Spring Semester**	**Fall Semester**	**Spring Semester**
3 unit course	3 unit course	3 unit course	3 unit course
3 unit course	3 unit course	3 unit course	3 unit course
3 unit course	3 unit course	3 unit course	3 unit course
3 unit course	3 unit course	3 unit course	3 unit course
3 unit course	3 unit course	3 unit course	3 unit course
--------------------	--------------------	-------------------	-------------------
15 units	**15 units**	**15 units**	**15 units**

Fig. 1-1. Typical two-year course sequence for Transfer based on Fall and Spring semesters.

In a perfect world, a two-year course sequence for Transfer would look like this (**fig. 1-1**): The nickname for community college as a **two-year** institution comes from this very idea of graduating in two years. The problem is that this formula assumes, for one, that every course a student takes will be a transferable course to the college they are applying to attend. That's why it is very important that students understand two things regarding transferable units:

1. **Not all courses offered at community colleges are transferable** to either the CSU or the UC campuses.

2. The **UCs and CSUs take different approaches to how they evaluate transfer credit** for CCC courses. Sometimes, a course that earns transferable units to the CSU may not count for the UC and vice versa.

Let me give an example of how easily this can confuse a student. Imagine that in one semester, you register for five classes, and based on the student portal at your CCC, it seems you have earned 15 units in one semester (**fig. 1-2**). Are all of those units transferable? In this case, the number of transferable units to CSU is nine, but only six transfer to UC. At the same time, this student would fulfill 15 units at their community college. While this example might look straightforward, a large part of what makes the Transfer planning process so confusing is that **no central place exists to view and verify the transferable units that count towards all systems of CA higher education across the CCC, CSU, and UC systems.**

Fall Semester	CCC Earned	CSU Transfer	UC Transfer
ESL 92 - Advanced ESL Course	3 units	0	0
CIS 44 - Web Development	3 units	3 units	0
SOC 10 - Intro to Sociology	3 units	3 units	3 units
MATH 63 - Intro to Statistics	3 units	3 units	3 units
MATH 120 - Tutoring for Statistics	3 units	0	0
	15 units	**9 units**	**6 units**

Fig. 1-2. CCC Earned versus Transferable Credits.

Also, there is no central system to integrate exam credits from AP and IB test scores against requirements for each of the three higher education systems. In fact, to make matters more confusing, each system and individual campuses will interpret AP and IB test scores differently and grant credits differently based on the subject test, the score, and how the course will be used. Finally, there is no central place that also integrates course credits completed at other colleges within California or the United States.

So, supposing a student completed six units of English in San Diego, then seven units of Science in Monterey, and now wants to enroll at Sacramento City College, that student will need to bring their official transcripts from each campus to be evaluated for credit. Much of that evaluation will involve combing through the transcripts to identify CCC and CSU credits but not necessarily UC credits. It's largely the work of counselors, articulation officers, evaluation specialists, and discipline faculty to verify the entire student coursework and how it counts differently across the CCC, CSU, or UC systems based on the student's goal. Additionally, private colleges and out-of-state universities have their own independent ways of evaluating and granting credit separate from this process.

Have I confused you yet? I'm sure I have because explanations are always confusing in the beginning. But here's some good news; several tools and resources are available for this process, and you do not need to do this alone. My main point was to show how complex the Transfer planning process can be, how easily students can misinterpret progress when only using the student portal, and why you need to lean on your community resources for help—starting with your Counselor.

Let's talk about Counselors and why they are your new BFF

First, let me say this. Counselors often get a bad rap. Part of this is because we are placed in the awkward position of being the go-between, the explainer of policies between the CCC, CSU, UC, and other partners. When the UC makes policies about transfer admissions, its main concern is the UC system, just as when the CSU makes policies about transfer, it focuses on its system. Community College Counselors, however, have to think about ALL of these systems together and how to best guide our students in planning when new policies are created, even ones we may not agree with personally. Still, we are more than messengers and must also consider our students' distinct needs. For instance, *military veterans* and how to navigate what credits will or won't count towards their GI bill, *undocumented students* and how to best navigate options for financial aid or questions related to career attainment, or *international students* with J-1 visa criteria they must meet. All of this activity and effort involves time to plan accordingly. We often have 30-minute appointment times or 60 minutes if we're lucky. So to be fair, know that the role of Counseling within our CCCs can get quite messy, even under the best of intentions.

Every counselor will vary and bring different strengths to the table. No one is perfect, and really, what you need above all is someone that gets you, is rooting for you, and you can talk with them honestly and meet regularly. So make sure you are working with at least one Counselor you can meet with at least once a semester and preferably *before* registration for the next term; you can check in with them for advice during the year you apply for transfer, and if you find a team of counselors that serve different needs, more power to you!

Why does this matter? It matters because there's no magic wand to integrate transferable units, GPA, and course requirements for transfer across higher education systems. That's what CA community Counselors do. That's what your educational plan will reflect. An educational plan is essentially a road map of the coursework you will need to complete to reach your educational goals based on your timeline. But it's also a projection of a pathway and is not set in stone. If you switch your classes, change your major or target Transfer college, or remember completing coursework at another college but haven't let your counselor know—all those things matter. It is always best to keep your Counselor informed as you go because that's what they need to provide accurate guidance for your situation.

A big obstacle in Counseling is that we are really at the mercy of our students to set appointments and remember to come to see us. We technically can't require students to attend a Counseling session (unless it's a special program like EOP&S). The issue is that students often do not know when they need to see a Counselor and might check in after taking a course they did not need or missed an important step. The rule of thumb is to meet with your Counselor at least once a semester, preferably before registering for classes. Also, check in with your Counselor when making big decisions like changing your major, taking a break from school, or dropping a course. You do not need to feel bad about asking for help with any of those kinds of choices, so don't avoid coming in for help. We can connect you to available tools and resources that you may not know about.

Set appointments with your counselor early and often. Stay organized during those appointments, and take notes of the questions you have so that you can make the most of the time together. Write down your next steps and make sure you understand what's being recommended to do. Prioritize those habits, and they will go a long way to helping you move through the transfer process in a way that doesn't waste time or money or have you take more courses than needed.

ASSIST and why it's way better than Instagram.

Another tool in your toolbox that you have for transfer is Assist.org. ASSIST is the "official course transfer and articulation system for California's public colleges and universities." But what does that mean? Well, first, let me ask: Can you guess how many community colleges, CSUs, and UCs there are in California? (Please take a minute to guess!)

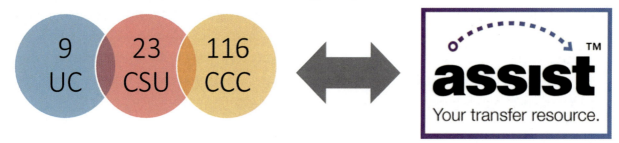

Fig. 1-3. Number of Campuses Available for Transfer via ASSIST.

Okay, so technically, there are 10 UC campuses in California if we include UC San Francisco. However, they do not offer Transfer baccalaureate programs, so only 9 UCs are available; there are 23 CSU campuses and a whopping 116 community colleges in California. The California community college system is, in fact, the largest system of higher education in the country. We have more community colleges than any other state, Texas is a close second, but California is still in the lead. Our size is, in many ways, our biggest strength because we can offer

students courses in nearly any subject they can imagine across our system. Another strength is that students can start their studies in San Diego and end them in San Jose, and much of that coursework will patch together to help save them both time and money. But here's the downside; with so many public colleges and universities in California, it's very confusing for a student to know how to navigate across systems, understand what courses count for what, and what each campus and each major requires for Transfer. That's where ASSIST comes in. Now, let's go through two step-by-step examples of searching ASSIST for transferable coursework.

ASSIST offers each students an up-front, public facing, totally accessible view to answer these questions:

1. Are my units transferable to the UC or to the CSU?
2. Do my courses count towards the CSU or UC general education requirements?
3. Beyond general education courses, what courses are required for my major that I should complete at my community college in order be eligible for transfer?
4. Is there a GPA or other kind of requirement for my major that I should be aware of in order to meet the transfer eligibility for my major at a specific campus?

Fig. 1-4. Transfer questions the Assist tool can answer.

How to use ASSIST to verify: CSU Transferable Units

A student can use ASSIST to independently check if a course completed at a CCC is **CSU transferable**. One minimum Transfer requirement for CSU is that CCC students complete 60 transferable units. This tool is especially helpful if students have completed courses at different CCCs and want to verify their transferable unit count directly. For example, suppose you took an advanced ESL course—ESL 99 (6 units)—and want to know if those course units can transfer to CSU. Follow these steps on ASSIST:

1. go to https://www.assist.org/;
2. use the dropdown menu to select the academic year you completed the course;
3. use the dropdown menu to select the college name where you completed the course;
4. select the type of transfer status you are seeking to find. In this case, CSU Transfer;
5. as shown in **fig. 1-5**, click on the button labeled **View Transferability Lists**;

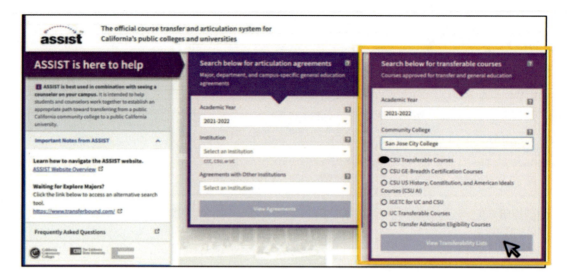

Fig. 1-5. Using ASSIST to Verify CSU Transferable Units: Steps 1 to 5.

6. a new menu pops up on the left side that lets you click the discipline name for the course you are searching, like ESL or English as a Second Language (**fig. 1-6**);

7. a list of transferable courses will appear on the right side for the chosen college and academic year;

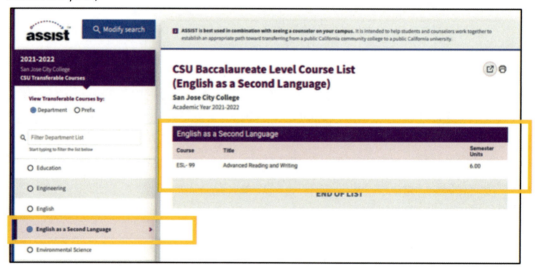

Fig. 1-6. Using ASSIST to Verify CSU Transferable Units: Steps 6 to 8.

8. Any non-transferable coursework will NOT appear.

Based on this example (**fig. 1-6**), if a student completed ESL 99 at San José City College during the 2021-2022 academic year, the six units for that course *ARE* transferable to CSU. *Any course not found in this list is NOT transferable to CSU for the 2021-2022 academic year.* For example, in this case—ESL 92—a different ESL course is not listed; therefore, ESL 92 does not provide transferable units to CSU for the 2021-2022 academic year. Courses may change transferable status from year to year, so always be sure to verify based on the academic year you completed the course.

How to use Assist to verify: UC Transferable Units

A student can use ASSIST to check independently if a course completed at a California community college is *UC transferable*. One minimum requirement for transferring to a University of California (UC) is that CCC students complete 60 transferable units. This tool is especially helpful if students have completed courses at different CCCs and want to verify their transferable unit count directly. For example, Let's say you took the Computer Information Systems course—CIS 41 (3 units)—and would like to know if the units for this course are transferable to the UC. Follow these steps on ASSIST.

1. go to https://www.assist.org/;
2. use the dropdown menu to select the academic year you completed the course;
3. use the dropdown menu to choose the college name where you completed the course;
4. select the type of transfer status you are seeking to find. In this case, UC Transfer;
5. as shown in **fig. 1-7**, click on the blue button, "View Transferability Lists";

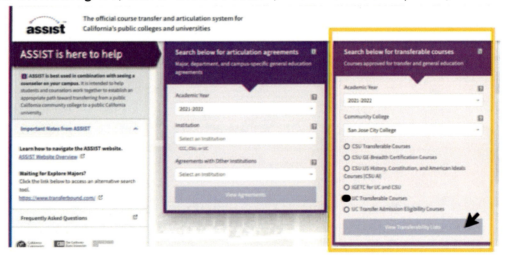

Fig. 1-7. Using ASSIST to Verify UC Transferable Units: Steps 1 to 5.

6. a new menu pops up on the left side that lets you click on the discipline name for the course you are searching, like CIS or Computer Information Systems (**fig. 1-8**);

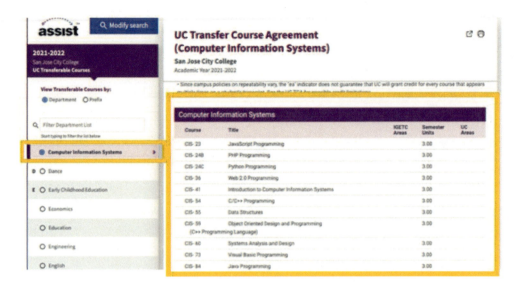

Fig. 1-8. Using ASSIST to Verify CSU Transferable Units: Steps 6 to 8.

7. a list of transferable courses will appear on the right side for the chosen college and academic year;

8. any non-transferable coursework will NOT appear.

Based on this example (**fig. 1-8**), if a student completed CIS 41 at San José City College during the 2021-2022 academic year, then the three units for this course *ARE* transferable to the UC. **Any course not shown on this screen list is NOT transferable to UC for the 2021-2022 academic year.** For example, in this case—CIS 47 Web Development—a different CIS course is not found; therefore, CIS 47 does not provide transferable units to UC for the 2021-2022 academic year. Since courses may change transferable status every year, always be sure to verify based on the academic year you completed the course.

Exams and Transferable Units — ¡Ay dios mío! It gets tricky.

Let's talk about AP and IB Exams

There are several ways for students can utilize exams to count towards transferable credit. However, students who work closely with their counselor and university admissions representative make better choices and get the best results. The UCs and CSUs will often take different approaches to evaluating exams, which ones they will admit for credit, and how they allow students to apply the exam credits toward Transfer. Those different approaches make it critical for students to work with university representatives to obtain accurate and up-to-date policies for their specific situations.

That said, the two most widely recognized exams for credit by universities and colleges in the United States, including the UC, CSU, and CCCs, are the AP and IB exams. In most cases, students would have taken these exams during high school and sought to apply the credit of passing scores toward college. Go to the College Board's AP Students page to learn more about the Advanced Placement (AP) exam and how to access your scores. Then, visit the International Baccalaureate's Assessment and Exams page for more information about the International Baccalaureate (IB) exams, including score access.

Here's the good news, generally speaking, a student with a passing score on an AP or IB exam will earn some form of transferable credit for the UC, CSU, private, out-of-state colleges, and CCCs. Yay! All that hard work was definitely *for* something, and it WILL save you money and time. In part, this means those exams can be applied as transferable credit towards reaching the 60 transferable units goal, potentially saving you from needing to complete certain elective units.

Here's the complicated news, where it gets well—ugly. Every single college and university will interpret your exam differently. Currently, there is no uniform way of interpreting how your AP or IB exams will count for Transfer across each higher education system. Although there are general patterns we lean on, there is no single answer key we can turn to for reference. In addition, colleges can and do change their policies year to year on how they interpret and apply the credit from AP or IB passing exam scores. Your counselor and an admissions representative are the best guides for helping determine how to use your exam scores as you plan for transfer. In **table 1-1**, you can see how varied AP and IB scores can be applied based on each student's goal. There are several lenses that your Counselor and admissions representative take on as they seek to best guide you on how your AP or IB exams may be applied.

Table 0-1. AP and IB Exam Credit Overview

CCC (116 campuses)	Advanced Placement (AP) Exam	International Baccalaureate (IB) Exam
CCC Credit	See the CCC catalog for lists of credit units applied for each course. Passing AP score is required.	See the CCC catalog for lists of credit units applied for each course. Passing IB score is required.
CSU GE Certification	See the CCC catalog for AP course listings that apply toward CSU GE certification. Decisions may be based on AP scores beyond the passing threshold.	See the CCC catalog for IB course listings that apply toward CSU GE certification. Decisions may be based on IB scores beyond the passing threshold.
IGETC Certification	See the CCC catalog for AP course listings that apply toward IGETC certification. Decisions may be based on AP scores beyond the passing threshold.	See the CCC catalog for IB course listings that apply toward IGETC certification. Decisions may be based on IB scores beyond the passing threshold.
Pre-Requisite	Work with a CCC counselor and instructional faculty to verify if AP exam substitutes for a course pre-requisite. Decisions may be based on AP scores beyond the passing threshold.	Work with a CCC counselor and instructional faculty to verify if IB exam substitutes for a course pre-requisite. Decisions may be based on IB scores beyond the passing threshold.
Associate Degree for Transfer	Work with a CCC counselor and articulation officer to verify if an AP exam may be applied toward ADT coursework. Only applies for CSU.	Work with a CCC counselor and articulation officer to verify if an IB exam may be applied toward ADT coursework. Only applies for CSU.

California State University (23 campuses)	Advanced Placement (AP) Exam	International Baccalaureate (IB) Exam
Transfer Credit	See each campus catalog to verify how transfer credits apply. A passing score is required.	See each campus catalog to verify how transfer credits apply. A passing score is required.
General Education	See each campus catalog to verify if an AP exam can apply toward the campus GE requirement. Ask a university admissions representative for more assistance.	See each campus catalog to verify if an IB exam can apply toward the campus GE requirement. Ask a university admissions representative for more assistance.
Pre-Requisite	Ask the university admissions representative for more assistance. Campuses vary widely.	Ask the university admissions representative for more assistance. Campuses vary widely.
Major Preparation Req	Ask a university admissions representative for more help. Sometimes **Limitations** are listed in ASSIST based on the major.	Ask a university admissions representative for more help. Sometimes **Limitations** are listed in ASSIST based on the major.

University of California (9 campuses)	Advanced Placement (AP) Exam	International Baccalaureate (IB) Exam
Transfer Credit	See each campus catalog to verify how transfer credits apply. Passing score required.	See each UC campus catalog to verify how transfer credits apply. Passing score required.
General Education	See each UC campus catalog to verify if AP exam can apply toward the campus GE requirement. Ask the university admissions representative for further assistance.	See each UC campus catalog to verify if AP exam can apply toward the campus GE requirement. Ask the university admissions representative for further assistance.
Pre-Requisite	Ask the university admissions representative for further assistance. Campuses vary widely.	Ask the university admissions representative for further assistance. Campuses vary widely.
Major Preparation Req	Ask the university admissions representative for further assistance. **Limitations** are sometimes listed in Assist based on the major.	Ask the university admissions representative for further assistance. **Limitations** are sometimes listed in Assist based on the major.

Table 1-1 is not meant to confuse you more, I promise. It is meant to give you a sense of how complicated a single AP or IB exam can become when planning your coursework. It's so important to use your resources like the campus catalog and the UC or CSU exams-for-credit sites (listed in the Appendix section of this guide), to carefully read through the fine print on ASSIST, and of course, work closely with your counselor and university representative to assess how your exams can be Transfer optimized.

Here are some examples of public-facing information available to you for researching these policies. By simply searching "AP Credit" and "San José State University" on Google, I could access the SJSU Advanced Placement (AP) page (**fig. 1-9**) with specific information about how SJSU will use each AP course for the 2021-2022 academic year.

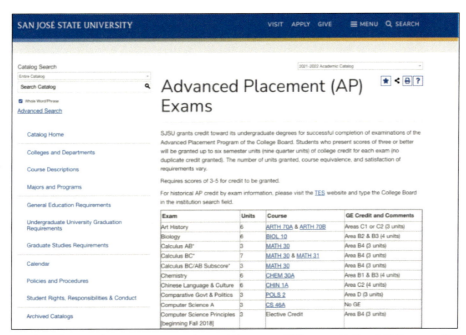

Fig. 1-9. Screenshot of San José State University Advanced Placement (AP) page with list of AP Exam credit acceptance.

Figure 1-10 shows a search result example for "IB credit" and "UC Santa Cruz" for 2021-2022.

In terms of major preparation requirements, **figure 1-11** is an example based on UC Berkeley's Psychology Lower Division B.A. articulation agreement on ASSIST for 2021-2022.

One of the Social Science requirements may be satisfied by a score of 4 or 5 on the AP US Government or Comparative Government exam. Students will be required to complete the second social science course from a department other than Political Science.

QUANTITATIVE: Two courses
The Psychology major does not accept AP or IBHL credits to fulfill any of the Quantitative requirements.

Only one introductory statistics course (Stat 2, 20 or 21) may be used to satisfy the requirement as these courses are credit restricted at UC Berkeley.

PSYCHOLOGY RESEARCH & DATA: One course at UC Berkeley
Psych 101 (Research and Data Analysis) must be taken at UC Berkeley the summer before or during the first semester.

NOTE: Different options may be available for satisfying certain requirements. Consult with the advisor in the Psychology department.

For more information:
For more information regarding applying to the major during your first semester at UC Berkeley, please see http://psychology.berkeley.edu or contact an undergraduate adviser at **psychsso@berkeley.edu.**

Fig. 1-11. Screenshot of ASSIST 2021-22 articulation agreement for UC Berkeley Major Prep for Psychology BA.

Compare this example with UC Riverside's articulation agreement (**fig. 1-12**) for the same major in the same academic year, and you'll find vastly different approaches for using AP credit based on the transfer major.

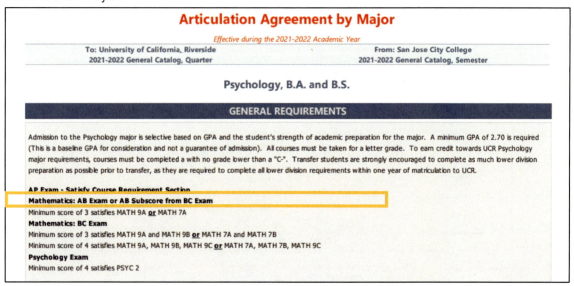

Fig. 1-12. Screenshot of ASSIST 2021-22 articulation agreement for UC Riverside's AP Exams for Psychology BA.

It's also quite important to take your time and read through the fine print on the ASSIST articulation agreements. **Figure 1-13** is another example of how to access information about AP or IB exams from a local CCC, Santa Monica College. They do a wonderful job of distinguishing for students what credit is applied locally for an Associate degree, the CSU GE, the IGETC, or towards Transfer units, while also noting many of the nuances and limitations associated with transferable credits.

I hope the key takeaway for students seeking to understand how to apply their AP and IB exam scores is this: work closely with your counselor and transfer admissions representative to ensure you get accurate and specific information based on your circumstances.

Credit by Exam: Advanced Placement (AP) Tests and SMC GE Chart

Students are granted units and subject credit for SMC degrees/certificates for College Entrance Examination Board (CEEB) Advanced Placement Tests with scores of 3, 4, or 5. Students must have the College Board send AP exam results to the SMC Admissions Office (hand carried copies will NOT be accepted).

AP credit can also be used to meet IGETC, CSU GE, and SMC Associate degree (majors and/or GE) requirements.
- AP credit granted at SMC does **NOT** reflect credit granted by a transfer institution.
- AP credit must be used in the IGETC area indicated, regardless of where the certifying institution's discipline is located.
- AP credit may be incorporated into the CSU GE certification by any certifying institution. All CSU campuses will accept the minimum units shown and apply them toward fulfillment of the designated CSU GE area if the examination is included as part of a full or subject-area certification. Please note that individual CSU campuses may choose to grant more units than those specified toward completion of CSU GE requirements.

Students interested in petitioning for AP credit should meet with a counselor. Students should be aware that AP test credit is evaluated by corresponding it to an equivalent SMC course, e.g., History 11. A student who receives AP credit and then takes the equivalent SMC course will have the unit credit for the duplication deducted prior to graduation. Credit by Advanced Placement exam is noted and listed first on a student's transcript, with units assigned and no grade.

Use of AP credit varies at each transfer institution. Please check the transfer institution's catalog for details.

UCLA will not grant AP credit if the exam is taken after the student has completed 24 semester units of college coursework.

EXAM	SMC ASSOCIATE DEGREE (MAJOR AND/OR GE)	CSU GE	CSU UNITS EARNED TOWARD TRANSFER	IGETC	UC UNITS EARNED TOWARD TRANSFER
Art History	AHIS 1 plus 3 elective units = 6 units: only 3 GE units Fulfills Global Citizen requirement	Area C1 or C2 3 semester units	6 semester units	Area 3A or 3B 3 semester units	8 quarter/ 5.3 semester units
Biology	BIOL 3 plus 2 elective units = 6 units; only 4 GE units	Area B2 and B3 4 semester units	6 semester units	Area 5B and 5C 4 semester units	8 quarter/ 5.3 semester units
Calculus AB	Score of 3: MATH 2* Score of 4 or 5: Math 7* 5 semester units	Area B4 3 semester units	3 semester units*	Area 2A 3 semester units	4 quarter/ 2.6 semester units**
Calculus BC	Score of 3: Math 7* Score of 4 or 5: Math 8* 5 semester units	Area B4 3 semester units	6 semester units*	Area 2A 3 semester units	8 quarter/ 5.3 semester units**
AP CALCULUS EXAM LIMITATIONS	*Qualifies student for next level of math		*Only one exam may be used toward transfer		**Maximum credit for both exams is 8 quarter/ 5.3 semester units
Chemistry	CHEM 10 5 semester units	Area B 1 and B3 4 semester units	6 semester units	Area 5A and 5C 4 semester units	8 quarter/ 5.3 semester units
Chinese Language & Culture	CHNESE 3 5 semester units	Area C2 3 semester units	6 semester units	Area 3B and 6A 3 semester units	8 quarter/ 5.3 semester units
Computer Science A	Score of 3 or 4: CS 55	N/A	3 semester units	N/A	8 quarter/ 5.3 semester units

Fig. 1-13. Screenshot of ASSIST 2021-22 Information from Santa Monica College about transferrable exams.

Let's talk about CLEP.

CLEP refers to the **College Level Examination Program**, a credit-by-examination program that measures a student's comprehension of introductory college-level material. Go to the College Board CLEP site to learn more details about the CLEP, including how to access your scores.

Transfer students can earn transferable college credit towards the California State University (CSU) system with passing scores on the CLEP exams. Each CSU campus, however, will determine for itself how they apply external exams toward the major. Some CLEP exam scores may be used towards the CSU GE Breadth fulfillment and CSU GE certification at your local community college. Use your campus catalog and work with your counselor to verify how your exams may or may not be used to this end. The **University of California (UC) does NOT recognize the CLEP**. Therefore, the CLEP may NOT be used towards the IGETC certification within the CCC system. **Figure 1-14** is an example taken from CSU's webpage College Level Examination Program (CLEP).

It's important to note that how the CLEP is used towards the CSU GE Breadth can vary from exam to exam. Also, how a local CCC uses CLEP may vary campus by campus and include additional policies given in their college catalog. That said, the CLEP offers a useful tool for students aiming to transfer to a CSU and seeking to save time.

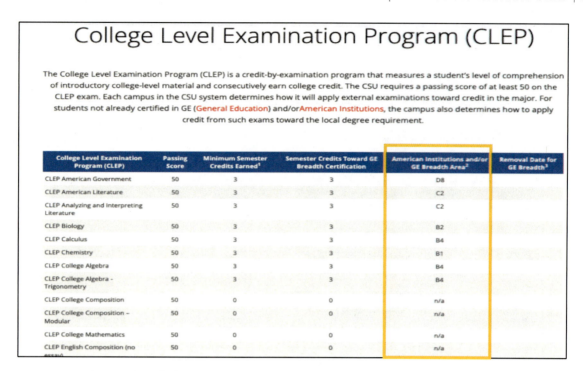

Fig. 1-14. Screenshot of information given on CSU's College Level Examination Program (CLEP) website.

Let's talk about Credit By Exam.

The current definition for the CCC system of Credit by Examination, also known as *Credit By Exam*, is located in Title 5, Section 55050 (e)—Credit for Prior Learning:

> The determination to offer credit by examination rests solely on the discretion of the discipline faculty. A separate examination shall be conducted for each course for which credit is to be granted. Credit may be granted only to a student who is registered at the college and in good standing and only for a course listed in the catalog of the community college. (California Code)

Each CCC offers *Credit by Exam* in some form. The idea is to offer community college students a way to earn college credit by demonstrating their knowledge and skills through locally designed exams. Every one of the 116 community college campuses in our system will take an individual approach in how they select courses that may utilize the credit-by-exam process as an option for students. They also differ in setting policies and limitations and defining the application process to complete a *Credit By Exam*. Many courses included in the list of *Credit By Exam* options will often include career readiness courses in disciplines such as Construction. In those cases, a student may enter college with a wealth of work experience that, with the *Credit By Exam* option, allows them to receive credit for knowledge, skills, and experience they have already attained.

For transfer students, work carefully with your counselor and university representative when selecting courses for the *Credit By Exam*. Many courses will not bare transferable credit when taken in this manner, especially to the UC, but some—such as a second language course— might be a great fit for this option.

There are also a new and evolving set of policies within California called Credit for Prior Learning (CPL). The idea behind CPL is very similar, to allow students to utilize prior knowledge for college credit. This *prior knowledge* can include work experience, portfolios, and locally designed assessments. CPL can be especially helpful for students with military training and experience by helping to better streamline their knowledge and skills into more appropriate levels of college standing. Once again, I would caution students to work with their counselor and admissions representatives to ensure that CPL is an appropriate tool for meeting their Transfer goals.

Let's talk about Cooperative Work Experience.

Cooperative Work Experience (CWE) is a program offered within the CCC system. It allows students to earn college credit for hands-on, work-based learning through paid or non-paid employment. There are, essentially, two kinds of **CWE: general or occupational**. General work experience means broader employment experience. Occupational work experience is intended to relate specifically to a student's educational or occupational goal and is meant to extend knowledge and skills learned in classrooms to application in a real employment environment.

To participate in CWE, students essentially register for the course at their local community college and work with their faculty instructor and employer to design and assess their learning outcomes. Students may earn a maximum of 16 units (semester) or 24 units (quarter) through general and occupational work experience. For example, a student working 20 hours per week can earn four units of college credit in one semester through this program.

It is important to note for transfer that **the UC does not recognize Cooperative Work Experience for transferable credit**. However, for students seeking a CSU Transfer, especially those already working full-time or completing a program that *requires* occupational work experience, the additional units earned through this program can be a valuable tool in helping to reach the 60 transferable unit threshold while also managing work schedules and responsibilities.

Figure 1-15 is an example from the Diablo Valley College (DVC) work experience program showing how varied the kinds of work experience options can be:

Work Experience Education (WRKX)

Work Experience is a course for students who already have a job/internship. It is an academic individualized work-based learning opportunity where you design your learning objectives. You earn credit for learning that takes place at your job or internship. This course can also help you to enhance your grade point average and maintain full-time college status.

There are three different Work Experience Education courses:

WRKX-160 (2-3 units): For students whose current job does not relate to their academic and/or career goal.

WRKX-170 (2-4 units): For students whose current job relates to their academic and/or career goal.

WRKX-180 (2-4 Units): For students working in a paid/unpaid internship or volunteer position that relates to their academic and/or career goal.

295 Course Series (2-4 Units): For students whose current degree/certificate requires a discipline-specific work-based learning course. (Example: CULN 295)

296 Course Series (2-4 Units): For students whose current degree/certificate requires a discipline-specific paid/unpaid internship or volunteer position. (Example: CULN 296)

Students complete orientation and schedule one teacher meeting per term and can earn up to a total of 16 units while enrolled at DVC.

Fig. 1 15. Screenshot of Diablo Valley College's "Work Experience Education (WRKX)" program information.

Works Cited

California State, Legislature. Credit for Prior Learning. Cal. Educ. Code, section 55050. *Legal*

   Information Institute, Cornell Law School, 21 Mar. 2020,

   www.law.cornell.edu/regulations/california/5-CCR-55050. Accessed 16 Jan. 2023.

California State University. "College Level Examination Program (CLEP)." *California State*

   University, www.calstate.edu/apply/transfer/pages/college-level-examination-

   program.aspx. Accessed 21 Jan. 2023.

Diablo Valley College. "Work Experience Education (WRKX)." *DVC Diablo Valley College*,

   www.dvc.edu/enrollment/career-employment/wrkx/index.html. Accessed 5 Feb. 2023.

Chapter 2: General Education

One of the first choices you will be asked to make as an incoming California Community College (CCC) student is deciding which GE pattern to follow as you prepare for transfer. So, let's unpack your options, how they differ, and why this process is crucial to transfer.

First, the options

Every CCC will hold two important documents for transfer in their catalog, on their website for download, and available in printed copies, usually through their counseling office. At every campus, they are referred to as the ***CSU GE Pattern*** and the ***IGETC GE Pattern***. Here's an example of each GE sheet from San Jose City College for the 2021-2022 academic year.

CSU GE Pattern Example

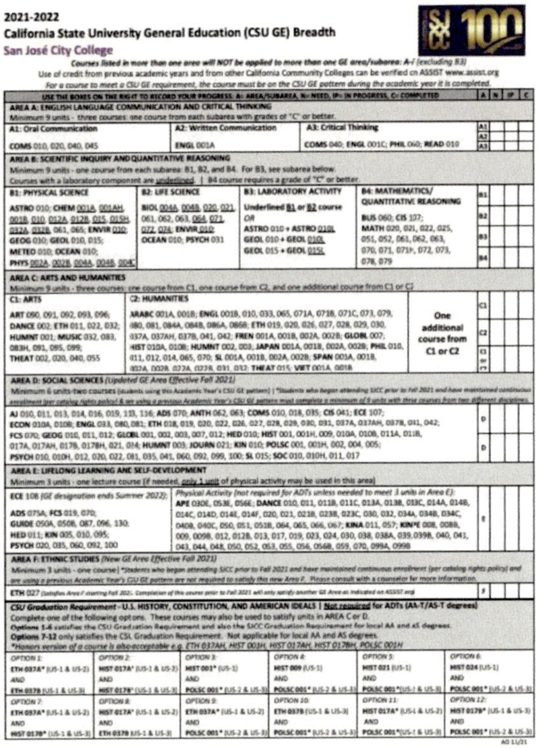
2021-2022
California State University General Education (CSU GE) Breadth
San José City College

Fig. 0-1. San José City College. "2021-2022 California State University General Education (CSU GE) Breadth."

IGETC GE Pattern Example

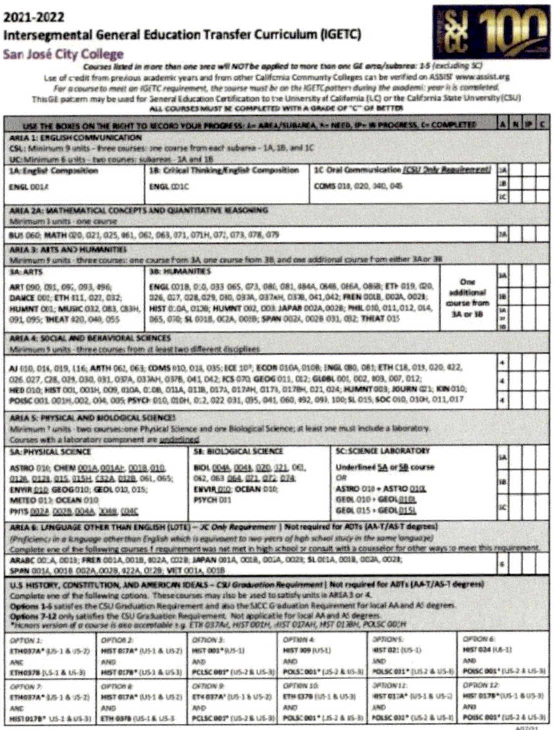
2021-2022
Intersegmental General Education Transfer Curriculum (IGETC)
San José City College

Fig. 0-2. San José City College. "2021-2022 Intersegmental General Education Transfer Curriculum (IGETC)."

Note that these GE sheets look very similar across CCC campuses.

The CSU General Education Pattern

The CSU GE Pattern is based on the California State University (CSU) general education requirements. The CSU system includes the 23 campuses listed below.

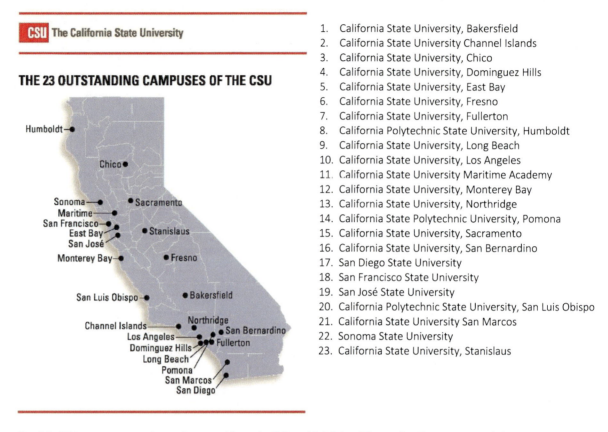

1. California State University, Bakersfield
2. California State University Channel Islands
3. California State University, Chico
4. California State University, Dominguez Hills
5. California State University, East Bay
6. California State University, Fresno
7. California State University, Fullerton
8. California Polytechnic State University, Humboldt
9. California State University, Long Beach
10. California State University, Los Angeles
11. California State University Maritime Academy
12. California State University, Monterey Bay
13. California State University, Northridge
14. California State Polytechnic University, Pomona
15. California State University, Sacramento
16. California State University, San Bernardino
17. San Diego State University
18. San Francisco State University
19. San José State University
20. California Polytechnic State University, San Luis Obispo
21. California State University San Marcos
22. Sonoma State University
23. California State University, Stanislaus

Fig. 0-3. CSU campuses map Image borrowed from the Edison High School Counseling Department website.

According to the CSU website, every CSU student, whether admitted as a Transfer or first-year student, will be required to complete a minimum of 48 units (semester) of GE requirements, including 39 units of lower division coursework ("Upper-Division Transfer"). So it's no coincidence that every single CCC offers students the option to complete the CSU GE Pattern. That pattern includes all the courses available at a CCC campus for that academic year that are currently approved for each CSU GE area to complete those 39 lower division GE units required to complete your bachelor's degree. You can find links to the CSU GE Pattern for every community college on the CCC Transfer Counselor Website.

Students who complete the CSU GE Pattern **must CERTIFY their GE requirements at their local CCC before Transfer**. That certification ensures they will not be required to repeat any lower division CSU GE requirements once they transfer. This process saves Transfer students both time and money so that rather than repeating GE courses taken at the CCC, they can focus instead on completing courses that fulfill requirements in their major or towards graduation.

Table 0-1. CSU Fall 2021 GE Subject Area Distribution

CSU GE Subject Area Distribution: Effective Fall 2021

Area A: English Language Communication and Critical Thinking

9 semester units (12 quarter units). One course in each Subarea.

A1	Oral Communication	(3 semester units or 4 quarter units)
A2	Written Communication	(3 semester units or 4 quarter units)
A3	Critical Thinking	(3 semester units or 4 quarter units)

Area B: Scientific Inquiry and Quantitative Reasoning

12 semester units (18 quarter units), with 3 semester units (4 quarter units) taken at the upper-divisional level. One course each in Subareas B1, B2, and B4, plus laboratory activity (B3) related to one of the completed science courses, and 3 additional semester units (4 quarter units) at the upper-division in one of the following Subareas.

B1	Physical Science	(3 semester units or 4 quarter units)
B2	Life Science	(3 semester units or 4 quarter units)
B3	Laboratory Science	A laboratory course of not more than 1 semester (2 quarter) unit value, associated with B1 or B2, may be required.
B4	Mathematics/Quantitative Reasoning	(3 semester units or 4 quarter units)

Area C: Arts and Humanities

12 semester units (18 quarter units), with 3 semester units (4 quarter units) taken at the upper-division level. At least one course completed in each of these 2 Subareas, and 3 additional semester units (4 quarter units) at the upper-division in one of the following Subareas.

C1	Arts: (e.g., Arts, Cinema, Dance, Music Theater)	
C2	Humanities: (e.g., Literature, Philosophy, Languages Other than English)	

Area D: Social Sciences

9 semester units (12 quarter units), with 3 semester units taken at the upper-division.

Courses shall be completed in at least 2 different disciplines among the 9 required semester units.

Area E: Lifelong Learning and Self-Development

3 semester units (4 quarter units) of study at the lower-division

Area F: Ethnic Studies

3 semester units (4 quarter units). This lower-division, 3 semester (4 quarter) unit requirement fulfills Education Code Section 89032. The requirement to take a 3 semester (4 quarter) unit course in Area F shall not be waived or substituted.

Source: CSU's General Education Policy webpage topic "Subject Area Distribution: Effective Fall 2021."

CSU GE Requirement – For CSU Only

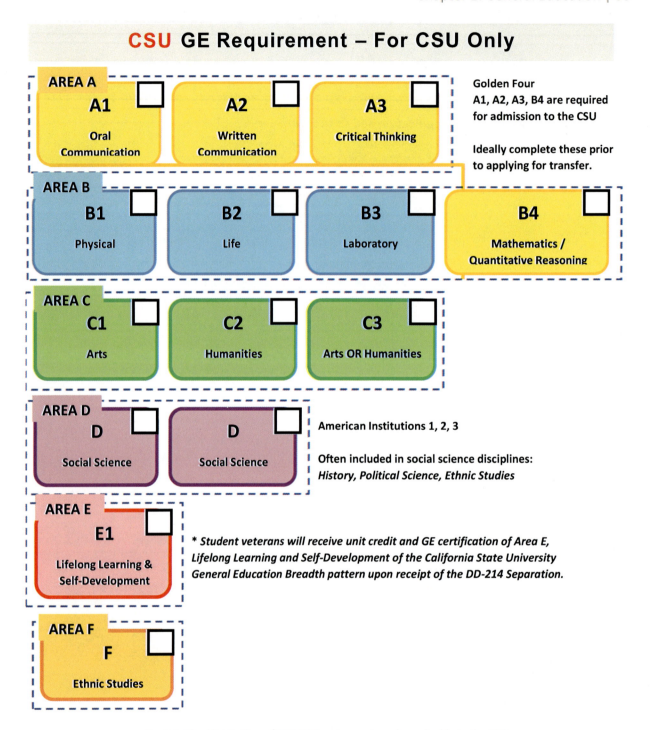

AREA A

A1 ☐	A2 ☐	A3 ☐
Oral Communication	Written Communication	Critical Thinking

Golden Four
A1, A2, A3, B4 are required
for admission to the CSU

Ideally complete these prior
to applying for transfer.

AREA B

B1 ☐	B2 ☐	B3 ☐	B4 ☐
Physical	Life	Laboratory	Mathematics / Quantitative Reasoning

AREA C

C1 ☐	C2 ☐	C3 ☐
Arts	Humanities	Arts OR Humanities

AREA D

D ☐	D ☐
Social Science	Social Science

American Institutions 1, 2, 3

Often included in social science disciplines:
History, Political Science, Ethnic Studies

AREA E

E1 ☐
Lifelong Learning & Self-Development

* Student veterans will receive unit credit and GE certification of Area E, Lifelong Learning and Self-Development of the California State University General Education Breadth pattern upon receipt of the DD-214 Separation.

AREA F

F ☐
Ethnic Studies

Fig. 0-4. Checklist Outline of CSU GE Requirements, only applicable to the CSU.

AI - American Institutions and Ideals Requirement for the CSU

Also included within the CSU GE Pattern at your local CCC is the American Institutions and Ideals (AI) requirement. The CSU Upper-Division Transfer webpage states that "every student receiving a baccalaureate degree [is required] to be knowledgeable about the Constitution of the United States, American history, and state and local government" (AI requirement from the Upper-Division Transfer page).

Most students will aim to complete the AI requirement at their local CCC, as it is more affordable, and the courses will also count towards the Area D Social Science GE. In most cases, completing these courses at your local CCC can be the most beneficial option. Still, it's important to point out that it is not required to complete the AI requirement for transfer admission, and students can complete this requirement after transferring to a CSU. In other words, the AI requirement is not a Transfer requirement; it's a requirement for CSU graduation and achievement of the baccalaureate degree. Students satisfy the AI CSU graduation requirement through coursework in three areas:

US-1: Historical development of American institutions and ideals

US-2: United States Constitution and government

US-3: California state and local government

Students can verify if a CCC course meets the AI requirement by looking at their CSU GE sheet for

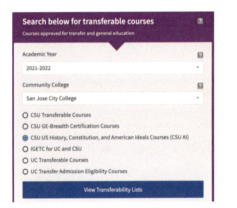

Fig. 0-5. Screenshots: ASSIST search results to verify if a CCC course meets CSU AI Requirements.

the academic year they are enrolling or by searching ASSIST, as seen below.

When searching out this information on ASSIST, the key areas you want to focus on are: US Areas 1, 2, 3, and Date Approved. Sometimes students will enroll in one AI course at one community college and then another at a separate community college. Please work with a counselor and verify on ASSIST that your courses will count towards US Areas 1, 2, and 3. I have often seen students make the error of not checking and taking two courses that count towards the same areas, like US Areas 2 and 3, but are still missing US Area 1. It's an easy mistake to make since courses can sound alike in title names; however, the only way to confirm is on ASSIST and with your Counselor's guidance.

Physical Activity for the CSU

Physical Activity courses can include disciplines in Physical Education, Kinesiology, Dance, Adapted Physical Education, or other related disciplines. These courses will fall within AREA E – Lifelong Learning for the CSU GE pattern. It's important to note that Physical Activity courses are not required for Transfer admission. However, they are often a graduation requirement at an individual campus and can be listed as *strongly recommended* or *strongly encouraged* for transfer admission to an individual CSU campus.

An important rule for transfer is when you see phrases such as ***strongly recommended***, treat it like a requirement whenever possible and aim to apply with that recommendation completed. That's one important way to remain competitive for Transfer admission that is especially true for highly competitive majors and campuses. **Figure 2.6** is an example of special guidance from San Jose State University (SJSU) included as part of their articulation report on ASSIST; in this case, two units of PE are "strongly encouraged."

IMPORTANT TRANSFER INFORMATION

Admission to San José State is competitive in all majors. SJSU continues to have more qualified applicants than available new student spaces. Because of this, SJSU is an impacted campus with impacted programs. For the most current information regarding admission impaction at SJSU please visit our website Admissions Impaction.

Prior to transferring to San José State University all transfers must earn at least 60 transferable semester units (90 quarter), including the CSU four basic skill courses required for CSU admission eligibility (except majors which have an approved CSU GE A3 waiver). Within those 60 semester/90 quarter units, students are strongly encouraged to complete the following:

1. Lower Division Major Course Requirements (especially for STEM Majors):
Complete as many of the lower division courses required for the major as possible. Many of these courses may be double counted as part of the CSU GE-Breadth 39 semester unit requirements. The lower division major courses for this major are shown below.

2. General Education (GE) Requirements:
Complete all the CSU GE Breadth requirements at the community college (39 semester units/58 quarter units). The approved courses for each area can be found at ASSIST.org under the link "CSU GE-Breadth Certification Courses" for your college. Many of these courses may be double counted to meet the major requirements shown below, so choose your courses wisely. Some SJSU majors which meet GE requirements within the majors are noted on the Exceptions for University Graduation Requirements page in our catalog. Please see your college counselor/advisor to review your general education in order to receive FULL OR PARTIAL CERTIFICATION PRIOR TO TRANSFER to San José State University.

3. Second Course in English Composition highly recommended:
All students are strongly encouraged to complete a second English composition course as part of their lower division GE prior to transferring to SJSU (either to meet CSU GE Area A3 or C2) for the greatest success in passing the Writing Skills Test (WST) at SJSU. Complete this course with a grade of "C" or better prior to registering for the WST at SJSU to avoid delays in enrollment for other SJSU courses. To register for the WST contact our Testing office at: http://testing.sjsu.edu/wst

4. American Institutions Requirement (US 1, US 2, and US 3 must be completed):
This requirement is normally two courses and can be taken as part of your CSU GE-Breadth 39 semester unit requirements (GE Area D and sometimes Area C). The approved courses can be found at ASSIST.org under the link "CSU US History, Constitution, and American Ideals Courses" for your college.

5. Graduation Requirement - Physical Education (PE): All undergraduate students who matriculate at SJSU are required to complete two units of physical education from Kinesiology/Dance activity courses, unless the major program has an approved PE waiver. Majors which have approved PE waivers are noted on the "Exceptions for University Graduation Requirements" page in our catalog.

Fig. 0-6. Screenshot: SJSU Articulation Report Special Guidance Information on ASSIST

Completion of the "Golden Four" for the CSU

Four courses are required for CSU Transfer admission listed under CSU Areas A1, A2, A3, and B4 of the CSU GE Pattern or as Areas 1A, 1B, 1C, or Area 2 under the IGETC pattern. These courses

General Education-Breadth	Intersegmental General Education Transfer Curriculum* (IGETC)
Area A - English Language Communication and Critical Thinking	Area 1 - English Communication
A1 - Oral Communication	1A - Written Communications
A2 - Written Communications	1B - Critical Thinking
A3 - Critical Thinking	1C - Oral Communications
Area B - Scientific Inquiry and Quantitative Reasoning	Area 2 - Mathematical Concept and Quantitative Reasoning

Fig. 0-7. Excerpt of the table from CSU's "Upper-Division Transfer" webpage showing the "Basic Four" areas.

are often called the "Golden Four" or the "Basic Four." All Transfer students must complete these courses with a passing grade; otherwise, they will be automatically disqualified for admission to a CSU. Here's the table from CSU's Upper-Division Transfer page showing those areas for the CSU GE and IGETC patterns (**fig. 2.7**).

Campuses will vary on how soon before Transfer they require those courses to be completed. Students can go to the CSU "Golden Four" Completion site for up-to-date campus-by-campus information, and of course, **work with your counselor** to ensure you are planning correctly.

One way to stay competitive for Transfer is to complete each "Golden Four" course with a passing grade **before** you begin filling out transfer applications. Waiting to complete those core requirement courses until the last semester or quarter before transferring means taking a big risk if you do not pass. You are also asking colleges to take a risk on you instead of admitting another student who has fulfilled their core requirements. Here's an example (**fig. 2.8**), based on a semester unit system, of what happens when a student waits to complete their transferable math course until the final semester before Transfer but they do not receive a passing grade in one of the Golden Four required courses.

Fall 2022   Spring 2023

October	February	April	May	June
Student applies to CSU Long Beach, their no. 1 choice	Student enrolls in GE Math course (CSU Area B4)	Student receives Conditional Admission to CSULB	Student receives a D grade in their GE Math course	CSULB rescinds admission offer, student is denied admission due to missing "Golden Four" core requirement for the CSU

Admissions decisions for the FALL are generally made between Feb – April for to the CSU. Colleges make those decisions with the student's Spring courses IN PROGRESS, without a student's final grades for the Spring. Therefore, if admission is granted it is CONDITIONAL pending final grades and unit completion. It is very risky to wait until the final semester to complete a core or major requirement for transfer. Offers of admission can be rescinded—withdrawn—if the requirements are not met at the end of Spring. Note, every CSU will vary – always work with your admissions representative for up-to-date information and your Transfer Center for added support.

Fig. 0-8. Example of the Result of receiving a D in a "Golden Four" course in the final semester before transfer.

The IGETC Pattern

The Intersegmental General Education Transfer Curriculum (IGETC) is the GE pattern available at the CCCs that is **_acceptable to both UC and CSU._**

Maps of all UC and CSU's across the state

Each of the 116 CCCs will offer students an option towards completing that campus's IGETC pattern. UC's pattern is different from CSU's as it captures requirements specific to UC, such as Foreign Language, and will only include GE courses that are transferable to both the CSU and the UC. You can compare CSU GE sheets with IGETC GE sheets at nearly any CCC and find noticeably fewer courses available on the IGETC. The UC generally has a narrower and stricter scope for what GEs will be allowable for each area. You can find links to the IGETC Pattern for each CCC on the CCC Transfer Counselor Website.

Students who complete the IGETC Pattern **must CERTIFY their GE requirements at their local CCC before transfer.** That certification ensures they will not be required to repeat any lower division UC requirements once they transfer. That action saves transfer students both time and money when they transfer so that rather than repeating GE courses completed at their CCC, they can instead focus on completing courses that fulfill requirements in their major or towards graduation.

Here's what is tricky about the IGETC and the UC. If you talk to most UC admissions representatives, they will tell you that the IGETC is not a Transfer requirement. Instead, Transfer students are required to complete what is called the "Seven-Course Pattern" for admission. **_That is true_**. However, completing the Seven-Course Pattern will get you in the door to a UC, but once there, the question is, do you still have to fulfill their campus GE courses to graduate? **_Yes!_** And, of course, completing the UC GE after Transfer is more costly and eats up the time needed for moving into your major coursework. For most students, the IGETC is ideal because it captures GEs for both the CSUs and UCs, and it's not a terribly long GE pattern to follow. So, let's look at the UC's IGETC subject and unit requirements table (**Table 2-2**) and UC's Basic Requirements 7-Course Pattern topic (**fig. 2-9**). Printable Version of UC's IGETC Subject and Unit Requirement and the 7-Course Pattern

Table 0-2. UC's IGETC Subject and Unit Requirement

Subject area	Required courses	Units required
1. English Communication One course in English composition and one course in critical thinking/English composition.	2 courses	6 semester units or 8-10 quarter units
2. Mathematical Concepts and Quantitative Reasoning	1 course	3 semester units or 4-5 quarter units
3. Arts and Humanities Three courses with at least one from the arts and one from the humanities	3 courses	9 semester units or 12-15 quarter units
4. Social and Behavioral Sciences Three courses from at least two disciplines or an interdisciplinary sequence	3 courses	9 semester units or 12-15 quarter units
5. Physical and Biological Sciences One physical science course and one biological science course, at least one of which includes a laboratory	2 courses	7-9 semester units or 9-12 quarter units
6. Language Other than English * Proficiency equivalent to two years of high school courses in the same language.	Proficiency	Proficiency
Total:	11 courses*	34 semester units

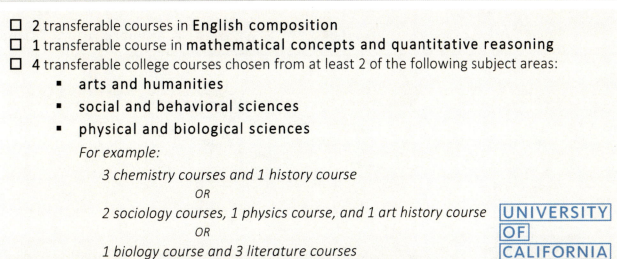

- ☐ 2 transferable courses in **English composition**
- ☐ 1 transferable course in **mathematical concepts and quantitative reasoning**
- ☐ 4 transferable college courses chosen from at least 2 of the following subject areas:
  - **arts and humanities**
  - **social and behavioral sciences**
  - **physical and biological sciences**

    For example:

    3 chemistry courses and 1 history course

    OR

    2 sociology courses, 1 physics course, and 1 art history course

    OR

    1 biology course and 3 literature courses

UNIVERSITY OF CALIFORNIA

Fig. 0-9. Adapted from UC's Basic Requirements webpage: "7-course pattern" topic.

IGETC GE Requirement – For UC & CSU

AREA 1

1A English Composition ☐	1B Critical Thinking/ English Composition ☐	1C Oral Communication ☐

1C is NOT required by the UC to fulfill the IGETC.

AREA 2

2A Mathematics / Quantitative Reasoning ☐

Golden Four
A1, A2, A3, B4 are required for admission to the CSU. Ideally complete these prior to applying for transfer for the most options at the UC & CSU combined.

AREA 3

3A Arts ☐	3B Humanities ☐	3 Arts OR Humanities ☐

AREA 4

4 Social Science ☐	4 Social Science ☐	4 Social Science ☐

American Institutions 1, 2, 3
Often included in social science disciplines:
History, Political Science, Ethnic Studies

AREA 5

5A Physical Science ☐	5B Biological Science ☐	5C Laboratory Science ☐

AREA 6

6 Language Other Than English (LOTE) ☐

* Language proficiency may be met by completion of an Area 6 course two years of high school language with C- or better, 2 year formal schooling in language that is not English, or verified competency by California Community College faculty member.

Fig. 0-10. Checklist Outline of UC and CSU IGETC Requirements – applicable to the UC and CSU.

IGETC for STEM

There is another option for the IGETC that is specific to STEM students. It's referred to as either IGETC for STEM or Partial IGETC at your local CCC. IGETC for STEM is a separate IGETC track available for students planning to major in science, technology, engineering, or mathematics (STEM). UC will accept the IGETC for STEM abbreviated courses pattern only if:

- you're earning an associate degree for transfer (ADT) at a California community college that offers IGETC for STEM as an option for those degrees AND
- the UC major program or college you're applying to accepts partial IGETC certification.

To learn more about this Transfer option, please work carefully with your CCC counselor and UC admissions representative because both those requirements can be quite narrow to fulfill. Importantly, you must ensure you are confirmed in both before assuming you can be certified for the IGETC for STEM *and* use it at the UC once you transfer (UC's IGETC for Stem abbreviated course pattern).

IGETC for CSU

IGETC for CSU simply includes the "1C: Oral Communications" GE area (**fig. 2-11**), which is a requirement for CSU and part of the CSU Golden Four.

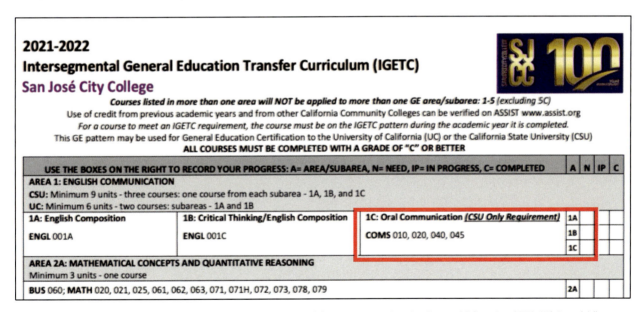

Fig. 0-11. Excerpt from: San José City College. "2021-2022 California State University General Education (CSU GE) Breadth" showing CSU Oral Communication transfer requirement.

IGETC based on Major Requirements

Every UC campus will consider the IGETC differently. Some campuses, like UC Berkeley, will build in the IGETC as a requirement for admission into any major under their College of Letters and Sciences (LAS). Although it can change at any time, this requirement has remained consistent for UC from year to year. Always check on ASSIST for up-to-date information and work with your counselor to ensure you meet all requirements for admission AND your major as shown on UC Berkeley's Articulation Agreement with San Jose City College (**fig. 2-12**).

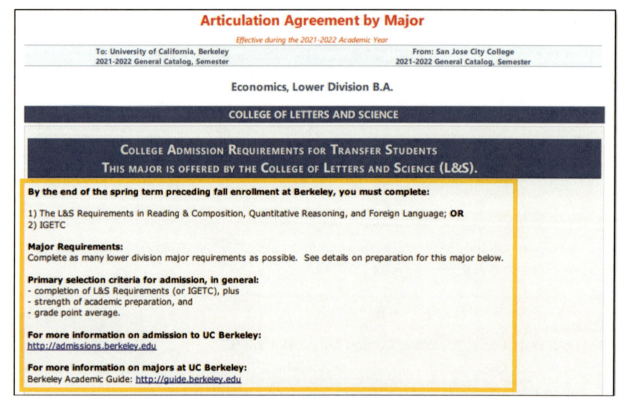

Fig. 0-12. Excerpt from UC Berkeley's Articulation Agreement with San Jose City College ASSIST report highlighting IGETC for admission to UC Berkeley.

How GE Certification Works

Let's take a moment to understand what GE Certification is. The CSU GE Pattern and the IGETC are evaluated and certified at your local CCC. That college will review your application and ensure that each standard, as defined by CSU or UC, has been fulfilled. At our college, San José City College, this is completed within the Admissions and Records (A&R) office and by evaluation specialists. Since every CCC may structure this process somewhat differently, always speak with your counselor and refer to the CCC catalog for specific information.

Usually, there is some type of form that you will need to complete to apply for GE certification. At some campuses, this may be completed online or via your student portal. In either case, you are essentially providing the following:

1. your student information;
2. the specific GE certification you are applying for (CSU GE, IGETC); and
3. the university or college you want this certification sent to

For example, you can download the San Jose City College form for General Education Certification Request (fig. 2-13). As part of this certification, it's critical that students provide official transcripts, exam scores, High School records, or any other documentation requested to confirm the fulfillment of the GE pattern.

Here are some tips to complete your GE Certification successfully.

1. Submit your request *after* you have decided which college you are transferring to and have submitted your Statement of Intent to Register (SIR) or confirmed this decision with your transfer college.
2. In many cases you *can* submit your request prior to completing your semester. It will be finalized once grades have posted for your final semester.
3. Check your email or portal for your transfer university for directions on where to send the GE certification to, campuses will vary on this.
4. Be sure to include updated official records with your GE certification request, such as official transcripts from other colleges or exam scores.
5. If you're not sure which GE certification to request, check with your counselor to ensure you are requesting the one that is appropriate to your transfer plan.

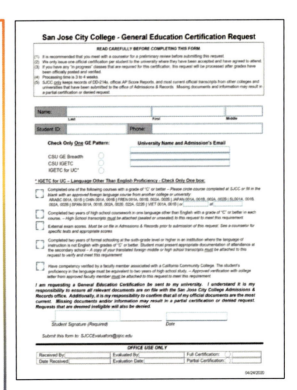

Fig. 0-13. Downloadable San Jose City College form for General Education Certification Request

So What Exactly Are AA and AS GE Patterns?

Every CCC offers students an option to complete what we call a 'local' degree program, namely either an Associate of Science (AS) or an Associate of Arts (AA) degree. Here's what's important to note about the AA and AS degree options for Transfer purposes—neither an AA nor AS degree is *required* for transfer. There are many reasons those degrees may be a great option for students to pursue, but neither is actually required for a Transfer admission.

In order to complete either the AA or AS degree programs, students are required to complete the corresponding AA GE or the AS GE pattern determined by their local CCC. Let's look at how these compare (**fig. 2-14**).

Associate of Arts (AA) GE Pattern	**Associate of Science (AS) GE Pattern**
▪ Designed to align requirements for **transfer**, at minimum to the CSU's ▪ Generally, includes **more GE requirements** as the focus is on fulfilling an academic pathway for transfer ▪ Can include **additional local requirements** set by the college or district, unrelated to transfer	▪ Designed to align with <u>**occupational**</u> degree programs and requirements ▪ Generally, **less GE requirements** allowing for more 'major' courses in occupational degree ▪ Can include GE's which are **not transferable**, but allowed as locally-based pre-requisites for occupational achievement ▪ Can include **additional local requirements** set by the college or district

Fig. 0-14. Comparison of GE Patterns for AA and AS degrees.

Here are the key points that students need to understand for Transfer purposes.

The Associate GE patterns for AA or AS are **not required for transfer, not recognized by our transfer partners**, including CSU and UC, and students **cannot receive GE certification** for transfer purposes using the Associate Degree pattern.

Since 2010, when the Associate Degree for Transfer (ADT) was first introduced into the CCC system, local degree programs have shifted a great deal. Some colleges stopped offering Associate of Arts (AA) degrees altogether, opting instead to use the ADT option for transfer students. Some colleges, like SJCC, have mainly kept AA degree programs not currently included in ADT options, such as Graphic Design or Engineering. Many colleges have done away with separate AA general education patterns and instead point transfer students to CSU GE or IGETC patterns to avoid confusion or taking additional courses. Every CCC is different, so when in doubt, ask your counselor and check your catalog.

AS degree programs operate differently from AA programs. These programs are, by nature, occupational degrees in areas like Dental Assisting, Construction, Early Childhood Education, or Automotive, and are continually focused on meeting the industry's requirements and responding to employers' feedback.

The Associate Degree for Transfer, aka the GAME CHANGER

In 2010 the earth shook, the plates shifted, and a new degree came to be within the California Community College system, commonly called the *ADT*, which is short for **Associate Degree for Transfer**. Students will see these degrees listed on their campus website or catalog as: AA-T (Associate of Arts Degree for Transfer) or the AS-T (Associate of Science Degree for Transfer). However, they all refer to the same idea; in this guide, I will refer to them all as the ADT.

In order to fully appreciate everything the ADT offers students, we must look back on how the transfer process happened before 2010, the *Old Way* to transfer. As shown in **figure 2-15**, a student would start by completing an assessment and then, in many cases, were placed into a remedial level of Math or English, which was intended to better prepare students to be successful in their transfer-level English and Math coursework. Some students could take 1-2 years to complete the remedial coursework alone. From there, the students would look to complete the General Education requirements for transfer, although in some cases, there were additional requirements to achieve an Associate degree at their college that we call *local requirements*. From there, the student would seek to complete the major requirements for the CSU campus they were seeking for a transfer. If a student were applying to more than one campus, they would follow a separate sequence of courses for each transfer campus. That's why achieving the simple goal of earning an Associate degree AND transferring could take a student 3-6 years, depending on their enrollment and assessment level.

I call the ADT the Transfer Game Changer because it did just that. As **figure 2-16** shows, students no longer take a different sequence of courses for each goal.

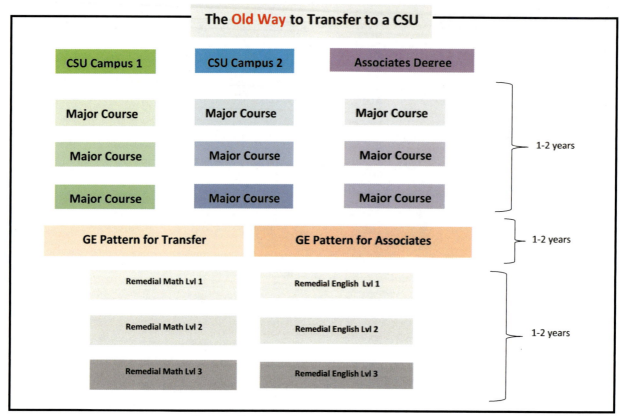

Fig. 0-15. Old Way to Transfer to a CSU.

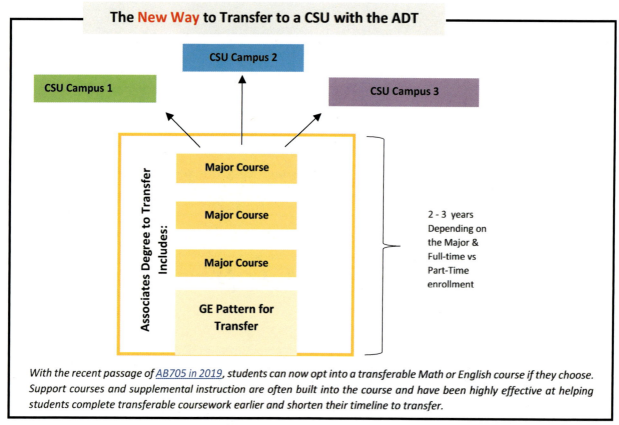

With the recent passage of *AB705 in 2019*, students can now opt into a transferable Math or English course if they choose. Support courses and supplemental instruction are often built into the course and have been highly effective at helping students complete transferable coursework earlier and shorten their timeline to transfer.

Fig. 0-16. New Way using ADT to Transfer to a CSU.

ADT required CSUs and CCCs to work together and align requirements for the major, then design Associate degrees specifically for Transfer and by major that provides students with one primary sequence or pathway of courses to meet multiple goals. One GE pattern for transfer, one set of courses for the major that would apply to *any* of the 23 CSUs, and one Associate degree that students would earn as a result. It also added other benefits, such as an additional GPA point to students applying who will have completed an ADT when they transfer. Once students transfer, the ADT holds the CSUs accountable for starting students as true Juniors. Meaning students are not moving backward when they transfer to retake GEs or lower-level major prep courses; they start as true college Juniors, which shortens and streamlines their path to graduation.

The passage of AB705 in 2019 means that students can now opt into a transferable Math or English course when they choose ADT. In addition, support courses and supplemental instruction are often built into the courses and have proven highly effective at helping students complete transferable coursework earlier and shorten their timeline to transfer.

So, is it possible to transfer in 2-years?

Answer: Yes! it's more possible now than ever before.

Works Cited

California State University. "General Education Policy." *CSU The California State University*, California State University Office of the Chancellor, www.calstate.edu/csu-system/administration/academic-and-student-affairs/academic-programs-innovations-and-faculty-development/faculty-development-and-innovative-pedagogy/Pages/general-education-policy.aspx. Accessed 28 Jan. 2023.

---. "'Golden Four' Completion." *CSU The California State University*, California State University Office of the Chancellor, Mar. 2021, www.calstate.edu/attend/student-services/casper/Pages/golden-four.aspx. Accessed 26 Feb. 2023.

---. "Introduction." *CSU The California State University*, California State University Office of the

    Chancellor, www.calstate.edu/csu-system/about-the-csu/facts-about-the-

    csu/Pages/introduction.aspx. Accessed 21 Jan. 2023.

---. "Upper-Division Transfer." *CSU The California State University*,

    www.calstate.edu/apply/transfer/Pages/upper-division-transfer.aspx.

San Jose City College. *San Jose City College - General Education Certification Request*. San Jose

    City College, 2022,

    sjcc.edu/_resources/PDF/admisssion_and_records/GE%20Certification%20Request%206.

    2022.pdf. Accessed 13 Feb. 2023.

San José State University. "Advanced Placement (AP) Exams." *San José State University.*,

    catalog.sjsu.edu/content.php?catoid=12&navoid=4077. Accessed 26 Feb. 2023. Table.

University of California Admissions. "Glossary: IGETC for Stem." *University of California*

    Admissions, admission.universityofcalifornia.edu/admission-requirements/transfer-

    requirements/glossary.html. Accessed 16 Jan. 2023.

---. "Glossary: Seven-Course Pattern." *University of California Admissions*, Regents of the U of

    California, admission.universityofcalifornia.edu/admission-requirements/transfer-

    requirements/preparing-to-transfer/general-education-igetc/igetc/. Accessed 16 Jan.

    2023.

---. "IGETC Subject and Unit Requirement." *IGETC*, Regents of the U of California,

    admission.universityofcalifornia.edu/admission-requirements/transfer-

    requirements/preparing-to-transfer/general-education-igetc/igetc/. Accessed 26 Feb.

    2023. Table.

University of California, Berkeley. "Articulation Agreement by Major: Economics, Lower Division

B.A." *ASSIST*, assist.org/transfer/report/25589110. Accessed 16 Jan. 2023.

Chapter 3: Major Prep

Major Preparation, also known as *Major Prep*, refers to lower division coursework, additional requirements, or both that transfer students will need to complete in order to fulfill Transfer admission eligibility for their major. Major Prep coursework will largely include lower division coursework required within the major at the transfer university. It may also include a GPA threshold or minimum Grade requirement to meet eligibility for the major. To fully understand Major Prep, let's take some big steps back and make sure we have a solid understanding of what a bachelor's degree is, how it's structured, and how transfer students enter their studies at a 4-year institution.

First, Degree Types.

There are essentially four levels of degree types in the United States: Associate Degree, Bachelor's Degree, Master's Degree, and Doctorate Degree. Each degree builds upon the previous level and must be completed sequentially (**fig. 3-1**).

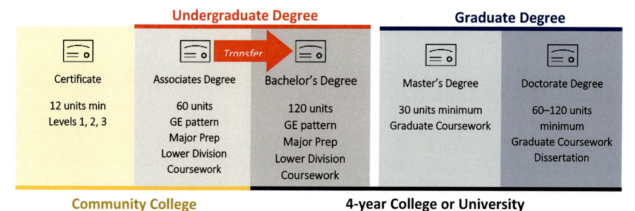

Fig. 0-1. Four Levels of Degree Types in the United States.

Community colleges differ from 4-year universities in that they can only offer lower-division coursework. **Lower division coursework** refers to the courses that match the first- and second-year student level of undergraduate study that include foundational subjects, survey courses, and introduction to the major types of courses. Generally speaking, CCC can confer certificates and Associate Degrees, but only the 4-year campuses can offer Bachelor's, Master's, and Doctoral degrees. There is an exception to this; in 2014, the CCC Board of Governors established a baccalaureate degree pilot program allowing 15 CCCs to develop bachelor's degree programs for high-demand occupational sectors ("Baccalaureate Degree").

To better understand Major Prep, let's review the parts of a bachelor's degree from a transfer perspective. In this example (**fig. 3-2**), the student is transferring from San José City College to San José State University with a major in Psychology in 2022.

120
Semester Units

Anatomy of a Bachelor's Degree

> **Example** of **Psychology Major** at San José State University

60 units – Upper Division Coursework

Upper Division — University Electives (27–28 units)

In this case elective units are built into the major. Students can use this option to pursue a minor or double major. AP or IB units can often also be applied towards graduation requirements.

Upper Division — Major Core Coursework (27 units)

Complete 1 Course From:
PSYC 100W - Writing Workshop *3 unit or* PSYC 118 - Adv Research Meth in Psych *3 unit*
Complete 1 Course From:
PSYC 102 - Psychology of Childhood *3 unit or* PSYC 112 – Psych of Adolescence *3 unit*
PSYC 114 - Psychology of Aging *3 unit*
Complete 2 Courses From:
PSYC 129 - Neuroscience *3 unit or* PSYC 135 - Cognition *3 unit*
PSYC 155 - Human Learning *3 unit. or* PSYC 158 - Perception *3 unit*
Complete 1 Course From:
PSYC 110 - Adult Psychopathology *3 unit or* PSYC 142 - Child Psychopathology *3 unit*
Complete 1 Course From:
PSYC 139 - Psychology of Personality *3 unit or* PSYC 154 - Social Psychology *3 unit*
Complete 1 Course From:
PSYC 117 - Psychological Tests & Measures *or* STAT 115 - Intermediate Statistics *3 unit*
Complete 1 Course From:
PSYC 190 - Current Issues Capstone *3 unit or* PSYC 195 - Honors Seminar in Psych *3 unit*
Psychology Electives (9 units)
Include, BIOL 129, ENGR 120, GERO 114, JS 161, KIN 167, PH 126, PH 145, POLS 177, SOCI 145.
3 units of upper or lower division psychology courses *3 unit*
6 units of upper division psychology courses *6 unit*

Each University will structure their graduation requirements in a major differently. In this example, SJSU has structured in flexibility for students to complete their major coursework with a series of options to meet their Core Requirements and has built in options for use of electives. Campuses will differ widely in how they structure graduation requirements and the kinds of upper division coursework they require. Some differences can include if they require a senior thesis, practicum hours, study abroad, lab requirements, or participation in a research project.

Be sure to study your options ahead of time and compare how your target transfer colleges differ in order to make an informed decision about which campus is a better fit for you and what to expect when you transfer.

GE and Major Preparation – Lower Division Coursework – Completed at CA community college

60 units – Lower Division Coursework

Lower Division Major Preparation
3 units	PSYCH 10 Intro to Psychology	*San Jose City College*
3 units	PSYCH 22 Intro to Research Methods	*San Jose City College*
3 units	PSYCH 31 Intro Psychobiology	*San Jose City College*
3 units	MATH 63 Elementary Statistics	*San Jose City College*

Example of required lower division coursework for a Major in Psychology at San Jose State University, completed at San Jose City College.

Lower Division — CSU General Education Pattern

1 course	3 units	Area A1	Communications
1 course	3 units	Area A2	English
1 course	3 units	Area A3	Critical Thinking
1 course	3 units	Area B4	Math/Quant Reason
1 course	3 units	Area B1	Physical Science
1 course	3 units	Area B2	Life Science
1 course	1 unit	Area B3	Science Lab
3 courses	9 units	Area C1 & 2	Arts & Humanities
2 courses	(6 units)	Area D	Social Science
1 course	3 units	Area E	Lifelong Learning
1 course	3 units	Area F	Ethnic Studies
2 courses	(6 units)	AI	American Institutions

16 courses 36 - 40 semester units

All CSU students must meet a minimum of 48 semester units of GE requirements to earn a Bachelor's Degree, including 39 units of lower division coursework and 9 units of upper division coursework

The CSU GE pattern completed at a local CA community college reflects the same areas required by the CSU system and the requirements for units.

Areas A1, A2, A3, B4 are required for admission with a passing grade of C or better. *(Note, some campuses will accept a grade of C- for these areas.)*

Fig. 0-3. San José State University Psychology, BA.

Fig. 0-2. SJSU Psychology Major with Major Prep and Lower Division Coursework Completed at a CCC.

This example (**fig. 3-3**) shows the required lower division coursework for a Major in Psychology at San José State University, completed at San José City College.

You Cannot Apply for Transfer as an Undecided Major

As you saw in **figures 3-2** and **3-3**, a bachelor's degree is a 120-units (semester) endeavor. About two-thirds of the total units will be related to your major. So, do majors matter? **They matter.** Unlike freshman-admitted students who can apply for admission as *undecided*, **transfer students cannot apply with an undecided major**; they must apply with a major declared for the UCs, the CSUs, and most private colleges and universities. They must demonstrate their readiness to transfer by completing the major prep work for *each* university to which they apply.

Of course, the follow-up question my students will pose is: "Can you change your major after your transfer?" In truth, it's tricky. At some campuses, depending on your major, that flexibility may exist. For example, I have had students transfer to a UC in one social science major, such as Community Studies, which had very little Major Prep required and was similar enough to another major, like Legal Studies, that switching early in the process was an option. In these cases, the students worked closely with their major adviser and switched early after transfer.

I've also seen the reverse hold true. I've had several students transfer to San José State University as social science majors and then decide to switch to a Business or Engineering major. Both majors include a good deal of Major Prep coursework. In a case like this, the student was advised to return to their local community college and complete the Major Prep for their new major and then come back for readmission options—which they did successfully. Each campus is different in how they handle this, but by and large, it's safer to assume for transfer that you will not be able to switch majors after transfer and so taking time to really determine which major is best for you will ultimately save you a good deal of money, time, and stress.

So—here's what's hard about that — the large majority of college students will change their major at least once as undergraduates. Changing majors as an undergraduate student is like a rite of passage in many ways; it's just part of the process of figuring out your path, and that's perfectly okay. How you overcome this situation for Transfer is to get hands-on about your choices and start EARLY in researching which majors suit you and which campuses offer them, and begin engaging with the 4-year universities.

The good news is that there are a dozen ways to start figuring out which major is best for you. One is going online and visiting university sites, the department sites for various majors, researching the coursework required to complete if you did transfer to that campus, and then comparing those results to another campus you like. Also, find ways to connect with a college by talking to their admissions representatives early. Visit the campuses you're considering when possible. Campuses hold weekly tours throughout the year that anyone can join if they call ahead. Also, be sure to visit your Career Center—there is a wealth of information, workshops, career assessments, and specialized career counselors to assist you. The point is this; it's important to move from the abstract to the practical and do so quickly. The sooner you do so, the sooner you will know what is and is not for you. That knowledge is really everything needed for transfer; it's the magic sauce. Once you have it, you can do almost anything to get where you want.

The Transfer Major Explorer tool, aka Candy for Transfer

Where to start when you are researching majors? Of course, the best place is with the Transfer Major Explorer or what I like to call Candy for Transfer.

The **Transfer Major Explorer** is graciously hosted by **Los Medanos College** and is available to ALL California community college students. It includes ALL majors listed on ASSIST by the CSU and the UC. It's a wonderful tool to use when you know what major you are looking to pursue and would like to know which campuses offer that major. And an even MORE wonderful tool when you have no idea what major you're going to decide on but need a place to start. Here's a step-by-step example of how to begin your Transfer Major Explorer search.

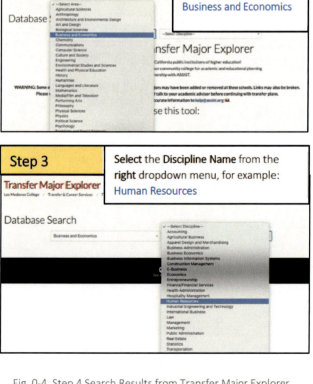

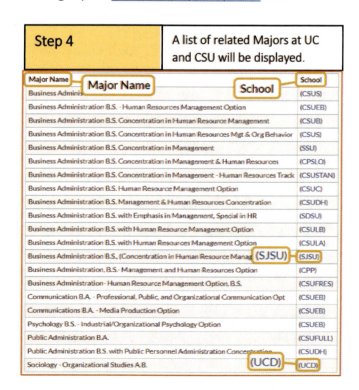

Fig. 0-4. Step 4 Search Results from Transfer Major Explorer.

Understanding Major Concentration and Degree Type

Every university will structure its degree programs in a way that is unique to them. Part of how these distinctions get communicated to students is in the Major name, the Major Concentration name, and the type of Degree. It's really important as a Transfer student to take time and really study these nuances to get clear about what to expect once you've transferred and ensure that the campus, the major, the concentration, and the degree type are a good fit.

Major Concentrations

Let's look at a major like Health Science. The names for this major do not vary much; most campuses will utilize the same major name: Health Science. However, they will differ widely in what concentrations they have structured into this major at their campus. For example, at CSU San Bernadino, there are three concentrations under Health Science: Environmental Health Concentration, Health Care Management Concentration, and Public Health Education Concentration (**fig. 3-6**).

Health Administration, B.S.	(CSUN)
Health Education B.S.	(SFSU)
Health Science (Environmental Health Concentration) B.S.	(CSUSB)
Health Science (Health Care Management Concentration) B.S.	(CSUSB)
Health Science (Public Health Education Concentration) B.S.	(CSUSB)
Health Science - Community Health Option, B.S.	(CSUFRES)
Health Science - Environmental/Occupational Health & Safety Option, B.S.	(CSUFRES)
Health Science - Health Administration Option, B.S.	(CSUFRES)
Health Science B.S.	(CSUCI) (CSUS) (SJSU)
Health Science B.S. Concentration in Community Health Education	(CSUS)
Health Science B.S. Concentration in Health Care Administration	(CSUS)
Health Science B.S. Concentration in Occupational Health and Safety	(CSUS)
Health Science B.S. with Community Health Education Option	(CSULB)
Health Science B.S. with Community Health Option	(CSUDH)
Health Science B.S. with Health Care Management Option	(CSUDH)
Health Science B.S. with Radiologic Technology Option	(CSUDH)

Fig. 0-5. Different Concentrations available for Health Science Majors found with Transfer Major Explorer.

Health Science B.S., (Concentration in Health Services Administration)	(SJSU)
Health Sciences B.S. - Administration and Management Option	(CSUEB)
Health Sciences B.S. - Community Health Option	(CSUEB)
Health Sciences B.S. - Environmental Health and Safety Option	(CSUEB)
Health Sciences B.S. - Pre-Clinical Preparation Option	(CSUEB)

The Transfer Major Explorer is the first tool students can utilize to understand which campuses offer which majors at CSU and UC. However, once you have that information, it's really important that you take time to research the upper-division course requirements for each major by its concentration. You can do this easily by typing the University name, Major name, and Concentration name into a search box. Here's an example of that (**fig. 3-7**).

Fig. 0-6. Google search results for a search phrase based on "University name_ Major name_ Concentration name."

What usually pops up at the top of your search is the Department website for this major or the university's catalog listing. The catalog listing really is the best place to find accurate information about the major and the concentration. It tends to be listed in a way that is readable and will include the full course names and descriptions, which is so important to fully understand what you'll be taking once you transfer and if it's a good fit for you. This information is *Transfer* GOLD. Another great tool for understanding the major, the concentration, and the road to graduation is the *graduation advising sheets*. Depending on the campus, those will look very different and often include a roadmap specific to transfer students. Here are some examples:

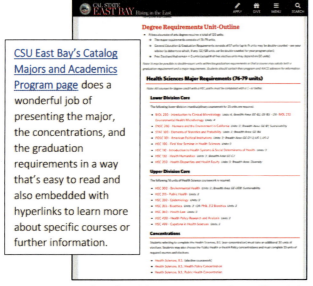

CSU East Bay's Catalog Majors and Academics Program page does a wonderful job of presenting the major, the concentrations, and the graduation requirements in a way that's easy to read and also embedded with hyperlinks to learn more about specific courses or further information.

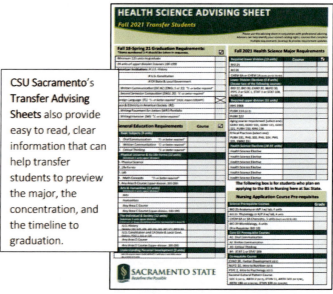

CSU Sacramento's Transfer Advising Sheets also provide easy to read, clear information that can help transfer students to preview the major, the concentration, and the timeline to graduation.

Fig. 0-7. Screenshot of Health Sciences, B.S webpage from Cal State East Bay Catalog Website.

Fig. 0-8. CSU Sacramento Health Science Transfer Advising Sheet.

As you read through the list of upper-division courses at each campus and within each concentration, you begin to see how different each option can be. For example, let's compare four main concentrations listed under a *Health Science* major from three universities (**fig. 3-1**).

Fig. 0-9. Health Science Major at Three Universities and Four Concentration Options.

Table 0-1 Comparison of Four Concentrations for Health Science Majors at CSU East Bay, CSU Sacramento, and CSU Fresno

Upper Division Coursework CSUEB Pre-Clinical Health ("Health Sciences")	Upper Division Coursework CSUS Public Health ("BS in Public Health").	Upper Division Coursework CSUF Health Admin. ("Health Science-Health").	Upper Division Coursework CSUF Envi./Occ. Health ("Health Science – Environmental").
Pre-Nursing Specialization or **Pre-Health Specialization** or **Pre-Doctoral Specialization** **Upper Division Coursework for these includes,** STAT 3031 **Statistical Methods in Biology** BIOL 3070 **Human Nutrition** ANTH 3720 **Medical Anthropology** OR SOC 4720 **Medical Sociology** HSC 3200 **Environmental Health** HSC 3300 **Health Care Systems in the U.S.** HSC 3350 **Health Legislation and Government Programs** HSC 3400 **Community Health** HSC 3550 **Health Care Law and Ethics** HSC 3800 **Multicultural Issues in Health Care**	**PUBH 112.** **Disease Prevention.** Surveys the current methods of promoting high-level wellness through a preventive medicine approach to promote more enjoyable and productive living. Attention is directed toward the specific methods of promoting personal health through various current methodologies, including the "holistic health" movement. Meets the needs of major students as well as those in allied fields such as nursing, social work, and other interested students. **PUBH 144.** **Community Health Planning and Evaluation.** Introduces students to the process and practice of program planning and evaluation. Examines the social and physical determinants of health, the impact of the community structure on health status, and the influence of personal health behavior on community health education practice. These concepts shall be applied in the planning, implementation, and evaluation of health education services.	**PH 151.** **Health Law and Legislation.** The theory and practice of managing inspection-based enforcement programs in health care and environmental health areas, with emphasis on legislation, procedure, and cases relating to public health. **PH 153.** **Principles of Healthcare Finance.** Provides foundational instruction in the practices and responsibilities of the finance function in the healthcare organization and a beginning look at the manager's role in the use of financial information. **PH 154.** **Health Care Administration.** Organizational design and managerial principles as they apply to the private sector of health care.	**PH 160.** **Principles of Toxicology.** Basic principles and concepts of toxicology with a particular emphasis on the regulation of environmental and industrial toxicants for men/women. **PH 162.** **Environmental Health Concepts.** Basic principles and concepts of environmental health with a particular emphasis on health hazards, communicable disease control, contamination control, food protection, rodent control, managing special environments, planned environments, and environmental health organizations. **PH 143.** **Occupational Safety.** Application of safety and accident prevention measures that provide a basis for insight into the hazards of occupational and industrial situations.

Table 3-1 shows how widely different each concentration can be within the Health Science major. A Pre-Clinical concentration (Col. 1) is designed for students pursuing graduate school in a health field like nursing, medical school, physical therapy, physician's assistant, and so on. A concentration in Public Health (Col. 2) is focused on education, community, and human behavior related to healthcare issues and promoting better health practices. Health Administration coursework (Col. 3) focuses on policies, regulations, finance, and other administration areas within a health provider's role. And last, Environmental/Occupational Health concentrations (Col. 4) are much more related to the hazards and safety side of health study

Types of Bachelor's Degrees

Another way that colleges will distinguish their majors is by degree type. Let's unpack what that means. Generally, most undergraduate degrees are offered as either a Bachelor of Arts (BA) or a Bachelor of Science (BS)—what's the difference? It's the coursework.

Bachelor of Arts (BA)	Bachelor of Science (BS)	Bachelor of Fine Arts
Examples:	Examples:	Examples:
▪ BA in Psychology ▪ BA in Sociology ▪ BA in English ▪ BA in Communications ▪ BA in Spanish	▪ BS in Nursing ▪ BS in Civil Engineering ▪ BS in Cellular Biology ▪ BS in Cognitive Psychology ▪ BS in Computer Science	▪ BFA in Animation ▪ BFA in Creative Writing ▪ BFA in Photography ▪ BFA in Dance ▪ BFA in Cinema

Fig. 0-10. BA Degree Examples. Fig. 0-12. BS Degree Examples. Fig. 0-13. BFA Degree Examples.

A Bachelor of Arts (BA) degree (**fig. 3-15**) will include humanities, behavior, and social sciences courses. Often the range of study is wider and allows broader options for coursework or can include a cross-disciplinary approach. *Cross-disciplinary* means that you can take courses from related majors as part of your path to graduation. So, if you are a Psychology major pursuing a BA in Psychology, you may be able to take a course in Child and Adolescent Development, Sociology, or Anthropology towards fulfilling your major requirements.

A Bachelor of Science (BS) degree (**fig. 3-16**) includes science, mathematics, engineering, or technology courses. The parameters for these majors are more structured and specialized within a specific area and, for the most part, do not offer much flexibility within the major. These courses often include lab work, **quantitative research, or technical electives. For example, a major in Software Engineering at SJSU will include technical electives in Autonomous Mobile Robots or** Cryptocurrencies and Blockchains ("SJSU BS Software Engineering Technical Electives").

Another undergraduate degree that is less common is a Bachelor of Fine Arts (BFA) degree (**fig. 3-17**). These degrees involve creative study and include areas like Dance, Drama, Music, Film, Creative Writing, and Visual Arts. Coursework in these areas is often limited within the major, highly specialized, and for the purpose of creative development in the field. Coursework may include performances, art installations, table readings, or film showings. Sometimes a bachelor's degree will include a name specific to that major. Examples include a Bachelor of Architecture (BArch) at Cal Poly San Luis Obispo, a Bachelor of Arts in Social Work (BASW) at San Jose State University, or the Bachelor of Science in Nursing available at most CSUs. These programs are similarly highly structured and specialized degrees tailored toward a specific career path.

Three Types of Majors

There are essentially three types of majors: **Career Specific Majors, Career Field Majors, and Foundation Majors**. Each type of major is structured differently and includes its own risks, challenges, benefits, and outcomes after graduation. Here's an overview of where many of our most popular majors will fall with the three types of majors (**fig. 3-14**).

Career Specific Majors	Career Field Majors	Foundation Major
- Nursing - Accounting - Finance - Engineering - Graphic Design - Social Work - Construction Management - Industrial Design - Computer Science - Dental Hygiene - Screenwriting - Game Design - Data Science - Agricultural Sciences - Viticulture (Wine Making) - Architecture - Landscape Architecture - Aviation - Horticulture - Radiology Technology - Animation	- Business - Communications - Journalism - Genetics - Health Science - Urban Studies - Legal Studies - Health Science - Kinesiology - Administration of Justice - Hospitality & Tourism - Nutrition - Pharmacology - Animal Science - Fashion Design - Teacher Credential Programs - Theater Arts - Creative Writing - Public Health - Marine Biology - Public Administration	- Sociology - Psychology - Anthropology - Biological Sciences - Literature - History - Spanish - Ethnic Studies - Linguistics - Political Science - Liberal Studies - Economics - Environmental Science - Mathematics - International Relations - Philosophy - Geology - Classics - Religious Studies - Critical Studies - American Studies - Humanities
Upside ↑ - Prepares you for a specific Career - High Paying - Training is often built into the Major - Often does not require Masters degree for career mobility	**Upside** ↑ - Prepares you for a Field with related Careers - Allows you to pivot within the field - Will often graduate faster - Allows for some exploration as part of your study	**Upside** ↑ - Prepares students in theoretical foundation of study - Allows for well-rounded exploration - Will often include research experience - Will often graduate faster
Downside ↓ - Can take longer to graduate - Less ability to explore, very structured programs - More pre-reqs required	**Downside** ↓ - Hands on experience often NOT built into the program - Getting hired, often requires experience the field - May require a Masters degree for career mobility	**Downside** ↓ - Will often require a Masters Doctorate degree for career entry - Less options for employment after graduation - Will often not include work experience

Fig. 0-11. Comparison of Three Types of Majors.

Career Specific Majors

Career Specific Majors are undergraduate majors that prepare you for a specific career. These majors require specialized training in the field. They often include some direct, hands-on work experience, training, internship, or practicum required to graduate that is built into the major. These majors may also necessitate that students pass an exam or gain licensure or certification in this specific career. For example, students who major in Nursing cannot become Registered Nurses by simply completing their BSN Coursework and graduating. At the end of their program, BSN graduates must also pass the NCLEX exam to attain RN status.

Career Specific majors often include more pre-requisite coursework, which can extend a student's timeline to graduation. For example, instead of a 4-year path, most Engineering majors average 5-6 years to graduate due to the pre-requisite courses required of their major. That added time pays off, however, as most Career Specific majors allow students to enter directly into high-demand jobs that tend to pay much higher than most other undergraduate majors. As an example, **Table 3-2**, based on the Indeed.com Salary Finder, shows the average entry-level salaries for these Career Specific Majors in California for 2022.

Table 0-2 Average Salary for Career-Specific Majors in California for 2022.

Entry Salary	Job Title	Career Specific Major
$87,000	Registered Nurse	Nursing
$99,000	CPA Accountant	Accounting
$80,000	Investment Adviser	Finance
$86-100,000	Biomedical Engineer	Engineering
$56-65,000	Graphic Designer	Graphic Design
$50-70,000	Social Worker I	Social Work
$93,000	Construction Manager	Construction Management
$84,000	Industrial Designer	Industrial Design
$122,000	Software Developer	Computer Science
$95,000	Dental Hygienist	Dental Hygiene
$67,000	Screenwriter* (Bureau of Labor Statistics)	Screenwriting
$104,000	Video Game Designer	Game Design
$119,000	Data Scientist	Data Science
$105,000	Agribusiness Manager	Agricultural Sciences
$61,000	Assistant Winemaker* (Comparably)	Viticulture (Wine Making)
$98,000	Junior Architect	Architecture
$87,000	Landscape Architect	Landscape Architecture
$121,000	Aircraft Pilot	Aviation
$68,000	Horticulture Manager	Horticulture
$71,000	Radiology Technologist	Radiology Technology
$61,000	3D Animator	Animation

Except as noted, the data presented was searched and compiled from Indeed.com's Salary Finder website.

Since these majors are specific to a career, they require very narrow, structured coursework and focus on employer needs. The downside to these majors is that there's little room for exploration; students often must commit early to this path as sophomores or even first-year students, and often the timeline to graduation is extended. However, the upside for students that enter with a great deal of clarity and commitment for these majors is that once you have completed your studies, you can truly enter these careers upon graduation, and in most cases— Social Work is one exception to this—graduate school is not required for career advancement.

Career Field Majors

Career Field Majors are undergraduate majors that prepare you to enter a career field or work sector. The coursework for these majors is focused on a field but also allows for exploring its different aspects. In addition, universities may offer concentrations within the major that relate to a specific career path. The benefit of this option is that studies are grounded in a career area, yet students can also explore and pivot inside of it.

Let's look at some examples of Career Field Majors, the common concentrations within these majors, and the typical entry salaries for these concentrations based on the Indeed.com Salary Finder for California in 2022 (**figs. 3-15–3-17**).

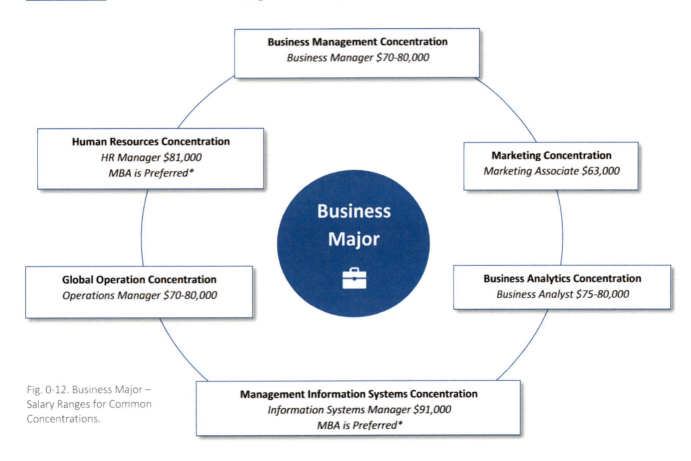

Business Management Concentration
Business Manager $70-80,000

Human Resources Concentration
HR Manager $81,000
MBA is Preferred*

Marketing Concentration
Marketing Associate $63,000

Business Major

Global Operation Concentration
Operations Manager $70-80,000

Business Analytics Concentration
Business Analyst $75-80,000

Management Information Systems Concentration
Information Systems Manager $91,000
MBA is Preferred*

Fig. 0-12. Business Major – Salary Ranges for Common Concentrations.

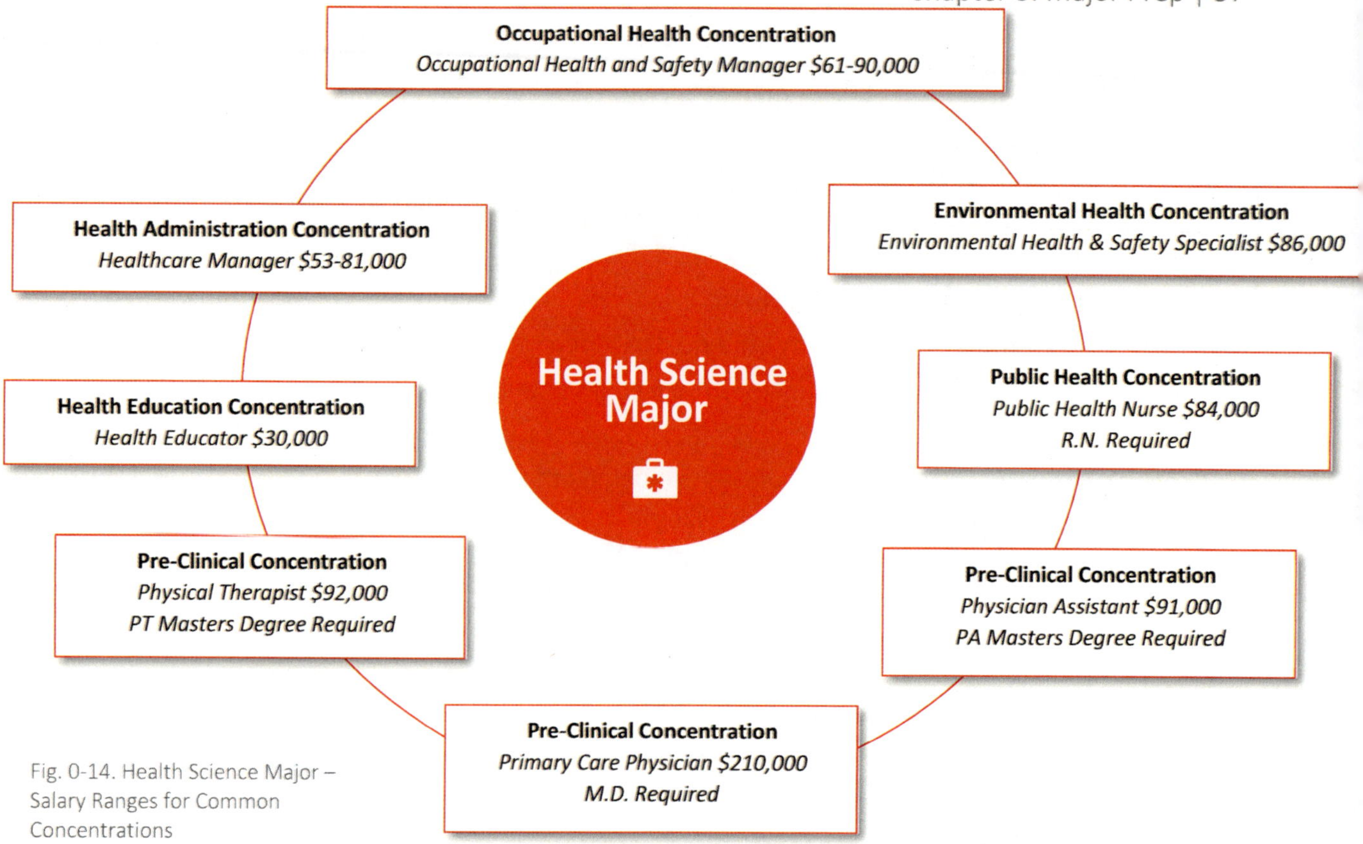

Occupational Health Concentration
Occupational Health and Safety Manager $61-90,000

Health Administration Concentration
Healthcare Manager $53-81,000

Environmental Health Concentration
Environmental Health & Safety Specialist $86,000

Health Science Major

Health Education Concentration
Health Educator $30,000

Public Health Concentration
Public Health Nurse $84,000
R.N. Required

Pre-Clinical Concentration
Physical Therapist $92,000
PT Masters Degree Required

Pre-Clinical Concentration
Physician Assistant $91,000
PA Masters Degree Required

Pre-Clinical Concentration
Primary Care Physician $210,000
M.D. Required

Fig. 0-14. Health Science Major –
Salary Ranges for Common
Concentrations

Preschool Teacher
$53,000

Elementary School Teacher
$72,000
Teacher Credential Required

Preschool Director
$62,000

Child Education Major

High School Counselor
$83,000
PPS Credential Required

School Principal
$133,000
Administrative Credential Required

Special Education Teacher
$69,000
Special Education Credential Required

Assistant Principal
$94,000
Administrative Credential Required

School Psychologist
$93,000
School Psychology Credential Required

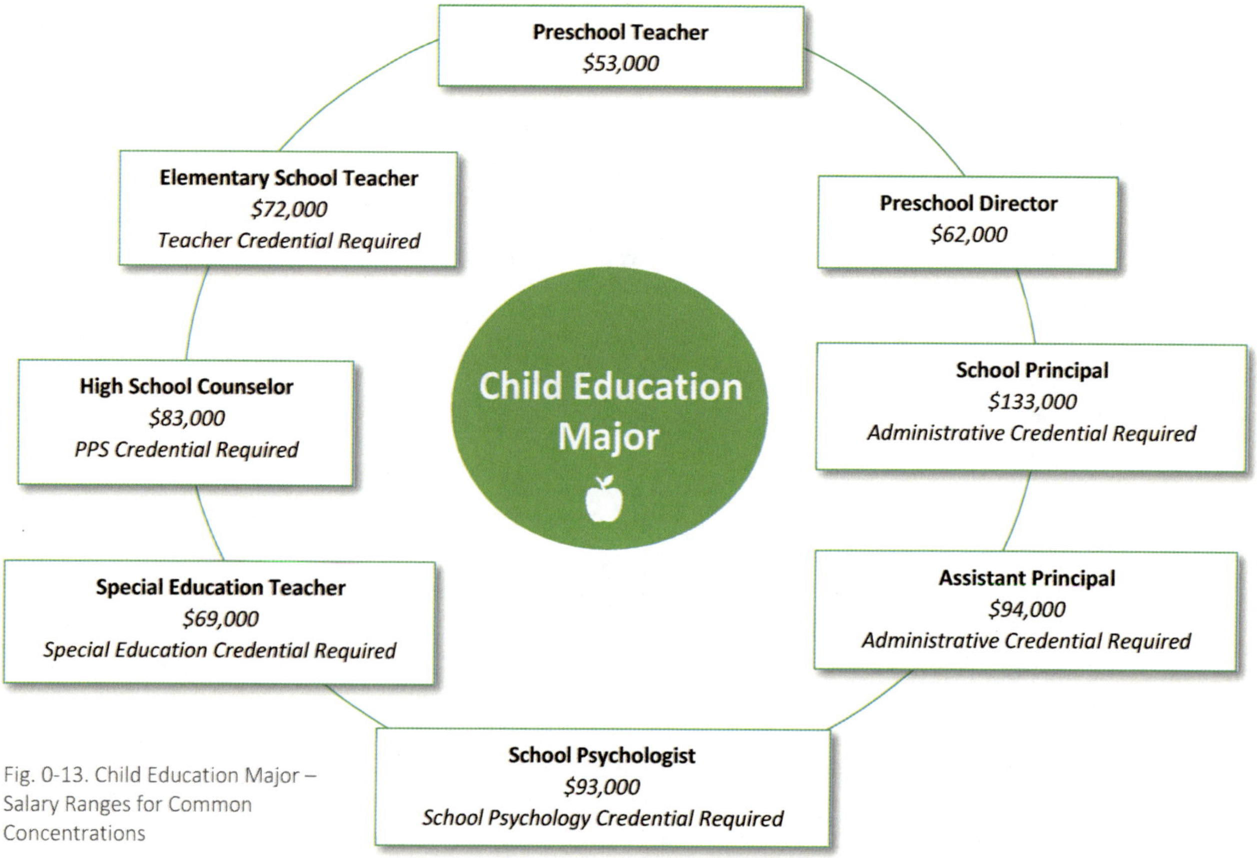

Fig. 0-13. Child Education Major –
Salary Ranges for Common
Concentrations

Career Field Majors offer students a great balance of career focus without too many prerequisites or an extended timeline toward graduation. One downside to a Career Field major is that often times to enter into the work field, graduates must have work experience or have completed internships in the field. A great example of this is Journalism or Fashion Design. Often students will need to pursue these opportunities on their own; they are not necessarily built into the major, as is the case with most Career Specific majors. Another downside is that depending on the field, further study is often required to either enter the field or to *move up* once you have begun your work experience. A Childhood Education major is a great example of a Career Field Major that will require graduate-level studies to enter the field with a credential in order to work with students in California K-12 school settings. By contrast, a student majoring in Business with a concentration in Human Resources will likely be able to enter the field without graduate-level studies, but career advancement in their field into Manager and higher-level positions will often prefer applicants with a Master's in Business Administration (MBA) if not ultimately require it.

Foundation Majors

Foundation Majors are undergraduate majors that prepare you for the theoretical foundation of studying. That is, they teach you how to think critically and to do so within a grounded academic discipline that can be applied to any number of career options. The upside of Foundation Majors is that they are popular, most colleges will include a wide umbrella of options, and they often include cross-disciplinary study or lend themselves more easily to the option of a double major or opportunities like study abroad.

I want to take a moment to give you a personal account of how *transformational* foundation majors can be. As an undergraduate student, I double majored in Gender Studies and International Relations. I was a young, queer woman coming out at 19 years of age when I began my major. My courses in Gender Studies gave me the language, history, and empowering examples I needed of women like bell hooks and Gloria Anzaldua—whose work I not only studied but completely internalized. I will forever be grateful for the Gender Studies community of students and scholars that made my coming out process an uplifting experience at a time that was very painful for LGBTQ communities.

My studies in International Relations taught me to view the complexities and interconnectedness of the world. I took courses in Systems Thinking, Economics, Microlending, Middle Eastern law, Environmental Policy, and Modern Conflict Negotiations. At face value, none of these studies directly applies to my work as a Counselor in any obvious way, and yet I can't imagine doing what I do without them. Those foundational studies gave me a way to see the world, a lens that I carry with me into everything I do. I tend to lean into the *grey areas* with comfort and find myself often probing the underlying systems that shape our work in education. I tend to value qualitative, grounded research types of evidence. These tendencies came directly from my foundational major in International Relations. I grew up in a small neighborhood in East

Los Angeles. We never left our little pocket of the city. Yet, my studies also helped me to see the world and to feel a part of it in a way that has never left me.

So — are Foundational Majors good? My goodness, YES. But — you have to have a GAME PLAN after graduation. These majors alone do not necessarily lead to a career or profession. Students can often get employed and *move up* at work based on their merit, but many careers require additional specialized study. In many cases, foundation majors are wonderful preparation for pursuing a Master's or Doctorate degree, which will prepare you for a specific profession. Let's look at an example in the diagram below for undergraduate foundation majors and their relationship to graduate school (**fig. 3-18**).

Fig. 0-15. Undergraduate Foundation Majors and Graduate School.

Here a Political Science major graduate can opt for any number of graduate school programs with their bachelor's degree. For instance, they can opt to become a Social Worker, an Attorney, or CFO. Of course, your bachelor's degree doesn't have to be the same as your graduate-level studies. It may help if it does, but generally speaking, it's not a requirement. And here's the good news about graduate school programs: students tend to like them a lot more. They are often shorter programs than a Bachelor's Degree; they are specialized and often include more applied and immersed learning opportunities. Another upside is that students with graduate-level degrees consistently show greater income levels and lower unemployment levels across the board. Here are some data tables (**figs. 3-19; 3-20**) from the U.S. Bureau of Labor Statistics that can best illustrate the differences from 2020 (Elka).

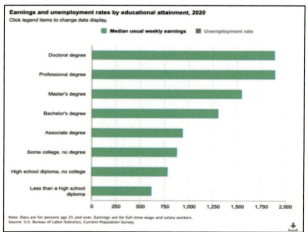

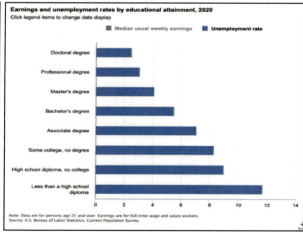

Fig. 0-16. Median Usual Weekly Earnings Data Display (Elka).　　Fig. 0-17. Unemployment Rate Data Display (Elka).

Using ASSIST for Major Prep Research

Major Prep requirements for all transfer majors at the UC and the CSU are found on Assist.org. One of the most important ways you demonstrate you are ready for your major as a transfer applicant and to make yourself the most competitive for transfer admissions is to fulfill the Major Prep coursework and requirements outlined on the ASSIST articulation reports. Let's walk through an example together. A student attending San José City College that would like to apply for transfer at CSU Pomona with a major in Business Administration and a concentration in Human Resources will complete these three steps (**figs. 3-21–3-23**).

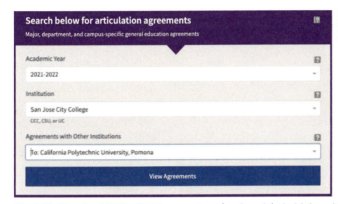

Step 1

1. Go to www.assist.org;
2. Select the current academic year in the drop down menu;
3. Select the community college you are currently attending and will transfer from;
4. Select the university you are exploring;
5. Click the bottom button that reads
6. *View Agreements*.

Fig. 3 21. Step 1 – SJCC to CSU Pomona transfer, Bus. Admin Major with Human Resources Concentration.

Step 2

1. Select the name of the Major under the list of majors.
2. Or type in the name of the Major in the search field as a shortcut to find your Major.

Fig. 0-19. Step 2 – SJCC to CSU Pomona transfer, Bus. Admin Major with Human Resources.

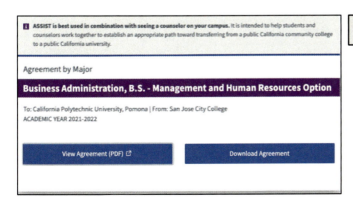

Step 3

1. Click on the bottom left button that reads *View Agreement*.
2. The Articulation Agreement by Major will then appear as a PDF that you can save or print this document for review.

Fig. 0-18. Step 3 – SJCC to CSU Pomona transfer, Bus. Admin Major with Human Resources Concentration.

How to read an Articulation Agreement by Major document from ASSIST

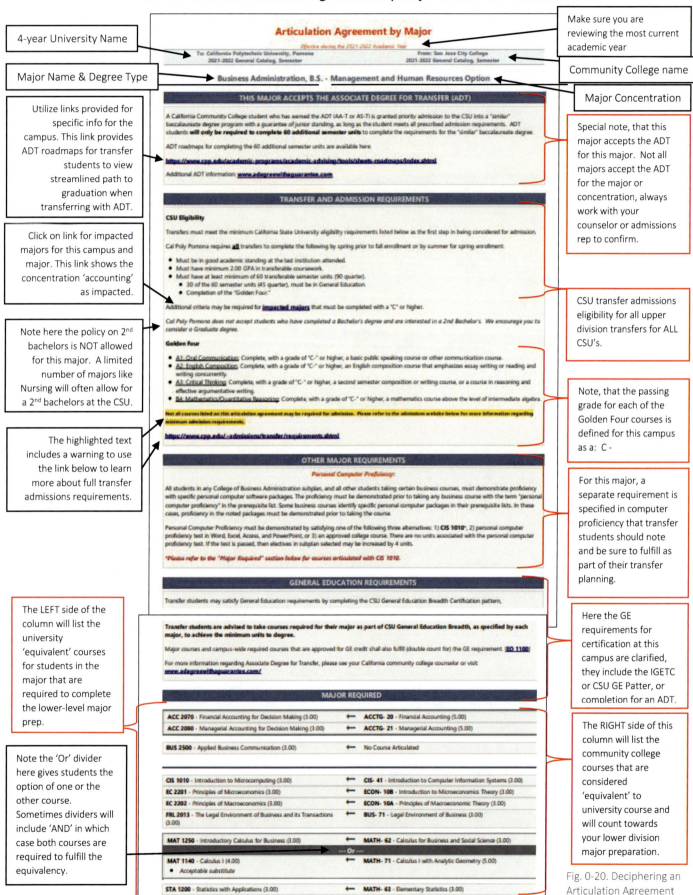

Fig. 0-20. Deciphering an Articulation Agreement from ASSIST.

Comparing Major Prep Across Campuses

Major Prep requirements for all transfer majors at each UC and CSU campus can be found on ASSIST. San Diego State University is one campus that does not post updated major prep data using ASSIST. Instead, SDSU uses its own tool called the Transfer Admission Planner to house this information. Once you have begun to identify a major or set of majors you're interested in exploring, your next step will be to compare the major prep requirements across different campuses for this major. Here's an example of the Major Prep coursework desired at three different campuses for a major in Psychology using ASSIST.

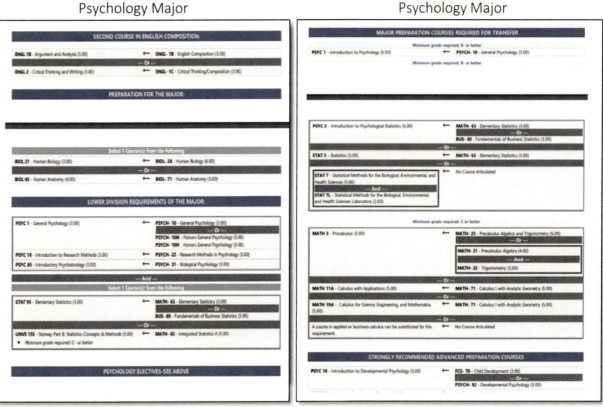

Fig. 0-21. SJSU Psychology Degree Major Prep report from ASSIST. Fig. 0-22. UCSC Psychology Degree Major Prep report from ASSIST.

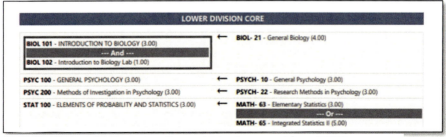

Fig. 0-23. CSU East Bay Psychology Degree Major Prep report from ASSIST.

Table 3-3 makes it easier to read the different Major Prep courses listed in ASSIST, requested by each campus for a Psychology major at San José City College. Unfortunately, there are only two courses— *General Psychology* and *Statistics*— that each of the three campuses has in common. Therefore, **it is critical to work with your counselor to plan for transfer, avoid taking more courses than you need, and ensure that the required courses and grades for transfer are met for your top campuses**. STEM majors especially are encouraged to plan carefully and early as the UC and CSU will differ widely in requirements.

Table 0-3 Same SJCC Psychology Major: Different CSU Campus Means Different Major Prep Requirements.

	1	2	3
	San Jose State Major: Psychology	UC Santa Cruz Major: Psychology	CSU East Bay Major: Psychology
ENGL 1B: English Comp OR ENGL 1C: Critical Thinking/Comp	ENGL 1B or ENGL 1C		
BIOL 20: Human Biology OR BIOL 71: Human Anatomy	BIOL 20 *or* BIOL 71		
BIOL 21: General Biology			BIOL 21
PSYCH 10: General Psychology OR PSYCH 10H: Honors Gen Psych	PSYCH 10 or PSYCH 10H	PSYCH 10 *Grade of B- or higher*	PSYCH 10
PSYCH 22: Research Methods in Psych	PSYCH 22		PSYCH 22
PSYCH 31: Biological Psychology	PSYCH 31		--
MATH 63: Elementary Statistics OR BUS 60: Fun. of Business Statistics OR MATH 65: Integrated Statistics	MATH 63 *or* BUS 60 *or* MATH 65	MATH 63 or BUS 60	MATH 63 or MATH 65
MATH 25: Precalculus / Trig OR MATH 21: Precalculus & MATH 22: Trig OR MATH 71: Calculus	--	MATH 25 *or* MATH 21 & 22 or MATH 71	
PSYCH 92: Developmental Psych. OR FCS 70: Child Development	--	*Strongly Recommended* PSYCH 92 *or* FCS 70	

Works Cited

"Assist IS Here To Help." *Assist*, California Community Colleges / California State U / U of

California, 2022, www.assist.org/. Accessed 26 Feb. 2023.

"Baccalaureate Degree Program." *California Community Colleges*, California Community Colleges

   Chancellor's Office, 2023, www.cccco.edu/About-Us/Chancellors-

   Office/Divisions/Educational-Services-and-Support/What-we-do/Curriculum-and-

   Instruction-Unit/Curriculum/Baccalaureate-Degree-Program. Accessed 17 Jan. 2023.

California Community Colleges Chancellor's Office. "Baccalaureate Degree Program." *California

   Community Colleges*, 2023, www.cccco.edu/About-Us/Chancellors-

   Office/Divisions/Educational-Services-and-Support/What-we-do/Curriculum-and-

   Instruction-Unit/Curriculum/Baccalaureate-Degree-Program. Accessed 17 Jan. 2023.

California State University. "Upper-Division Transfer." *CSU The California State University*,

   www.calstate.edu/apply/transfer/Pages/upper-division-transfer.aspx.

CAL State East Bay. "Health Sciences, B.S." *CAL State East Bay*, 2023,

   catalog.csueastbay.edu/preview_program.php?catoid=31&poid=13304&returnto=26833

   . Accessed 26 Feb. 2023.

---. "Majors and Academic Programs." *CAL State East Bay*, 023,

   catalog.csueastbay.edu/content.php?catoid=31&navoid=26892. Accessed 26 Feb. 2023.

---. "Health Sciences, Pre-Clinical Preparation Option, B.S." *Cal State East Bay: Catalog Search*,

   CSU East Bay, 2023,

   catalog.csueastbay.edu/preview_degree_planner.php?catoid=2&poid=450&print.

   Accessed 18 Jan. 2023.

Comparably. "Assistant Winemaker Salary." *Comparably*, 2022,

   www.comparably.com/salaries/salaries-for-assistant-winemaker. Accessed 18 Jan. 2023.

Elka, Torpey. "Education Pays, 2020." *U.S. Bureau of Labor Statistics: Career Outlook*, U.S. Bureau

    of Labor Statistics, June 2021, www.bls.gov/careeroutlook/2021/data-on-

    display/education-pays.htm. Accessed 19 Jan. 2023.

Fresno State. "Health Science – Environmental/Occupational Health and Safety Option, B.S."

    Fresno State: General Catalog, 2 Nov. 2022,

    www.fresnostate.edu/catalog/subjects/public-health/hseohs.html. Accessed 18 Jan.

    2023.

---. "Health Science – Health Administration Option, B.S." *Fresno State: General Catalog*, 2 Nov.

    2022, www.fresnostate.edu/catalog/subjects/public-health/hs-

    admin.html#requirements. Accessed 18 Jan. 2023.

Sacramento State. "BS in Public Health (Community Health Education)." *Sacramento State*,

    California State U, Sacramento, catalog.csus.edu/colleges/health-human-services/public-

    health/bs-in-public-health/.

---. *Health Science Advising Sheet: Fall 2021 Transfer Students*. California State University,

    Sacramento, 2021. *Sacramento State*, www.csus.edu/college/health-human-

    services/health-science/_internal/_documents/hlsc_2021transfer_advisingsheet_3.pdf.

    Accessed 26 Feb. 2023.

San José State University. "Bachelor of Science in Software Engineering: Technical Electives." *San

    José State University*, 9 Feb. 2022, www.sjsu.edu/bsse/about-bsse/technical-

    electives.php. Accessed 18 Jan. 2023.

---. "Psychology, BA." *San José State University: Catalog Search*, 2023,

catalog.sjsu.edu/preview_program.php?catoid=12&poid=3979&returnto=4146. Accessed

17 Jan. 2023.

U. S. Bureau of Labor Statistics. "Writers and Authors." *U.S. Bureau of Labor Statistics:*

Occupational Outlook Handbook, 8 Sept. 2022, www.bls.gov/ooh/media-and-

communication/writers-and-authors.htm. Accessed 18 Jan. 2023.

Chapter 4: GPA

Okay, much like the movie *Fight Club*, I'm going to ask you to repeat after me:

> The first rule of transfer: **Protect Your GPA.**

> The second rule of transfer: **Protect your GPA.**

You DO NOT need a perfect GPA to transfer successfully, *but you do need to be competitive* as an applicant, and your GPA is an important way to do that for transfer admission. So let's unpack how each system views student GPAs when evaluating transfer applications, starting with the CSU system.

Understanding Impaction at the CSU

Let's ensure we understand *impaction* and how it impacts transfer admission. *Impaction* is a term the CSUs use to describe the dynamic of what happens **when a college receives more eligible applications for admission than it has space for in the major or the campus.**

For example, suppose ten applicants are applying for Animation at a CSU, but only six seats are available in this major. The department may increase the GPA eligibility beyond the CSU entry requirement of 2.0 as part of their admissions criteria to fill these spots. Here's an example of what the looks like.

GPA Ranges at the CSU

CSU has two kinds of impaction: **Major Impaction** and **Campus Impaction.**

Figure 4-1 shows an example of *Major Impaction*, meaning a major receives more eligible applicants than there are spaces available. *Campus Impaction* is that same dynamic when there are more qualified applicants for the campus than there are spaces—in this case, usually most, if not all, majors at these campuses are impacted.

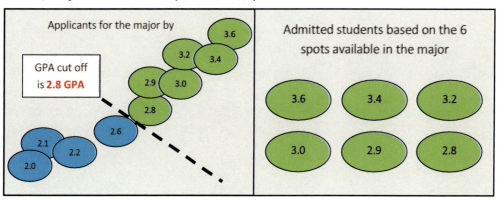

Fig. **Error! No text of specified style in document.**-1. Major Impaction - More

If we take a general view of CSU as a whole, here's a sketch of how impaction works along GPA ranges. **Non-impacted majors** tend to lay anywhere from the 2.0 to 2.8 GPA range. **Impacted majors** tend to sit between the 2.8 to 3.6 range. And some majors, like Nursing, are considered **Highly Impacted Majors**, with GPA ranges that sit around 3.6 to 4.0 depending on the campus (**fig. 4-2**).

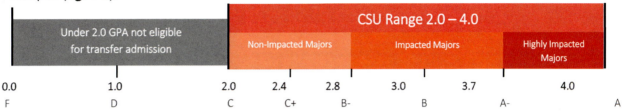

Fig. Error! No text of specified style in document.-2. Grade Ranges at CSU.

Please know this snapshot varies from campus to campus and is intended to give Transfer students a general idea of how to understand your GPA as it relates to their major, its impaction, and the chances of being competitive for your major at each campus. *Note that this GPA range is not in an official CSU guide. It is based on my knowledge and research of the general CSU GPA data available and is meant to provide a range and framework for students to see a general range of how impaction can vary by GPA.*

The difficulty in understanding CSU impaction is that, as a system, the CSUs do not provide GPA data from previous admission cycles—as the UCs do. What does that mean in practice? It means that when our students apply for CSU Transfer, to some extent, they are applying blindly. They may know that a major is impacted, but if a CSU campus does not provide GPA data from previous admissions cycles, how can students be fully informed about their options and, ultimately, which campuses and majors they are competitive to apply for? This lack of information is a critical issue of equity that our CCC counselors have been advocating about for years.

The result is that popular campuses like San Diego State University or CSU Long Beach—beautiful campuses by the beach that do not need help recruiting students—are inundated with applicants and ultimately only admit a limited number of those that apply. Yet, other wonderful CSU campuses like Cal Poly Humboldt, CSU Channel Islands, CSU Monterey Bay, San Francisco State, and even mid-range ones like CSU Fullerton, Chico, or Sonoma fly under the radar. These are great campuses with solid programs that students likely know little about and yet would have a good chance of admission if they had access to that data and could make better-informed choices.

CSU GPA threshold data for 2021-2022.

Thankfully, some CSU campuses share their GPA data for admission, which makes a world of difference for us, as CCC counselors, in helping our students. CSU Long Beach, Cal Poly San Luis Obispo, and our partner campus at SJCC, San Jose State University—each share their GPA threshold for each major or department that students should aim for as they prepare to apply. Let's take a look at how that information can make a difference in practice. **Figure 4-3** shows three campuses a Transfer student might consider for a Psychology major.

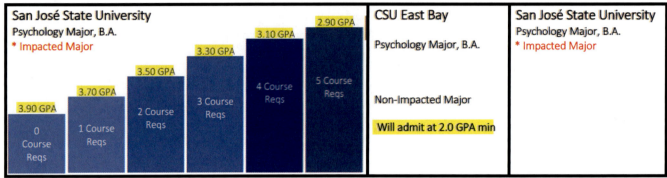

Fig. 4 3. Psychology Major GPA Threshold Comparison.

SJSU has provided details on how the number of Major Prep courses completed by the student in this major will impact how they evaluate the student's GPA. For SJSU, the more courses completed at Transfer time, the lower the GPA threshold the student needs to meet. CSU East Bay's Psychology major is non-impacted, which essentially means they will admit students for this major using the CSU Transfer minimum admission requirement of a 2.0 GPA. However, San Diego State University has listed this major as Impacted without details. Since we do not know where impaction begins along the GPA range—we don't know if a student with a 3.0, 3.2, or 3.4 would be competitive at this campus under this major. GPA is a vital factor when selecting which campuses to apply for Transfer, and that's why it is so important that our partners at CSU aid students by providing this information upfront.

In Chapter 6, we go into greater detail to understand CSU's terrain for transfer, impaction, and local vs. non-local applicants. For now, search CSU's Impacted Majors website to see if the CSU major that interests you is impacted at any CSU campus.

Understanding Impaction at the UC

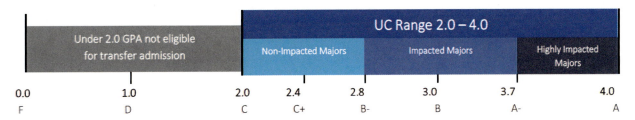

Fig. Error! No text of specified style in document.-3. Grade Ranges at the University of California.

GPA Ranges at the UC

The UC minimum GPA for transfer admission is 2.4. However, the UCs are highly sought-after Universities, so the GPA realistically needed for entry is currently more like a 2.8 GPA for non-selective majors (**fig. 4-4**).

Like Impaction at the CSUs, the UCs utilize the terms *Selective* and *Non-Selective* majors to describe the same dynamic. When there is an abundance of eligible applicants for the major, it becomes a **selective major,** or at UCSC, they call it a **screening major**. What this means for UC is the admission GPA for those majors will be higher than the 2.4 entry GPA and more along the lines of a 3.0 minimum. The UCs will also screen carefully for students who have completed the Major Prep sequence for their campus. *Again, the GPA range provided above is not an official UC range. It is, however, based on data from the UC Data Center and individual campus sites that will often share their guidelines for GPA entry.* The idea again is to provide our transfer students with a big-picture look at where selective and non-selective majors often lay. Always reference the individual UC sites for the most accurate information about your major. Below is an example from UC Santa Cruz of the screening (**fig. 4-5**) and non-screening majors (**fig. 4-6**) available to transfer.

Fig. Error! No text of specified style in document.-5. UC Santa Cruz Fall 2023 Screening Majors for Transfers Selection

Fig. Error! No text of specified style in document.-4. UC Santa Cruz Fall 2023, Non-Screening Majors for Transfer Students

In order to further examine these options, the UC provides a great tool that can't recommend enough for transfer students; it's the UC Data Center Transfer Admissions profile from each admissions cycle. Students can basically look to see the GPA range where transfer students were previously admitted, how many applications were received for their major, and the overall rate of acceptances. If you know of a campus you really want to attend, this is an excellent way to start planning early and getting a clear-eyed sense of marks you need to hit, in terms of your GPA, to get there.

Here's a snapshot of the Fall 2021 transfer admissions cycle at UCSC using the UC Data Center Transfer Admission profiles (**fig. 4-7**).

Broad discipline	College/ School	Major name	Applicants	Admits	Enrolls	Admit GPA range	Enroll GPA range	Admit rate	Yield rate
		Theater arts	109	81	17	3.27 - 3.78	2.88 - 3.64	74%	21%
Foreign Languages & Lilterature	Not applicable	Language studies	60	42	9	3.02 - 3.48	2.86 - 3.12	70%	21%
		Linguistics	86	74	13	3.14 - 3.80	3.17 - 3.80	86%	18%
Interdisciplinary Studies	Not applicable	Cognitive science	140	52	17	3.07 - 3.76	2.59 - 3.46	37%	33%
		Undeclared	283	114	21	3.20 - 3.72	3.07 - 3.48	40%	18%
Law	Not applicable	Legal studies	187	143	35	2.97 - 3.62	2.76 - 3.54	76%	24%
Letters	Not applicable	History	293	241	52	3.05 - 3.72	2.86 - 3.52	82%	22%
		Literature	346	282	55	3.03 - 3.71	2.91 - 3.67	82%	20%
		Philosophy	187	152	26	3.07 - 3.73	2.78 - 3.38	81%	17%
Mathematics	Not applicable	Mathematics	212	166	27	3.17 - 3.80	2.84 - 3.50	78%	16%
		Mathematics education	21	13	3	3.33 - 3.92	masked	62%	23%
Physical Sciences	Not applicable	Astrophysics	73	52	18	3.16 - 3.65	2.84 - 3.56	71%	35%
		Chemistry	185	84	12	3.16 - 3.76	2.75 - 3.20	45%	14%
		Earth science	137	117	32	3.03 - 3.51	3.04 - 3.37	85%	27%
		Earth science/anthropology	16	14	3	2.96 - 3.39	masked	88%	21%
		Physics	86	61	14	3.29 - 3.74	2.97 - 3.43	71%	23%
Psychology	Not applicable	Psychology	1,483	542	154	3.20 - 3.81	3.08 - 3.66	37%	28%
Public Admin & Social Serv ..	Not applicable	Community studies	159	126	29	2.99 - 3.59	2.96 - 3.63	79%	23%
Social Sciences	Not applicable	Anthropology	325	258	77	3.05 - 3.73	2.86 - 3.69	79%	30%
		Economics	708	525	62	3.15 - 3.74	2.82 - 3.32	74%	12%
		Global economics	55	23	3	3.37 - 3.81	masked	42%	13%
		Politics	568	439	85	3.09 - 3.76	2.76 - 3.34	77%	19%
		Sociology	756	505	108	3.06 - 3.72	2.88 - 3.51	67%	21%

Totals may vary slightly from data elsewhere because this dashboard uses applicant level provided by the evaluating campus, rather than at the time of application.

Fig. Error! No text of specified style in document.-6. UC Santa Clara Fall 2021 UC Data for Transfers by Major

In this case, you can see the difference between the screening major (Psychology) and the non-screening major (Anthropology). Psychology received 1,483 applications and admitted 37% of those applicants within a GPA range of 3.2 to 3.81. In contrast, the non-screening major, Anthropology, received 325 applications and admitted 79% of those applicants within a 3.05 to 3.73 GPA range.

As a Transfer student, you can spend time exploring your options and using these tools to be savvy about your choices and prepare to apply for majors you know you either already satisfy the GPA eligibility or are within reach. Especially for students that know the campus they want to attend 100%. I've had many

2020 Highly Selective Majors" in the UCLA College				
SELECTIVE MAJOR	APPLIED	ADMITTED	ALTERNATIVE MAJORS	RELATED MINOR
Biochemistry	362	37%	Math/Applied Science, Biophysics	Public Health
Biology	955	21%	Computational and Systems Biology, Anthropology B.S.	Biomedical Research
Business Economics	2,077	12%	Applied Mathematics, Asian Studies	Entrepreneurship
Communication	1,185	9%	Linguistics, Comparative Literature	Digital Humanities
Economics	1,271	17%	Math/Economics, African and Middle Eastern Studies	Accounting
Human Biology and Society B.S	136	17%	Psychobiology, Anthropology B.A	Public Health
Microbiology, Immunology and Molecular Genetics	216	27%	Molecular, Cellular and Development Biology, Physiological Science	Biomedical Research
Political Science	1,377	39%	History, Philosophy	Public Affairs
Psychology	2,243	19%	Cognitive Science, Linguistics and Psychology	Applied Developmental Psychology
Sociology	1,650	38%	Gender Studies, African American Studies	LGBTQ Studies

* The demand for the major significantly exceeds the space available. This list does not include all highly selective majors. Majors within our specialty schools are considered highly selective and some require supplemental applications and/or auditions/interviews.

Fig. Error! No text of specified style in document.-7. UCLA Comparison of Highly Selective

diehard students seeking to transfer to UCLA or UCB. In this case, if you know that your GPA is vulnerable, then you may want to spend time reviewing similar majors. In fact, UCLA speaks openly about this dynamic, where they receive as many as 30,000 applications and most of those to their top 20 majors, yet they have 125 major options for students. They are literally asking applicants to consider *alternative majors*. Many of these majors are quite interesting and usually fall under the umbrella of the bigger-named majors (**fig. 4-8**).

The TAG GPA for Transfer

The UC shares the updated TAG GPAs for its campuses each year using the UC TAG Matrix. Although the information is written in a very technical way—mostly as a cheat sheet to aid counselors, it is also available at each UCs' TAG site (there's a table with links in Chapter 7 to aid you with this).

Basically, the TAG GPA is a separate GPA for students applying to UCs with the **TAG**. The TAG, which stands for ***Transfer Admission Guarantee***, is a separate application that CCC students can use in tandem with their UC application. Students are required to meet additional criteria, such as taking their Math and English required courses early, but on the flip side, they benefit from a guaranteed admission if they meet the TAG eligibility and complete the requirements. That's why the TAG GPA is a huge benefit.

As you can see from **figure 4-9**, a CCC applying to UC Davis into a highly selective major like Engineering would benefit greatly from applying with the TAG, especially if they are applying with a GPA closer to 3.5 or 3.6—it removes some of that vulnerability for the student.

UC Davis – TAG GPA Range 2022-2023 (Based on the UC TAG Matrix)

2.4	3.0	3.2	3.5	4.0
C+	B	B	B+	A

- College of Agricultural and Environmental Sciences: 3.2
- College of Biological Sciences: 3.2
- College of Letters and Science: 3.2

College of Engineering: 3.5

Fig. Error! No text of specified style in document.-9. UC Davis TAG GPA Range Adapted from the 2022-23 UC TAG Matrix data.

UCDAVIS
COLLEGE of ENGINEERING

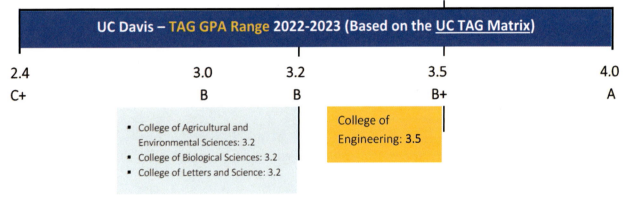

UC Transfer Admission Data Fall 2021

Major name	Applicants	Admits	Enrolls	Admit GPA range	Enroll GPA range	Admit rate	Yield rate
Aerospace science and engineering	171	23	5	3.58 - 3.87	3.58 - 3.76	13%	22%
Biomedical engineering	132	22	6	3.68 - 4.00	3.63 - 3.95	17%	27%
Chemical engineering	112	20	6	3.61 - 3.92	3.62 - 3.76	18%	30%
Civil engineering	245	62	18	3.59 - 3.94	3.45 - 3.82	25%	29%
Computer engineering	172	16	9	3.72 - 3.94	3.67 - 3.98	9%	56%
Computer science & engineering	572	19	4	3.70 - 3.99	masked	3%	21%
Engineering	232	76	21	3.58 - 3.91	3.58 - 3.80	33%	28%
Environmental engineering	32	6	4	3.69 - 3.94	masked	19%	67%
Mechanical engineering	425	83	24	3.60 - 3.89	3.43 - 3.76	20%	29%

Fig. Error! No text of specified style in document.-8. UC Davis College of Engineering Fall 2021 Transfer Admission Data from UC "Transfers by Major."

I encourage students to take time to really study the individual UC TAG sites by campus and the UC TAG matrix. Students will often get confused about the TAG and think they can TAG to several campuses or that it's automatic when they apply for transfer. It's not, and there are a lot of criteria, like the student's GPA, which qualify students for the TAG at each campus. We'll discuss this more in chapter 7.

Types of GPAs

Let's take time to fully understand the kinds of GPAs considered for Transfer admission. One is the *Overall GPA* or the *Cumulative GPA*. That GPA is calculated based on ALL of the student's coursework together. The other kind of GPA that's key to transfer admission is the *Major GPA* or the GPA for the major prep coursework as outlined by the University. Here's an example of these two at work. Let's look at the full coursework for a student seeking to transfer into a *Civil Engineering major* at a UC or CSU (**fig. 4-11**).

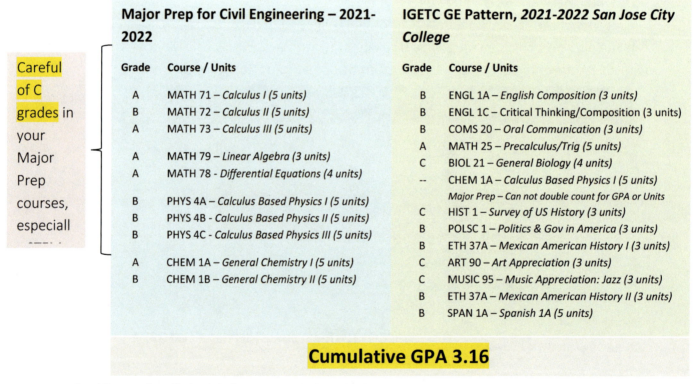

Fig. Error! No text of specified style in document.-10. Civil Engineering: Major Prep vs IGETC GE Pattern. Printable Version [link]

The cumulative GPA in this example is the total GPA for the entire transferable coursework of the student. It can all differ between CSU and UC cumulative GPAs if there is coursework included that is transferable to the CSU and not to the UC. One strategy to stay on top of that nuance is using the UC TAP account (which we'll discuss in Chapter 7) to calculate your UC transferable units and GPA.

Major Prep GPA will differ based on the university since each campus may count different courses towards the major prep for that same major. This nuance can get tricky; work with your CCC Counselor and Admissions representative for assistance to make sure you are calculating this GPA correctly. Also, be sure to read ASSIST major preparation reports carefully; they will list if a campus will NOT accept a C grade for their major prep. It's often UC campuses and STEM majors that will include these kinds of limitations. In those cases, a C grade can compromise your acceptance even if your Major Prep GPA still meets the requirements.

Transferable GPA's

Student GPAs get especially tricky once we start looking at the transfer status for each course. When you view your coursework on your student portal, it may list the units of each course under the *unofficial transcript* or *degree progress* section. However, these are not always the most accurate views for calculating **either units or GPA for transfer**. That's because each course you take could have a different transfer status. There are three main kinds of transfer status for CCC courses:

☐ UC and CSU transferable
☐ Only CSU transferable
☐ Non-transferable.

When the CSU and UC calculate your GPA for transfer, they ONLY INCLUDE the courses transferable to their system. So CSU will only include CSU transferable courses, and UC will only include UC transferable courses. Let's look at an example from a student's Fall semester coursework and grades. In this semester, one student can have three different GPAs based on the transfer status of their courses (**Table 4-1**).

Table Error! No text of specified style in document.-1. Sample CCC Student Fall Semester Courses and Grades

Fall Semester		CCC Earned	CSU Transfer	UC Transfer
ESL 92 - Advanced ESL Course	A grade	3 units	0	0
CIS 44 - Web Development	B grade	3 units	3 units	0
SOC 10 - Intro to Sociology	C grade	3 units	3 units	3 units
MATH 63 - Intro to Statistics	B grade	3 units	3 units	3 units
MATH 120 - Tutoring for Statistics	A grade	3 units	0	0
		15 units 3.0 GPA	9 units 2.67 GPA	6 units 2.5 GPA

In this case, two courses (6 units) are UC transferable, so the grades for those two courses make up the UC transferable GPA. The same is true for the CSU transferable courses. Most students see only the first column in their student portal, which lists CCC units. However, those units include transferable AND non-transferable coursework. We use these units for wider purposes, such as qualifying for financial aid, occupational courses, and non-credit courses that can benefit our students. You do not have to calculate these courses yourself, but you should know there's a difference. Many students I meet with are unaware of this difference. Sometimes they assume their GPA is higher than it is, and we must work closely to determine eligibility for the UC or impacted programs at the CSU. In other cases, students may not know how high their GPA is, and the reverse can be true. For example, I've had students with low grades in non-transferable math courses like a 5-unit Beginning Algebra course that weighed down their CCC GPA. However, their UC and CSU GPAs were quite strong.

How to calculate your UC transferable GPA

Summary—Based on Self-Reported Certified (ASSIST/UC) Data

GPA & Units:

	GPA:(Grd Pts/Units)	Units(Sem/Qtr) Complete:	IP/PL:	Total:
ASSIST Certified Courses:	3.48 (183.0/52.5)	35.00/52.50	21.00/31.50	56.00/84.00
Total Courses:	3.48 (183.0/52.5)	35.00/52.50	21.00/31.50	56.00/84.00
Total Exams:		0.00/0.00		0.00/0.00
Overall Total:	**3.48**	**35.00/52.50**		**56.00/84.00**

Fig. Error! No text of specified style in document.-11. Using the UC TAP to Obtain A True UC GPA for Transfer.

In truth, the CSU GPA for transfer is much easier to calculate since a larger portion of the CCC courses will transfer to the CSU. The UC is much more selective in which courses are permitted for transferable credit. To assist with this, UC provides a wonderful tool called the UC TAP which stands for Transfer Admission Planner (we discuss this more in Chapter 7.)

Using the UC TAP, students enter their coursework which is ASSIST-verified for UC transfer status and are then given their true UC GPA under the summary section (**fig. 4-12**, blue box); this weeds out the non-transferable and CSU-only courses. Note that only courses taken at a CCC are vetted through the UC TAP. For students starting out, it's a great way to track progress as you go, and for students preparing to transfer, it's an equally great tool for gauging their UC GPA and eligible majors.

GPA Calculator Tool

For students interested in tracking their GPA, especially those who have attended multiple CCCs and are seeking to find their combined GPA, SJCC Counselor Beverley Stewart has shared a tool for students that is a wonderful help. It's a GPA Calculator Excel spreadsheet that allows students to enter their courses, the units, and grades received, then calculates the combined semester units and GPA (**fig. 4-13**). It's very helpful when seeking to combine courses from different colleges or especially to project your future grades and see how quickly your GPA can gain points in one or two semesters/quarters.

College	Class	Quarter Units	Semester Units	Standard Units	Grade	Grade Value	Grade Points
De Anza CC	EWRT 1A	4		2.67	B-	2.7	7.20
De Anza CC	MET 10	5		3.33	A-	3.7	12.33
De Anza CC	MET 10L	1		1.67	C+	2.3	1.53
De Anza CC	SOC 15	4		2.67	B+	3.3	8.80
San Jose City College	MATH 63		3	3.00	B	3.0	9.00
San Jose City College	COMS 20		3	3.00	A	4.0	12.00
San Jose City College	ETH 37A		3	3.00	B	3.0	9.00
San Jose City College	OCEAN 10		3	3.00	B	3.0	9.00
				0.00		0.0	0.00
				0.00		0.0	0.00
				0.00		0.0	0.00
				0.00		0.0	0.00
				0.00		0.0	0.00
				0.00		0.0	0.00
				0.00		0.0	0.00
				0.00		0.0	0.00
				0.00		0.0	0.00
				0.00		0.0	0.00

Total Units: 21.33   Total Grade Points: 68.87

GPA: 3.2281

Fig. Error! No text of specified style in document.-12. Screenshot of Downloadable GPA Calculator.

Everyone Arrives at College with a different Academic Story

As a counselor, one of the hardest conversations I have with students is about their grades. Students pile a lot of judgment on themselves when they don't pass a course, have to withdraw from a course, or when they just know the grade doesn't reflect what they could have earned. **Everyone arrives at college with a different academic story. But almost no one is immune from having felt burned by a school in some way growing up.** Maybe it was an instructor that you had a conflict with or that didn't really see you and your potential, or a counselor that didn't really listen or make that extra effort, or the overall system of education that felt like you just rolled through it. There are absolute rock star educators, people that change lives every day—yes. But, if we're honest, we have to acknowledge that at all levels of education, there are folks that, through direct or indirect behaviors, through intentional or nonintentional avoidance, have caused hurt and distrust in our students, and that shows up with every student that has ever stepped onto a college campus.

Some of the most powerful conversations I've had with my students, in class or counseling sessions, have been unpacking the shame they carry around their grades as a reflection of somehow falling short or a reflection of a teacher that let them down. The whole process of grading itself can't help but make any student feel like they are being judged. **There's a power dynamic to grading that is embedded in every course**. When instruction is done well, the student knows with certainty what is expected and how to achieve the grade they're aiming for, and it's an affirming experience. You feel proud of the grade, or if it's not what you hoped for, at least it feels fair, and you know how to do better next time. When instruction is not done well, the assessments feel confusing, you feel lost trying to understand how you're being graded, the instructor may not communicate well, or worse makes you feel like they don't care about you or your *situation,* the grading itself seems unfair and afterward leaves you feeling distrustful.

I can definitely relate to both experiences. I've had incredible teachers and ones that left me feeling confused and upset. I totally get that. What helped me recover from the not-so-great teachers were those wonderful and caring instructors that restored my faith in the system. It's hard, though, if you haven't had a truly great instructor who pours their love for learning into you. The ones that are not just teaching the content of their course but lighting that fire inside you, bringing joy to learning; they make you feel smart and seen and give hope that you CAN do this. **Why does this experience matter?** Because it affects how you see yourself profoundly, how open you can be to looking for and finding the good in your college, and how hard you can hang on to your own sense of hope will make all the difference in your grades and, ultimately, in your opportunities for transfer.

One of the biggest ways students hurt themselves for transfer is getting by with more Cs than Bs. You don't have to have all As to transfer--that's great if you do. A's help, and yes, some highly competitive majors might require that—but most majors don't. Yet, if you were to receive all Bs for every single class you take at your community college, you would have a 3.0 GPA and qualify for honors status. And is that enough to transfer well? More than enough, it's enough to qualify for scholarships and be the one that's picking the college rather than hoping the college will pick you. **Your GPA gives you POWER.** Even though it is in no way a measure of how smart or capable you are, it does give you **CHOICE** and **OPPORTUNITY**.

How do C grades hurt you for transfer?

The thing about C grades that's more difficult than D or F grades **is that you cannot retake a course with a C grade.** You can't remove a C grade from your transcript. Even if you retook the same class for transfer, CSU or UC would only count the first passing grade—the C—over the following grade. The result is that C grades hang on your overall transcript like a big weight holding it down. One C grade or two is not the end of the world, yet once you start gathering your fair share of C's, it's like plucking the wings off a butterfly and expecting it to fly—it can only go so high.

If I have one message for transfer students, it's to **avoid C grades as much as possible so that you have the MOST options when you apply for transfer.** Now, let's say a student applies for transfer with all C grades. Can that student still apply for a transfer? Absolutely, *BUT* it limits your options—in some cases greatly—as to what majors or campuses might grant you Transfer admission.

Let's talk about the fine line between a B grade and a C grade.

As an instructor, I have to tell you I don't know that students are fully aware of how closely the line can fall between earning a B grade over a C grade. It can come down to one too many absences, not submitting a late assignment, even for partial credit, or not tracking your grade on Canvas from the start to avoid dipping below a B grade. Here's a general list of things that students earning a B grade over a C will do with some consistency that can make all the difference. These are not perfect students, but they are effective students who have formed habits or a mindset that helps them make those little, everyday wins that add up.

- ☐ They **monitor their grades on CANVAS** or check in with their instructor to get a sense of their grade.
- ☐ They **ask questions in class**, especially about assignments, to make sure they complete them correctly.
- ☐ They might miss a class or two, but they **try to make up their absence** by getting copies of notes or making up any lost points.
- ☐ They **show up to class on time** and aim not missing classes often.
- ☐ They **buy their books** for class, and they **read their materials** for class regularly.
- ☐ They **stay focused in class**, don't get distracted by their phones, and **take notes.**
- ☐ They **rewrite their notes** after class as a way to study, especially for their most difficult classes.
- ☐ They try to **hold boundaries with loved ones** and let others know that school is a priority.
- ☐ They **hold boundaries with work** and talk to their supervisor about their school schedule.
- ☐ They **try not to procrastinate** on assignments; they **utilize school resources** like the library for quiet spaces or computer access, laptop lending, or book lending.
- ☐ They **give themselves enough time** to study for tests and form study groups when needed.
- ☐ They **use tutoring and writing center resources** when they need them, especially if they're falling behind.
- ☐ They **participate in student programs** like EOP&S, PUENTE, UMOJA, or disability services that help them stay on track and connect with other students.
- ☐ They **avoid taking more classes than they can manage** and take a long view of their progress.
- ☐ They **read their emails, download CANVAS** to their phone, keep a **student calendar** to track their assignments and plan ahead.
- ☐ They're realistic when scheduling their courses and **try not to overestimate their time.**
- ☐ They **stay on top of their financial aid, apply for scholarships, and seek** resources.
- ☐ They talk to other students about **recommended instructors** and follow instructors that are a great fit.

What I hope you get from these examples is that these actions are all simple small habits, behaviors, or a mindset that anyone can take on. **I can tell you with 100% certainty that this is where your power lies as a student to change the narrative about college and to transfer on YOUR terms.** Your GPA does not have to be perfect, but it does need to be competitive. Small wins really do add up, so take time to reflect on the little changes you can make to gain that extra edge and position yourself to have the most options when applying for Transfer admission.

D and F grades

First, it's important to note that courses with *D* or *F* grades are repeatable. A **D** indicates a **less-than-satisfactory** grade, and **F's** indicates **unsatisfactory grades**.

The UC system campuses, without exception, do not accept *D* grades for any transferable coursework. The CSU, in contrast, will accept a *D* grade in a course – with some limitations. For example, several campuses will ask that students receive a passing score or a C or above grade in their major prep coursework. For students seeking to transfer to the CSU for non-impacted majors, it may be feasible to carry *Ds'* and still keep moving forward so long as your transferable GPA is 2.0 or above. As always, check with your counselor and admissions representative to help vet your coursework to ensure you meet the eligibility GPA for your Transfer major and campus.

Academic Renewal – Type I

There are two ways to remove *D* and *F* grades from holding down your GPA. The first one is familiar to most students--that is, to *retake the course and score a passing grade that will replace the D or F grade*. Once the course is retaken, your transcript will adjust to look something like this (**fig. 4-14**). Note that your transcript will still list the first time the course was taken and the original grade; however, it will also list *AR* or *E* or some other variation that indicates the grade is not factored into the student's GPA.

First Semester

ENGL 1A — English Composition I	3.0 Units	**(D) AR**

Second Semester

ENGL 1A — English Composition I	3.0 Units	A

Academic Renewal – Type II

There is a second type of Academic Renewal option for students that allows them to remove *D* or *F* grades WITHOUT having to retake these courses. The method isn't as well-known as Type I despite being such an important tool for transfer. If there were a meme or tweet I could send

Fig. Error! No text of specified style in document.-13. Example of Type I Academic Transcript Renewal – Removing Ds and Fs from GPA Calculation by retaking the course.

around the world, it would be about Academic Renewal—Type II.

Here's how Type II works. A student will apply with the help of their Counselor to submit an application for Academic Renewal. Together they will identify the courses requested to be removed from their GPA. Some campuses will allow as many as 24 units worth of grades to be removed, while others will allow for as limited an amount as 12 units. The campus will have some version of a GPA policy; for example, the applicant will have to demonstrate they have improved their GPA with either 12 units of a 3.0 GPA or 24 units of a 2.0 GPA since the last course seeking to be removed. Campuses will also differ as to when they allow students to apply for Academic Renewal. Some campuses will ask students to apply as early as one year since the last course they are seeking to remove or as many as three years since the final course. At most campuses, Academic Renewal is a tool that can be utilized once, so doing so at the right time and with the right guidance is very important.

Let's look at an example of how Academic Renewal—Type II—can work. Imagine a student that began their first semester as a nursing student. That student loaded up on science courses only to find it was not a good fit. That student then changed their major to Business and was now flourishing. It would make no sense to have the student retake the preparation for nursing courses in order to move forward toward their goals. So, in this example (**fig. 4-15**), the student is applying to have their entire first semester of courses or a total of 14 units removed from their cumulative GPA.

First Semester

CHEM 15 – Chemistry Fundamentals	(4.0 Units) (0.00)	(D) AR
BIOL 20 – General Biology	(4.0 Units) (0.00)	(F) AR
HSCI 8 - Medical Terminology	(3.0 Units) (0.00)	(D) AR
FCS 19 – Nutrition	(3.0 Units) (0.00)	(F) AR

Fig. Error! No text of specified style in document.-14. Example of

As you can see, it works the same way as Academic Renewal—Type I. The courses are listed, but **the units and grades do not calculate into the cumulative GPA or unit count**.

For a list of Academic Renewal applications offered within each CCC, visit the CCC Transfer Counselor site to help navigate these applications across different campuses (**fig. 4-16**).

Students can apply for academic renewal at *multiple colleges*. So, for example, if you were enrolled at De Anza College over ten years ago and received your share of D and F grades. Years later, you enrolled at SJCC, and this time you did well and earned a GPA of at least 2.0 and above for 24 units. I would advise you to use your SJCC transcript to apply for Academic Renewal at De Anza College in order to repair your GPA and prepare for transfer. In fact, this is an important step to take before completing the transfer admissions applications so that students are applying with the best possible GPA. The process can take weeks, so the best advice is to start early and work with your Counselor to plan for the best time to apply.

Fig. Error! No text of specified style in document.-15. Example of an Academic Renewal

Let's talk about: Withdraw (W)

I once had a former student who transferred to UCLA come to talk to my current Transfer students about his journey. He called himself a *late bloomer* and was so generous with his time and his story. He began his studies at a local community college straight out of high school and didn't do well. He would hop in and out of school. It wasn't until he'd lived more and worked a lot more that he decided to go back to school in his mid 20's—when as he put it, he felt like an old man. To his surprise, he did amazing. He enjoyed school this time around. He even became a journalist for the campus paper and earned awards for his work. His new GPA this time around was nearly 4.0. His life still carried its share of challenges, but what had changed when he returned to school was him. He knew *why* he was there and had become passionate about learning for its own sake. My students loved hearing him speak, but they still felt like his journey was different from theirs. He could sense their resistance when finally he blurted out to them,

"Look, guys, I got into UCLA, and I had 16 W's. If I can do this, you can do this."
I'll never forget that moment. How much my students gasped from shock and how relieved it made them feel. The first thing to know about W's is that, yes, you can transfer successfully with W's! Even as many as 16.

What is a W? A 'W' on your transcript stands for Withdraw. It means you started a course and did not finish the course, that's all. It is not factored into your GPA and, in many cases, can be a good tool to protect your GPA if used cautiously. Although W's may not impact your transfer admissions options, they will most certainly impact your eligibility for financial aid if you earn too many of them. If you'd like to know how many are too many, ask your financial aid office for more information.

How to avoid a Withdraw? Students usually have the first two weeks of school to try their courses out. After that, there's a deadline at each campus; at San José City College, we call it *Census Day*. Students that officially drop their course before or on Census Day will not receive a Withdraw on their transcript.

Let's talk about: Excused Withdraw (EW)
In many cases, students find they must drop out to manage the personal challenges they face. The pandemic has made us all greatly aware of the critical situations and life events that can interrupt our plans for school. It is so important that when these events arise, students know how best to go about this process so that it does not penalize them in the future. This situation is where Excused Withdraw (EW) comes into play. It allows students to withdraw from their course(s) for excused emergency situations without hurting their access to financial aid or compromising their ability to re-enroll at a subsequent time. For assistance with these options, reach out to your Counselor, the Admissions Office, Records Office, or all three for assistance.

Let's Talk about: Incomplete (I)
An Incomplete (I) is an option for students that are not able to complete the final assignment(s) or exam(s) for the course but, **with the approval and collaboration of their instructor**, are provided extended time after the course to complete the course requirements. The student's grade is

marked as an 'I' on their transcript temporarily until the requirements have been satisfied and the instructor can update the student's grade.

At our college, students have a year to complete the requirements agreed upon with their instructor. Not doing so in time could result in an F grade. I have worked with students in the past who were very close to completing the semester of a class in good standing before life took a turn. That's when the additional time to complete an assignment or project in the course made all the difference. Please note that each class is different. Some courses might lend themselves more easily to this option. In any event, it is a policy that students should be aware of and in contact with their instructional faculty to learn more. Again, each college may vary in terms of how they structure this policy, but each CCC will offer this option in some form.

Let's Talk about: Pass / No Pass (P/NP)

Another option for students seeking to protect their GPA is to take a course with a Pass/No Pass grade. That means if a student earns the equivalent of an A, B, or C grade, it will show on their transcript as a P. If the student earns a grade of D or F, it will likewise show on their transcript as an NP. In either case, the passing or non-passing grade will be noted but not calculated into their GPA. Taking a course as a P/NP can be a good strategy to relieve the pressure of a grade. Still, it should always be decided upon with your counselor's guidance since colleges will often not want major prep coursework to be taken as a Pass/No Pass option. During the pandemic, this was one form of relief offered to students that suddenly had to take courses remotely and, as a result, hurt their GPA. However, since life is slowly shifting passed the pandemic, this remains a helpful option for students that should also be taken cautiously and in consultation with a Counselor or admissions representative.

GPA, like a Credit Score, can quickly shift in your favor with a few right moves.

I cannot overemphasize how quickly your student GPA can shift in your favor with some simple but powerful changes. Let's look at a few examples.

Carrying a D and C grade

Class	Quarter Units	Semester Units	Standard Units	Grade	Grade Value	Grade Points
PE Course		1	1.00	B	3.0	3.00
PE Course		1	1.00	B	3.0	3.00
Science Course		3	3.00	D	1.0	3.00
English Course		3	3.00	A	4.0	12.00
Math Course		3	3.00	C	2.0	6.00
			0.00		0.0	0.00
			0.00		0.0	0.00
		Total Units:	11.00	Total Grade Points:		27.00
				GPA:		2.4545

Academic Renewal for a D grade

Class	Quarter Units	Semester Units	Standard Units	Grade	Grade Value	Grade Points
PE Course		1	1.00	B	3.0	3.00
PE Course		1	1.00	B	3.0	3.00
Science Course			0.00	AR	0.0	0.00
English Course		3	3.00	A	4.0	12.00
Math Course		3	3.00	C	2.0	6.00
			0.00		0.0	0.00
			0.00		0.0	0.00
		Total Units:	8.00	Total Grade Points:		24.00
				GPA:		3.0000

Fig. Error! No text of specified style in document.-16. Using Academic Renewal to Flip the D grade.

Here's an example of a student *using Academic Renewal to flip their D grade* (fig. 4-17), moving their GPA from 2.45 to 3.0 for this semester.

Carrying a D and C grade

Class	Quarter Units	Semester Units	Standard Units	Grade	Grade Value	Grade Points
PE Course		1	1.00	B	3.0	3.00
PE Course		1	1.00	B	3.0	3.00
Science Course		3	3.00	D	1.0	3.00
English Course		3	3.00	A	4.0	12.00
Math Course		3	3.00	C	2.0	6.00
			0.00		0.0	0.00
			0.00		0.0	0.00
		Total Units:	11.00	Total Grade Points:		27.00
				GPA:		2.4545

Flipping a D grade to an A

Class	Quarter Units	Semester Units	Standard Units	Grade	Grade Value	Grade Points
PE Course		1	1.00	B	3.0	3.00
PE Course		1	1.00	B	3.0	3.00
Science Course		3	3.00	A	4.0	12.00
English Course		3	3.00	A	4.0	12.00
Math Course		3	3.00	C	2.0	6.00
			0.00		0.0	0.00
			0.00		0.0	0.00
		Total Units:	11.00	Total Grade Points:		36.00
				GPA:		3.2727

Fig. Error! No text of specified style in document.-17. Retake the Course to Flip the D Grade to an A Grade.

Using the example above, here's how a GPA can dramatically increase when a student *retakes a course to flip their D grade to an A grade* (fig. 4-18).

At the same time, imagine the same student taking the required Math course as a P/NP to protect their GPA and then using a Withdraw to protect their GPA in their Science course. That student would have earned a 4.0 GPA for the same semester versus the first example of earning a 2.45 GPA (**fig. 4-19**). Again, this is a great example of options students can use to be strategic and cautious in order to protect their GPA and their eligibility for transfer admissions.

Carrying a D and C grade

Class	Quarter Units	Semester Units	Standard Units	Grade	Grade Value	Grade Points
PE Course		1	1.00	B	3.0	3.00
PE Course		1	1.00	B	3.0	3.00
Science Course		3	3.00	D	1.0	3.00
English Course		3	3.00	A	4.0	12.00
Math Course		3	3.00	C	2.0	6.00
			0.00		0.0	0.00
			0.00		0.0	0.00
		Total Units:	11.00	Total Grade Points:		27.00
				GPA:		2.4545

Use of a W and a P/NP

Class	Quarter Units	Semester Units	Standard Units	Grade	Grade Value	Grade Points
PE Course		1	1.00	A	4.0	4.00
PE Course		1	1.00	A	4.0	4.00
Science Course			0.00	W	0.0	0.00
English Course		3	3.00	A	4.0	12.00
Math Course			0.00	P	0.0	0.00
			0.00		0.0	0.00
			0.00		0.0	0.00
		Total Units:	5.00	Total Grade Points:		20.00
				GPA:		4.0000

Fig. Error! No text of specified style in document.-18. Using a W and a P-NP to Protect GPA.

Last, **figure 4-20** is an example of a student who used a P/NP option for their Math course and then an Incomplete in their Science course. This student did not have to retake the Science course but instead gained an extension to complete their assignment and was able to protect their GPA.

Use of an IC and P/NP

Class	Quarter Units	Semester Units	Standard Units	Grade	Grade Value	Grade Points
PE Course		1	1.00	A	4.0	4.00
PE Course		1	1.00	A	4.0	4.00
Science Course			0.00	IC	0.0	0.00
English Course		3	3.00	A	4.0	12.00
Math Course			0.00	P	0.0	0.00
			0.00		0.0	0.00
			0.00		0.0	0.00
		Total Units:	5.00	Total Grade Points:		20.00
				GPA:		4.0000

Flipping an Incomplete

Class	Quarter Units	Semester Units	Standard Units	Grade	Grade Value	Grade Points
PE Course		1	1.00	A	4.0	4.00
PE Course		1	1.00	A	4.0	4.00
Science Course		3	3.00	A	4.0	12.00
English Course		3	3.00	A	4.0	12.00
Math Course			0.00	P	0.0	0.00
			0.00		0.0	0.00
			0.00		0.0	0.00
		Total Units:	8.00	Total Grade Points:		32.00
				GPA:		4.0000

Fig. Error! No text of specified style in document.-19. Using an IC and P-NP to Protect GPA.

These are some simple examples that I hope illustrate a larger point, that your GPA can be repaired and protected with the use of a few policies like Academic Renewal, Incomplete, Withdraw, Excused Withdraw, and Pass/No Pass when used in collaboration with your Counselor or instructional faculty.

When is your GPA evaluated for transfer admission?

A final point regarding your GPA that is especially important when applying for transfer admission is knowing when the admissions office will review your GPA. Let's explore how a GPA can shift drastically for a student applying for Fall admissions.

In the case shown below (**fig. 4-21**), the student ended the Summer before application season with a 2.4 GPA. The student then applied for academic renewal at two different colleges to remove D and F grades and received a GPA boost to 2.8 GPA. That updated coursework and GPA were submitted during the Fall application period ending Nov. 30th.

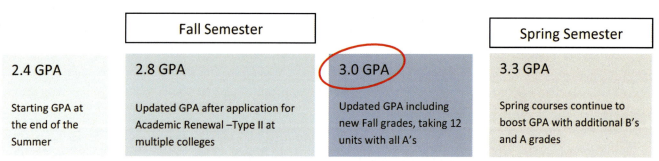

Fig. Error! No text of specified style in document.-20. GPA Evaluation Periods for Transfer Admission.

After submitting that application, the student also did incredibly well during their Fall semester and opted to take additional units to increase their GPA further, earning all A's in 12 units. By January, that student would report their Fall grades to the CSU and UC. And ultimately, the January updated GPA, the 3.0, is the one ultimately evaluated for their Transfer major and admissions. So, even if the student went on to achieve an even higher GPA by performing well in the Spring, the 3.0 GPA earned for Fall grades becomes ultimately the one that the admissions decision is based on.

The final, final points on GPA for transfer?
1. Avoid C's as much as possible.
2. Use AR, W, EW, I, and P/NP options with your counselor's guidance as a tool to protect your GPA.
3. **Protect** Your GPA.
4. **Protect Your** GPA.
5. **Protect Your GPA.**

Works Cited

Board of Governors of the California Community Colleges. Academic Record Symbols and Grade

Point Average – § 55023 Withdrawal– § 55024. California Community Colleges

Chancellor's Office, [2018]. California Community Colleges, www.ccccо.edu/-

/media/CCCCO-Website/About-Us/Divisions/Office-of-the-General-Counsel/Regulation-

Notices/Excused_Withdrawal_AS_FILED_Regs.pdf. Accessed 4 Mar. 2023.

California Community Colleges. "GE, Academic Renewal, ADT, Catalogs and Centers." *CCC

Transfer Counselor Website*, ccctransfer.org/ge/. Accessed 26 Feb. 2023.

California State University. "Impacted Undergraduate Majors and Universities, 2023-24." *CSU The

California State University*, California State University Office of the Chancellor,

www.calstate.edu/attend/degrees-certificates-credentials/Pages/impacted-degrees.aspx.

Accessed 22 Jan. 2023.

UCLA Undergraduate Admission. "Highly Selective Majors* in the UCLA College." *UCLA

Undergraduate Admission*, Regents of the U of California, 2023,

admission.ucla.edu/apply/transfer/deciding-on-major. Accessed 12 Feb. 2023. Chart.

UC Santa Cruz. "Non-Screening Majors for Transfer Students: Non-Screening Majors." *UC Santa

Cruz | Undergraduate Admissions*, Regents of the U of California, 2023,

admissions.ucsc.edu/posts/non-screening-majors. Accessed 12 Feb. 2023.

---. "Screening Majors for Transfers: Screening Major Selection Criteria." *UC Santa Cruz |

Undergraduate Admissions*, Reagents of the U of California, 2023,

admissions.ucsc.edu/posts/screening-major-selection-criteria. Accessed 12 Feb. 2023.

University of California. "Transfers by Major." *University of California*, Regents of the U of California, 9 Feb. 2023, www.universityofcalifornia.edu/about-us/information-center/transfers-major. Accessed 12 Feb. 2023.

University of California Admissions. "Transfer Admission Guarantee (TAG)." *University of California Admissions*, Regents of the U Of California, admission.universityofcalifornia.edu/admission-requirements/transfer-requirements/uc-transfer-programs/transfer-admission-guarantee-tag.html. Accessed 25 Jan. 2023.

---. *Transfer Admissions Guarantee (TAG) Matrix 2022-2023*. Regents U of the California, 2022, admission.universityofcalifornia.edu/counselors/_files/tag-matrix.pdf. Accessed 13 Jan. 2023.

---. "Transfer Admission Planner." *University of California Admissions*, Regents of the U of California, uctap.universityofcalifornia.edu/students/. Accessed 25 Jan. 2023.

Chapter 5: Application

How do you know when you're ready to apply for transfer?

Working with your Counselor, you will identify together when you are ready to apply for transfer based on how close you are to finishing your coursework. Using your **Student Education Plan (SEP)** is helpful because it's broken down semester by semester (or quarter by quarter), and you can begin to see the finish line as you cross out courses completed.

In truth, the final year of enrollment is the most difficult because that's when you usually take the hardest courses. During that final year, it is also more difficult to register for courses because you need to find the exact remaining courses that align with your schedule, and it's also the year you actively apply for Transfer. **Figure 5-1** shows how to use your remaining units to estimate when to apply for transfer based on full-time or part-time enrollment.

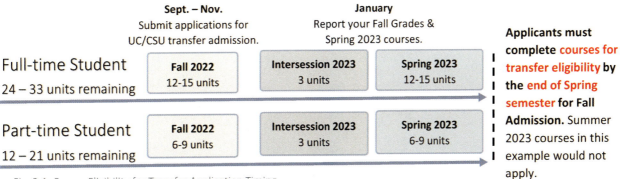

Fig. 0-1. Course Eligibility for Transfer Application Timing.

I include here the use of our Intersession term at San José City College that begins and ends in January. Other colleges may include their own version of an Intersession, like a Winter session that operates similarly, allowing students to space out their units. Additionally, you can see below that *when* you're ready to transfer is based largely on how many units you can complete in the final year to satisfy the 60 transferable units required and also fulfill the GE pattern and Major Prep requirements. Note that the application cycle involves the entire year. It includes *two application submissions* to the CSU and the UC, one in the Fall and again in January. Also, note how important Fall grades are in the year you apply because they get factored into your final cumulative and major GPA.

When you apply to transfer depends on which transfer admissions cycle you will enter. The **transfer admissions cycle** is *the process from the start to finish of applying to transfer for any one season.* There are four main admissions cycles for transfer admission: **Fall, Winter, Spring, and Rolling Admissions.**

Fall Admissions Cycle

The main application cycle for CCC students applying for transfer to nearly any system is the **Fall Admissions Cycle (fig. 5-2)**. This cycle includes the UC, the CSU, California private colleges, and out-of-state options. **The biggest benefit to focusing your application on Fall Admissions is that the most campuses AND the most majors are open for transfer,** which means you have the most chances for admission and the most options available!

| Apply Fall **2022** | → | Attend Fall **2023** | Fig. 0-2. Apply in Fall 2022 to attend college in Fall 2023. |

Figure 5-3 shows how the **Fall admissions cycle for** *the CSU system* looks throughout the year.

CSU Fall Admissions Cycle for Transfer

August	September	October	November	December
		CSU Application Opens Oct. 1st	CSU Application Deadline is Nov.	Some CSU's offer extended deadlines in Dec. & Jan.

January	February March April	May	June	July	August
CSU Supplemental Applications are due throughout January. Each application &	CSU's start to review transfer applications using student's Fall Grades and reported Spring coursework. Notifications of CSU admission happen between Feb-April.	May 1st is the deadline to SIR, or accept admissions offer to 1 CSU and pay deposit. Students register for summer orientations and other next steps to begin classes in the		Official College Transcripts & AP/IB scores due in July to the CSU. Dates will vary at each campus.	Fig. 0-3. CSU Fall Admissions Cycle.

In contrast, **figure 5-4** shows a breakdown of how the **Fall admissions cycle for** *the UC system* looks throughout the year.

UC Fall Admissions Cycle for Transfer

August	September	October	November	December
UC Application is open to begin entry on Aug.	UC TAG Opens for submission on Sept. 1st Deadline to Apply for the UC TAG is Sept. 30th	UC Application is open for Submission Oct. 1st	Deadline to submit application is Nov. 30th	Some UC's offer extended deadlines in Dec. & Jan.

January	February March April May	June	July	August
The UC's Transfer Academic Update (TAU) is due Jan. 31st One submission goes to ALL UC campuses.	UC's start to review transfer applications using student's Fall Grades and reported Spring coursework. Notifications of UC admission happen between Mar.-May.	June 1st is the deadline to SIR, or accept admissions offer to 1 UC and pay deposit. Students register for summer orientations and other next steps to begin classes in the	Official College Transcripts to the UC are due July 1st AP/IB scores to the UC are due July 15th	Fig. 0-4. UC Fall Admissions Cycle.

Spring Admissions Cycle

As you can see, during the Fall Admissions Cycle, the UC and CSU deadlines operate fairly similarly. This changes for Spring Admission (**fig. 5-5**). Here's an overview of those differences.

The CSU Spring Admission Cycle varies greatly from campus to campus. Figure 5-5 is an example of San José State University's Spring Admissions cycle.

Apply Summer **2022** → Attend Spring **2023**

Fig. 0-5. Apply in Summer 2022 to attend college in Spring 2023.

CSU Spring Admissions Cycle

August	September	October	November	December	January
CSU Application Opens Aug. 1st Closes Aug. 31st	After Aug. 31st, students will receive notice of admission sometime between Sept.-Dec., it varies. Some campuses will request official transcripts during this period, others will wait until January.				Official College Transcripts & AP/IB scores are generally due in January after Fall grades have posted.

Once offered admission, students will need to submit their SIR-statement of intent to register to 1 CSU —confirming their acceptance, and be prepared to pay the admissions deposit.

Note - only courses completed up to the end of the Fall Semester can be used for admissions eligibility (Transferable Units, GPA, Golden Four, Major Prep).

Fig. 0-5. SJSU Spring Admissions Cycle.

There are two UCs with admit cycles for Spring / Winter Admissions: **UC Merced and UC Riverside**. Here's an overview of their admissions cycle (**fig. 5-7**).

UC Fall Admissions Cycle for Transfer

April	May	June	July	August
	UC TAG Opens for submission on May 1st Deadline to Apply for the UC TAG is May 31st		UC Application is open for Submission July. 1st Deadline to submit application is July. 31st	

September	October	November	December	January
The UC's Transfer Academic Update (TAU) is due Mid September One submission goes to ALL UC campuses.	Oct. 15th is the deadline to SIR for UC Riverside	SIR to UC Merced is due in November Official College Transcripts & Scores of coursework up to the end of the Summer is due for UC Riverside Nov. 1st		Final Transcripts with Fall Grades is due in Jan. for UCM, and for UCR Jan. 15th

Fig. 0-7. UC Spring/Winter Admission Cycles for UC Merced and UC Riverside.

The Transfer Center is HOME BASE.

The Transfer Center is your hub throughout the transfer process, but most especially when you begin the actual application process. It is where you can connect with your local UC, CSU, and Private college admissions representatives—and *you should* connect with them. In addition, the Transfer Center is where you can learn about scholarships for transfer students. But most importantly, this is where you can begin your application materials and have them reviewed by others to ensure there are no errors to troubleshoot or any other issues. Each application—the UC, CSU, or the Common Application—is intensive and based on self-reported data. In order to make admissions determinations, the applications asks students to enter their entire coursework and grades. **Now, is it easy to make errors when reading through the application and entering one's entire transcript? YES. A BIG BIG YES.**

Why does this matter? **Making an error in your application can lead to *automatic disqualification*.** Here's a common example of how easy it is to make an error in your application. Let's say you took SPANISH 1A for five units. The first time taking the course, you received an F grade. The next semester you retook the same course and received a B grade. If you enter an F AND a B, your self-reported GPA will be a 1.5 GPA (D+) instead of your true 3.0 GPA (B). Students need to know how to enter courses retaken with AR, W, IC, or AP scores.

				Incorrect Entry	Correct Entry
1st attempt	SPANISH 1A	5 units	Grade	F	AR
2nd attempt	SPANISH 1A	5 units	Grade	B	B
				1.5 GPA	3.0 GPA

Fig. 0-6. Example of Fatal Application Errors

Each application has simple pitfalls that can determine whether or not you qualify for the fee waiver, if your ADT is accepted for your major, or listing the correct ADT; in other areas, like the UC Insight Questions or Common Application essays, the pitfalls include whether you're fully presenting your strengths and speaking to admissions criteria such as the UC's comprehensive review factors. You do not need to be an expert on these applications, but you do need to turn to your campus experts for help. So let's talk more explicitly about what kinds of help Transfer Centers provide. Each CCC Transfer Center might vary in size or offerings, but they all generally follow similar support patterns across campuses.

1. Application Workshops

Transfer Centers provide several kinds of workshops to aid students with transfer admissions applications. Sometimes these are presented by UC or CSU representatives, Counselors, or other staff. They will likely be offered a few weeks before the deadlines for each. Be sure you stop by your Transfer Center to pick up a calendar of events or look on their website for one to download. Here are some titles of common workshop names to look out for that support the application process.

- ☐ CSU Application Workshop
- ☐ CSU EOP&S Application Workshop
- ☐ UC TAP to TAG Workshop
- ☐ UC Application Workshop
- ☐ UC Insight Questions Workshop
- ☐ Common Application Workshop

Fig. 0-7. CSU and UC Application Workshop Posters.

2. UC TAU and the CSU Supplemental Application Workshops & Support

In January, the UCs and CSUs ask students to submit their Fall grades and coursework pending during the Spring. This submission is very important for evaluating your admissions application and is something you want to be sure is completed correctly and on time. Here's the issue, they are due in January, following the winter break when most campus operations are either closed or partially open. Check with your Transfer Center to ensure you know the best way to access their support—whether limited hours, use of drop-ins, appointments, or workshops that require sign-up. The UCs' TAU and the CSUs' Supplemental Applications do not necessarily take long to complete, but they're each different, they can read confusing, and you want to be sure your entry is correct. It is very common for students to make simple errors when entering this information, which can lead to having to appeal their admission status. Also, if you received a low grade or there's a course you did not pass, or in the Fall, you want to be sure to work with your Transfer Center for any added guidance to avoid hurting your application.

3. Scholarships and Financial Aid Workshops

Throughout the year, but especially in Winter and Spring, there are incredible scholarships for transfer that you can apply for. Often the organizations promoting these scholarships will send the information to your Transfer Center or might even participate in presentations or workshops about these awards. Often, the Financial Aid centers offer workshops on submitting your FAFSA or CADA applications to qualify for financial aid. So be sure to stay connected to your Transfer Center throughout the year, not only in the Fall, to avoid missing out on the opportunities.

4. University Visits, Tours, and Conferences

Often Transfer Centers assist in coordinating visits to local Universities and partner campuses for the day or even overnight. These will often include an admissions tour and a chance to preview your options in person and get a sense of what it would be like to be a student there. Sometimes campuses might hold a special program like a Transfer Conference and invite students to their campus for a special events program. These are truly golden opportunities to learn and gain exposure to the campus, your major, and other opportunities available at each campus. These are highly impactful for students, and I

Fig. 0-8. Southern California College Tour Poster.

can't recommend them enough. For example, at San José City College, we've offered our students a 4-day visit to 7 Universities in Southern California each year during Spring Break. And every year, I saw each of the 50 students who participated return completely transformed and incredibly motivated to earn high grades, finish their coursework strong, and get to that University experience they had tasted.

5. Make time for your Transfer Fair

Each Transfer Center will host a transfer fair for their students that nearly all UC, CSU, and many private college and out-of-state campus admission representatives attend. They usually last 3-4 hours and include anywhere from 20-50 campus representatives. Do yourself a favor and make time to attend these fairs for at least one hour. Take time to engage with the campuses you know you want to attend, but also to learn about the ones that you didn't know existed. This guide's Appendix section includes a list of questions you can ask transfer admissions representatives to get you started. One of the greatest benefits of attending your campus Transfer Fair is meeting the incredible admission representatives from the UC, the CSU, private colleges, and out-of-state campuses. The representatives provide transfer students with incredible service and are available to assist throughout your process. They are the experts on admission to their campus and will often help transfer students after admission in their next-steps process of beginning attendance at their campus.

Fig. 0-9. SJCC Alumni McArthur Hoang at the SJCC Transfer Fair. He later transferred to UC Berkeley and graduated with distinction.

In Summary

Some takeaways I hope you have gained from this chapter are the importance of

- completing the appropriate GE pattern,
- completing your Major Prep coursework,
- finishing a minimum of 60 transferable units,
- attaining a GPA competitive for the Transfer campus and major that you want to attend, and
- utilizing your campus Transfer Center.

Part II: Different System, Different Strategy

At heart, Transfer is two things: a **PLAN** and a **PROCESS**. As a plan, you can begin planning for transfer the minute you register for your first class. Ideally, that planning is exactly what happens when you meet with your California Community College (CCC) Counselor and draft your first educational plan together. *The planning for transfer happens entirely at the CCC level,* and there are so many resources and special support programs to help you along the way.

The *process of transfer*, however, **begins with the admissions applications for transfer**. It can be confusing and will differ across campuses, and it involves students working outside of community college and deciphering the different University applications, platforms, connecting with University admissions offices and representatives, and— most importantly—utilizing the full resources of your CCC Transfer Center. Timelines and applications will differ between the CSUs, UCs, Private colleges, HBCUs, and out-of-state campuses. The months between applying for transfer and committing to a campus can be some of the most emotional, stressful, and culminating sense of accomplishment and celebration beyond what you can imagine. This thing you've been working for is finally happening, you're taking real steps at the start, and then once the waiting period begins, anxiety sets in for ALL students—no matter how they wear it. Then, once you hear back, there's a rush of next steps, perhaps choosing between colleges, weighing financial options or living situations, or completing the last steps in the application process like submitting transcripts, completing your coursework with high grades, signing up for housing or orientations. The process of transfer can be A LOT. And yet, each year, we have incredible stories of resilience, acceptance, graduation, and yes—Transfer. The main takeaway here: *Si se puede*!! *You can do it*!!

We'll spend time on the *Transfer Process* in another section. For this section, let's turn our attention to *Transfer Planning*. The first step to planning is understanding that each higher education system operates differently. Preparing to apply to each system is like being an astronaut preparing to travel to different planets or, in this case, different systems of higher education that include the CSU, the UC, Private colleges, HBCUs, or out-of-state campuses. Each voyage to these different planets requires a different path, an understanding of each planet's atmosphere, and a different distance to travel. How do you get there? Follow the golden rule: *Different system, different strategy*!

Chapter 6:
California State University (CSU)

First, what is the CSU?

CSU stands for the *California State University* system of higher education. CSU is one of the three branches of higher education in California with a focus designed to "help meet California's workforce demands for skilled professionals" ("Introduction"). As noted on CSU's "Introduction" webpage, there are 23 CSU campuses and seven off-campus centers making CSU "the nation's **largest** *four-year public university system* (emphasis added). It produces **nearly half** of California's bachelor's degree graduates, with nearly one-third of CSU students being the first in their families to attend college. CSU also notes that its campuses educate "the **most ethnically, economically, and academically diverse student body** in the nation" (emphasis added). It's an impressive system that is deeply connected to values of equity that mirror our CA community college system and makes it a wonderful fit for our students.

The following is a list of CSU campuses with the corresponding map.

1. California State University, Bakersfield
2. California State University Channel Islands
3. California State University, Chico
4. California State University, Dominguez Hills
5. California State University, East Bay
6. California State University, Fresno
7. California State University, Fullerton
8. California Polytechnic State University, Humboldt
9. California State University, Long Beach
10. California State University, Los Angeles
11. California State University Maritime Academy
12. California State University, Monterey Bay
13. California State University, Northridge
14. California State Polytechnic University, Pomona
15. California State University, Sacramento
16. California State University, San Bernardino
17. San Diego State University
18. San Francisco State University
19. San José State University
20. California Polytechnic State University, San Luis Obispo
21. California State University San Marcos
22. Sonoma State University
23. California State University, Stanislaus

Fig. 0-1. Map of California State Universities (CSU).

Students will often ask about the differences between the CSUs and the UCs and if one system is *better*. In truth, many students will often assume that the UCs are better because they can be harder to get into, are more expensive, or carry a reputation of prestige. I think it's really important to challenge some of those assumptions. In fact, the CSUs and the UCs have different *missions* in California that shape how students experience them, and what they have to offer is unique to each system.

As mentioned earlier, CSU acknowledges its task of meeting the state's needs for skilled workforce professionals: Teachers, Nurses, Police Officers, Social Workers, Accountants, Engineers, Counselors, Licensed Therapists, Physical and Occupational Therapists, Business Managers, Administrators, Nutritionists, Fire and Forrest Managers, Probation Officers, Dental Hygienists, Environmental Resource Managers, Computer Scientists, Data Analysts, Graphic Designers, and many more! In addition, each CSU campus offers several majors that are rare, if not completely absent, at the UCs. Some of those include Nursing, Social Worker, or Teaching Credential Majors. As a counselor, my guidance to students is comparing colleges isn't a question of which one is better, but rather **which one is better for YOU**.

CSU Admissions Eligibility

First, let's talk about what you need to Transfer to a CSU campus. For all of the 23 CSU campuses, there is an overall admission eligibility that all Upper-Division Transfer (UDT) students need to meet to qualify for admission. Those requirements are:

1. To complete a minimum of **60 semester or 90 quarter units of transferable coursework**

2. To have an **overall college GPA of at least 2.00**. (*Your GPA is calculated using all your transfer units attempted. In high-demand majors and campuses, a GPA of 2.00 may not be sufficient to be admitted.*)

General Education-Breadth	Intersegmental General Education Transfer Curriculum* (IGETC)
Area A - English Language Communication and Critical Thinking	Area 1 - English Communication
A1 - Oral Communication	1A - Written Communications
A2 - Written Communications	1B - Critical Thinking
A3 - Critical Thinking	1C - Oral Communications
Area B - Scientific Inquiry and Quantitative Reasoning	Area 2 - Mathematical Concept and Quantitative Reasoning
B4 - Mathematics/Quantitative Reasoning	

Fig. 6 2. CSU Upper-Division Transfer webpage graphic: admission requirements.

3. To be in **good standing** at the last college or university attended. (*In simple terms, "good standing" means you can re-enroll at your last college or university.*)

4. To have completed **ten general education courses** (30 *semester-based* units or 45 *quarter-based* units), also called *basic skills* courses, **with a grade of C- or better**, and, specifically, four courses completed in the following areas known as the *Golden Four*:

What do Impaction and Non-Impaction Mean for CSU Transfer?

For some Non-Impacted CSU campuses and majors, meeting the CSU admission eligibility criteria listed above (**fig. 6-2**), Upper-Division Transfer (UDT) is sufficient for admission. However, for several campuses with Impacted majors, there are additional requirements transfer students must complete for transfer admission. Let's unpack this.

First, what is Major Impaction?

As mentioned in Chapter 4, *Major Impaction* means **there are more qualified student applicants for the major than there are spaces for admission,** so the major is called *impacted*. Since there isn't enough space in the major, departments must create additional criteria for admission. In most cases, that means increasing the GPA for admission. However, in some cases, like Nursing, there are several other criteria that applicants must meet to qualify for admission into their major.

Figure 4-1 from Chapter 4, shown below, helps us visualize how impaction and GPAs work. For example, if ten applicants apply for the Animation Major at a CSU, but only six seats are available in that major, the department may increase the GPA eligibility beyond the CSU entry requirement from 2.0 to 2.8 to fill these spots.

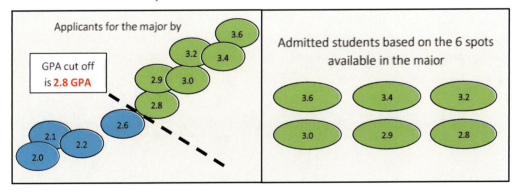

Fig. 4-1. Major Impaction - More Eligible Applicants Than Spaces Available.

What is Campus Impaction at the CSU?

Campus Impaction is very similar. CSU states that a campus is considered impacted when a campus receives more applications from qualified applicants than the available number of spaces, and that designation applies to "undergraduate degree programs or for undergraduate students who apply from outside the local admission area (California State University, "Impacted"). Naturally, popular CSU campuses, like San Diego State University, CSU Long Beach, San José State University, or Cal Poly San Luis Obispo, receive the most CSU applications and reach Campus Impaction regularly.

Yet, the reverse is also true. *Non-Impaction* means majors or campuses that have not surpassed their limit of eligible applicants for the major or the campus. Non-Impacted campuses will widely admit students that meet the basic CSU Upper-Division Transfer Admission Requirements listed earlier. Examples may include campuses like CSU Bakersfield, CSU Channel Islands, CSU Stanislaus, CSU Maritime Academy, Cal Poly Humboldt, or CSU Dominguez Hills. Those excellent campuses fly under the radar because they might be less accessible regionally or locations students are unfamiliar with. Yet, they offer great facilities and programs for study. For students who are open to moving, especially students applying with lower GPAs and seeking out competitive majors, those campuses can offer an excellent option for Transfer.

Where can you find out which campuses and majors are impacted?

CSU's Apply "Transfer" is the admissions site for the CSU system. Here you will find a wide range of tools for transfer, including the application, deadlines, and also information on impaction. Each year, the campus and major impaction designations may change, but you can find them by visiting CSU's "Impacted Undergraduate Majors and Universities" and using the online tool located at the bottom of the webpage (**fig. 6-3**).

CSU Campus	Applicant Level
Choose a ⌄	○ First-time freshmen ◉ Upper-division transfers
No campus impaction at the upper-division transfer level. Open to all CSU-eligible applicants.	

Fig. 6-3. Image: CSU's impaction database search tool found on the "Impacted Undergraduate Majors and Universities" webpage.

CSU's "Transfer" webpage also provides access to the **current** annual report called the CSU Undergraduate Impacted Programs Matrix, which lists the overall impacted majors by campus name for the given year, as shown (**fig. 6-4**).

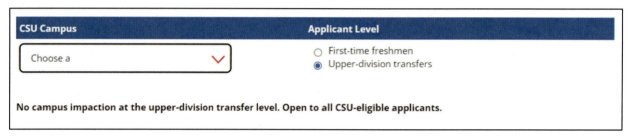

2022-2023 CSU Undergraduate Impacted Programs Matrix																						
	Bakersfield	Channel Islands	Chico	Dominguez Hills	East Bay	Fresno*	Fullerton*	Humboldt	Long Beach*	Los Angeles*	Maritime Academy N	Monterey Bay	Northridge	Pomona	Sacramento	San Bernardino	San Diego*	San Francisco	San Jose*	San Luis Obispo*	San Marcos	Sonoma	Stanislaus
Apparel Design & Merchandising														O	O		O						
Architecture														I						I			
Art	O	O	O	O	O	I	I	O	I	I		O	O	O	O	O	I	N	I	I	O	O	O
Biological Sciences**	O	O	O	O	O	I	I	O	I	I		N	I	I	O	O	I	O	I	I	I	O	O
Business	O	O	O	O	O	I	I	O	I	I	O	N	N	N	I	O	I	N	I	I	I	O	O
Chemistry/Biochemistry	O	O	O	O	O	I	I	O	I	I			O	I	O	O	I	O	I	I	O	O	O
Child/Human Development	O		O	O	O	I	I	O	I	I		O	O		O	O	I	O	I	I	O	I	O
Communication	O	O	O	O	O	I	I	O	I	I		O	I	I	O	O	I	O	I	I	I	O	O
Computer Science	O	O	O	O	O	I	I	O	I	I			I	O	I	O	O	I	O	I	I	O	O	O
Criminology/Criminal Justice	O		O	O	O	I	I	O	I	I			I		I	I	I	O	I	I	O	I	O
Economics	O	O	O	O	O	I	I	O	I	I		O	O	O	O	O	I	O	I	I	O	O	O
Engineering	O	I	O	O	O	I	I	O	I	I			O	N	O	O	I	O	I			O	O

Codes: *= All programs are impacted   I = Programs Impacted at the campus   N = See notes for the campus on the next page
O = Programs offered at the campus but not impacted   ☐ = A blank cell indicates that the program is not offered at this campus
**Biological Sciences should include Biology, Biotechnology, Microbiology, and Medical Technology

Fig. 0-2. Excerpt from 2022-2023 CSU Undergraduate Impacted Programs Matrix PDF.

Local vs. Non-Local Applicants

Each CSU reviews transfer student applications as either **Local or Non-Local Applicants**. For example, in the case of San José State University, transfer student applicants from Santa Clara County and Santa Cruz County are considered *local applicants*. The CSU system requires "that every impacted program to all CSU campuses provide first priority to local applicants" . . . [and] is provided to all CSU-eligible undergraduate applicants over non-local applicants" (Muñoz-Murillo 2). This provision is not an admissions guarantee for local students but does provide eligible local students with a substantial advantage. The flip side, of course, is students applying as non-local students, especially into impacted campuses or majors, are at a disadvantage.

To find a PDF of the local service areas for each campus, like the excerpt below (**fig. 6-5**), utilize the CSU Local Admission and Service Areas list. Under the *Upper-Division Transfer Admission* column, you can see how differently each CSU campus defines *local*. Non-Impacted campuses are very open. As you can see below, San Francisco State University reads "Non-Impacted: State of California," meaning open to all eligible transfer students from the entire State of California. In contrast, San Diego State University, which is highly impacted, defines local admission as students earning an ADT from specific CCCs within the San Diego region.

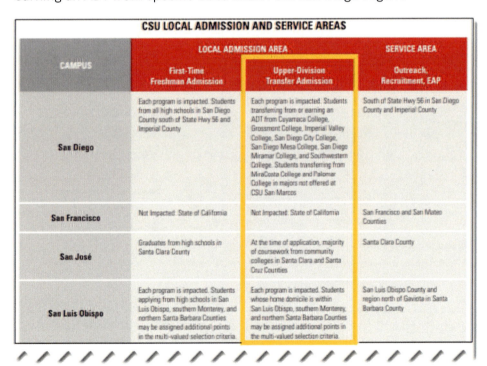

Fig. 0-3. Excerpt from CSU Local Admission and Service Areas PDF

Impaction and Local Area for CSU Admission

The combined effect of Impaction and Local Area priority will surely impact students applying to CSU. **Figure 6-6**, based on 2020-21 data, helps clarify how campuses approach admission by combining impaction and local area (Lozano and Prado). Campuses in Column 1 have ALL majors impacted AND utilized local area priority. Those were the most competitive CSU campuses for the 2020-21 admissions cycle. Column 2 campuses had SOME Impacted majors AND used local priority. In this case, it depended on the major. For example, Impacted majors like Nursing or Computer Science can be highly competitive, especially for non-local students. However, campuses with Non-Impacted majors, such as Human Development, could have been open and accessible to non-local students. In Column 3, we see the lists of CSU campuses that did not utilize local priority AND listed some Impacted majors. For students with lower GPAs in particular, those campuses offered great options for admission, especially if students were non-local applicants. Use the Impacted Undergraduate

2020-2021 CSU IMPACTION & LOCAL AREA

ALL MAJORS IMPACTED LOCAL AREA PRIORITY	SOME MAJORS IMPACTED LOCAL AREA PRIORITY	SOME MAJORS IMPACTED NO LOCAL AREA
LONG BEACH (local area priority based on high school of graduation and military veteran status)	**CAL POLY POMONA**	**DOMINGUEZ HILLS** (No majors are impacted)
FRESNO	**CHICO**	**BAKERSFIELD** (only Nursing impacted)
FULLERTON	**MONTEREY BAY**	**CHANNEL ISLANDS** (only Nursing impacted)
LOS ANGELES (Military veterans are considered local)	**NORTHRIDGE** (ECC is considered a local campus)	**EAST BAY** (only Nuring impacted)
SAN DIEGO	**SACRAMENTO**	**HUMBOLDT**
SAN LUIS OBISPO (SLO) (local area priority based on home address)	**SAN BERNARDINO**	**MARITIME ACADEMY**
SAN JOSE	**SAN MARCOS**	**SAN FRANCISCO**
1	2	**SONOMA** (No majors are impacted)
		STANISLAUS (only Nursing impacted)

Impacted major/campus: When the number of applications received is expected to be larger than the number of spaces available.

Local Area: A CSU admissions policy that offers priority to students that attend a "local" community college determined by the individual CSU campus.

Online CSU Impaction Search: https://www2.calstate.edu/attend/impaction-at-the-csu

Updated 3/17/20   Created for El Camino College by Rene Lozano and Blanca Prado

Majors and Universities database search tool to check current CSU admission information about Impaction and Local Area Priority.

Fig. 0-4. Examples of 2020-2021 CSU Impaction using Local Area information adapted from Lozano and Prado.

ADT Admissions Guarantee & Redirection

ADT stands for **Associate Degree for Transfer**; it sounds like essentially what it is: an Associate degree granted by a local CCC designed to satisfy requirements for transfer. This degree program was introduced as part of transfer reform and enacted by the California State Legislature as Senate Bill (SB) 1440 to amend the State's Educational Code; that is to say, *ADT is the law*. Since its introduction in 2010, incredible progress has been made to streamline the process to transfer for CCC students. For one, instead of students having to choose between different goals—achieving an Associate's degree OR completing the admission requirements to transfer—students can now accomplish both with the same coursework.

A benefit of the ADT Admissions option for students is that applicants to the CSU with an ADT are guaranteed admission to **ONE** of the 23 CSU campuses. This option works as a benefit because, on the CSU application, students will be asked to select from a list of CSU campuses where they would like their application *redirected* if they are not admitted to their first choice. In this case, the CSU will offer options to non-impacted campuses. These campuses can change from year to year based on the student's preferences. For example, if a student applied to SJSU and was not admitted, that application could be redirected to CSU Stanislaus for guaranteed admission. Therefore, it's important that students take time to truly explore non-impacted campuses to select a campus for redirection that's a good fit should that option come to pass.

So, how does it work? First, let's start with the options. **Table 6-1** shows all the options listed as either Associate of Arts (AA-T) or Associate of Science (AS-T) Transfer degrees. Students can find a listing of their CCC's ADT options using the Transfer Tool on the California Community Colleges Associate Degree for Transfer webpage.

Table 0-1. List of Associate of Arts or Associate of Science Transfer Degree Options.

Associate of Arts for Transfer (AA-T)	Associate of Science for Transfer (AS-T)
1. Anthropology	1. Administration of Justice
2. Art History	2. Agriculture Animal Sciences
3. Child and Adolescent Development	3. Agriculture Business
4. Communication Studies	4. Agriculture Plant Science
5. Early Childhood Education	5. Biology
6. Economics	6. Business Administration & Business Administration 2.0
7. English	7. Chemistry
8. Film, Television, and Electronic Media	8. Computer Science
9. Geography	9. Elementary Teacher Education
10. Global Studies	10. Environmental Science
11. History	11. Geology
12. Journalism	12. Hospitality Management
13. Law, Public Policy, and Society	13. Kinesiology
14. Music	14. Mathematics
15. Philosophy	15. Nutrition and Dietetics
16. Political Science	16. Physics

17. Psychology	17. Public Health Science
18. Social Justice Studies, African American Studies	
19. Social Justice Studies, Asian American Studies	
20. Social Justice Studies, Chicano Studies	
21. Social Justice Studies, Ethnic Studies	
22. Social Justice Studies, Gender Studies	
23. Social Justice Studies, General	
24. Social Justice Studies, LGBTQ Studies	
25. Social Justice Studies, Native American Studies	
26. Social Justice Studies, African American Studies	
27. Social Justice Studies, Asian American Studies	
28. Social Work and Human Services	
29. Sociology	
30. Spanish	
31. Studio Arts	
32. Theatre Arts	

As shown, each degree name pretty much sounds like the name of a Major. You can imagine a student majoring in Communication would pursue an AA-T in Communication, and that would be correct. However, **many CSUs have ALSO allowed students to use *similar* ADTs** for majors that may not seem as obvious. For example, **Figure 6-7** shows three such San José City College AA-Ts, based on San José State University's list of options for 2021-2022.

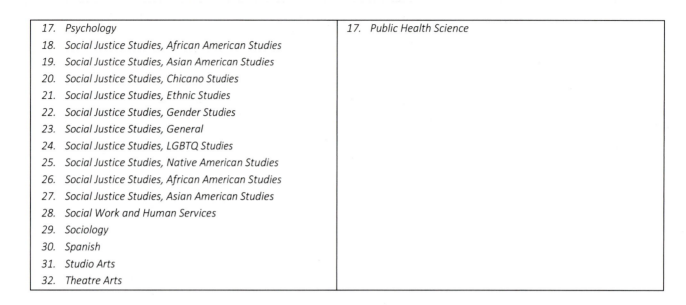

Associates Degree for Transfer is completed at the community college level.

Different ADT's can be used to transfer into the same or similar majors, depending on what the CSU decides. In this example from 2021, SJSU allowed students with ADT's in Global Studies and in Social Justice Studies to be used towards their Communications Major. *Note, CSU's can change these options from year to year.*

Fig. 0-5. Example of Three SJCC ADTs Used For an SJSU Communication Major.

It's so important that students work with their CCC Counselor and CSU transfer admissions representative to gain up-to-date information about these options. They do change from year to year, usually by adding pathways to similar majors but sometimes by removing them.

Where to get more information about ADTs at your CCC

In addition to your CCC's website, catalog, Counselor, and Admissions representative, there is a tool provided by the CCC Chancellor's office for students to navigate and compare their options at different community colleges at icangotocollege.com. Students can search ADT using the Transfer Tool (**fig. 6-8**) while seeing which CSU majors may be linked to these degrees.

Select the Transfer Tool

Select Community College

Find your CA community College

Select the ADT desired and then Select the CSU campus of interest.

See the majors listed as possible options for this ADT to then ask your Counselor & Admissions representative about.

Fig. 0-6. Steps to Search ADT Programs Using the CCC Transfer Tool.

A closer look at ADTs and why they are better than a perfect Boba drink.
There are some fundamental ways that the Associate Degree for Transfer (ADT) helps students
to transfer and ultimately saves them a lot of time, money, and stress in the transfer process.

1. ADTs provide students with a path to transfer. They **lay out the Major Prep coursework** available at their CCC required for their major at the CSU, eliminating confusion for students applying to more than one CSU.

2. ADTs require students to complete at least one of the **GE patterns for transfer** (CSU GE pattern or the IGETC for CSU pattern), thereby satisfying the CSU GE requirement for admission.

3. ADTs ensure students have completed **60 transferable units**.

4. ADTs ensure students have met the **minimum 2.0 GPA for transfer**.

5. ADTs provide students with an **Associate degree** at their local CCC related to their Transfer major and allow them to participate in graduation without having to choose between completing an Associate degree OR meeting transfer requirements. With the ADT options, students can achieve both.

6. ADTs provide students with **an added GPA point that assists with CSU impaction**, which can aid in admissions to competitive campuses or majors.

7. ADTs ensure transfer students are **guaranteed admission to at least one CSU campus**.

8. ADTs require CSU to **admit Transfer students to their campuses as true juniors**, which streamlines their path to graduation for their Bachelor's degree.

Benefits at the CA community college when preparing to transfer:

- The Associates Degree for Transfer (ADT) ensure 60 transferable units, GE requirements, good standing, minimum GPA of 2.0, and major prep is achieved prior to transfer.
- Participate in CCC graduation, earn an Associates with transfer coursework.

Benefits when applying for transfer:

- Added GPA Point when applying for transfer
- Guaranteed admission to 1 CSU campus through redirection.
- Impacted campuses & majors prioritize students applying with an ADT.

Benefits at the CSU after transferring:

- Enter CSU as a true Junior, no going backwards and taking CSU GE's once you transfer.
- Pathway to graduation is streamlined, programs like San Jose Promise at SJSU, allow for full-time transfer students to have

| **California Community College (CCC)** | | **California State University (CSU)** |

Fig. 0-7. Summary of ADT Benefits Before, During, and After the Transfer Process.

Using a degree sheet, let's look at what an [AA-T from San José City College](#) looks like up close (**fig. 6-10**).

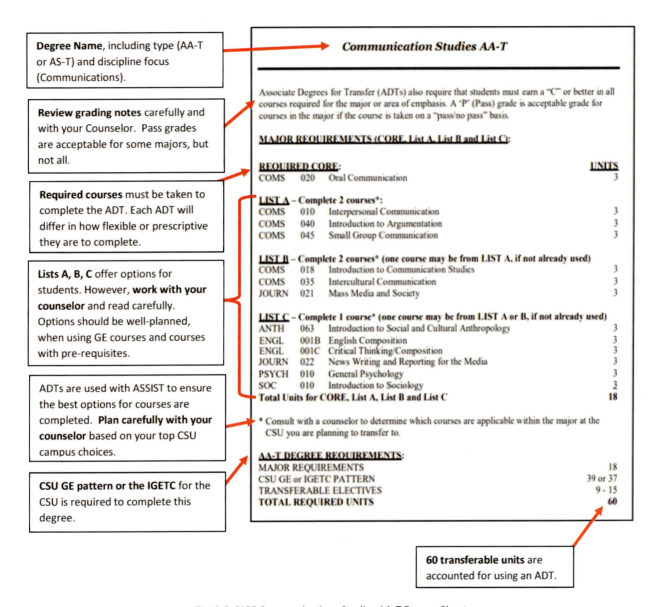

Degree Name, including type (AA-T or AS-T) and discipline focus (Communications).

Review grading notes carefully and with your Counselor. Pass grades are acceptable for some majors, but not all.

Required courses must be taken to complete the ADT. Each ADT will differ in how flexible or prescriptive they are to complete.

Lists A, B, C offer options for students. However, **work with your counselor** and read carefully. Options should be well-planned, when using GE courses and courses with pre-requisites.

ADTs are used with ASSIST to ensure the best options for courses are completed. **Plan carefully with your counselor** based on your top CSU campus choices.

CSU GE pattern or the IGETC for the CSU is required to complete this degree.

Communication Studies AA-T

Associate Degrees for Transfer (ADTs) also require that students must earn a "C" or better in all courses required for the major or area of emphasis. A 'P' (Pass) grade is acceptable grade for courses in the major if the course is taken on a "pass/no pass" basis.

MAJOR REQUIREMENTS (CORE, List A, List B and List C):

REQUIRED CORE:			UNITS
COMS	020	Oral Communication	3

LIST A – Complete 2 courses*:

COMS	010	Interpersonal Communication	3
COMS	040	Introduction to Argumentation	3
COMS	045	Small Group Communication	3

LIST B – Complete 2 courses* (one course may be from LIST A, if not already used)

COMS	018	Introduction to Communication Studies	3
COMS	035	Intercultural Communication	3
JOURN	021	Mass Media and Society	3

LIST C – Complete 1 course* (one course may be from LIST A or B, if not already used)

ANTH	063	Introduction to Social and Cultural Anthropology	3
ENGL	001B	English Composition	3
ENGL	001C	Critical Thinking/Composition	3
JOURN	022	News Writing and Reporting for the Media	3
PSYCH	010	General Psychology	3
SOC	010	Introduction to Sociology	3
Total Units for CORE, List A, List B and List C			**18**

* Consult with a counselor to determine which courses are applicable within the major at the CSU you are planning to transfer to.

AA-T DEGREE REQUIREMENTS:

MAJOR REQUIREMENTS	18
CSU GE or IGETC PATTERN	39 or 37
TRANSFERABLE ELECTIVES	9 - 15
TOTAL REQUIRED UNITS	**60**

---

60 transferable units are accounted for using an ADT.

Fig. 0-8. SJCC Communications Studies AA-T Degree Sheet.

Three steps to plan for the CSU with an ADT

In some ways, planning for the ADT has been simplified down to three easy steps:

| 1. Complete the Transfer GE Patten | 2. Fulfill the ADT Requirements | 3. Meet the Campus & Major GPA based on CSU Impaction |

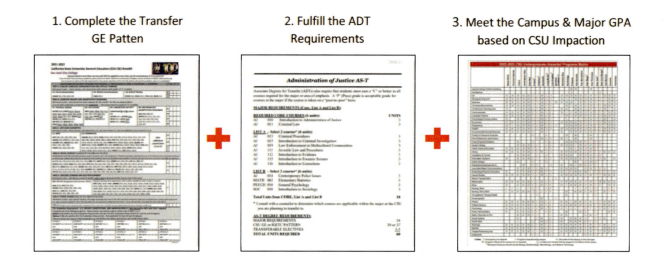

For some students, those steps really are that easy, and when that's the case, I can promise that your Counselor will rejoice! However, there are still important questions that can continue complicating the process when applying to CSU. The most important one for Transfer admissions is GPA.

Unlike our UC partners, the CSU system does NOT let students know the GPA and Admit rate from the prior admissions cycle. So even though Transfer students might know that a major or campus is *impacted,* they would not have a clear understanding of the GPA cut-off, meaning they are largely *applying blind*. So again, that issue is why it's so important to plan with your Counselor and utilize your Transfer Center and your CSU Admissions representatives. They will often have information that is not always made public on a website and understand how majors and GPAs trend at different campuses. Thankfully some campuses like San José State University, CSU Long Beach, and Cal Poly San Luis Obispo do share their GPA data. When students have access to this data, I have seen first-hand the phenomenal difference this makes in helping them make empowered choices about their future.

Alternate Majors & GPA

Here's an example of how much difference shared GPA data can make for CSU Transfer admission. Some CSUs, like SJSU, will ask students to select an alternate major. An alternate major is an option when a student is not admitted into their first choice of major due to impaction. At that point, the student would be admitted into the alternate major so long as they meet the eligibility for that major.

Suppose a student with a 2.4 GPA applied to SJSU for Psychology (**fig. 6-11**). Even with the ADT and local area status they'd most likely not be admitted to the major due to impaction. However, using the GPA data provided by SJSU the student can select a similar major like Behavioral Science (**fig. 6-12**) that admits students using basic eligibility of 2.0 GPA. A common mistake students make when applying with a vulnerable GPA is selecting an alternate major that is similarly highly impacted. That vulnerability is why it's so important to work with your CCC counselor, Transfer Center, and CSU admissions rep for assistance.

Psychology

Applicants who completed five course requirements were admitted above a 2.90 GPA.

Applicants who completed four course requirements were admitted above a 3.10 GPA.

Applicants who completed three course requirements were admitted above a 3.30 GPA.

Applicants who completed two course requirements were admitted above a 3.50 GPA.

Fig. 0-9. SJSU Psychology Major GPA Requirements.

SAN JOSÉ STATE UNIVERSITY

Program (Major)	Admit to Program Threshold
Advertising	2.00
Aerospace Engineering^	See below
African-American Studies	2.10
Animation and Illustration^	See below
Anthropology	2.10
Applied Math - Applied & Computational	See below
Applied Math - Statistics	See below
Art History and Visual Culture	2.00
Art - Digital Media Art	2.00
Art - Photography	2.00
Art - Pictorial Arts	2.00
Art - Spatial Arts	2.00
Art - Studio - Prep for Teaching, SS	2.00
Art - Studio Practice	2.00
Aviation^	See below
Behavioral Science	2.00
Biological Sciences^	See below
Biological Sciences - Microbiology^	See below

Fig. 0-10. Alternate Major Option GPA

What's a Cal Poly Technical Campus?

Now that we've talked about admissions eligibility, impaction, and GPA, let's dig deeper into understanding the CSU campuses. With 23 different colleges, there's a lot available to our students. To start with, the three Cal Poly Technical options within the CSU system across California are,

- Cal Poly Humboldt
- Cal Poly San Luis Obispo
- Cal Poly Pomona

A Cal Poly Technical campus is a CSU focusing *on technical and applied science degrees*. The majority of majors at each of these campuses will focus on math, engineering, or science. Both Cal Poly San Luis Obispo and Cal Poly Pomona have several highly ranked STEM programs and are competitive campuses to apply to. Cal Poly Humboldt, as of 2022, is the newest Cal Poly in the system with a wealth of technical and STEM majors and a learn-by-doing philosophy.

Cal Poly Humboldt: *Forestry Majors*

Fig. 0-13. Forestry Hands-on learning, Cal Poly Humboldt.

Cal Poly San Luis Obispo: *Construction Management*

Fig. 0-12. Construction Mgmt. Hands-on Learning Cal Poly SLO

Cal Poly Pomona: *Engineering Majors*

Fig. 0-11. Engineering Hands-on

What's a CSU Maritime?

Cal State University Maritime Academy is one of only seven maritime academies in the United States and the only one on the West Coast. It's the smallest CSU, with only 1,000 students and seven majors for degrees in technical fields like Mechanical Engineering, Marine Transportation, Oceanography, Facilities Engineering Technology, Global Studies, Maritime Affairs, and Business Administration. Participation in the military is not a requirement for students. However, the academy's basic organizational structure operates through a *Corps of Cadets* that stresses "soft" skills such as responsibility, accountability, leadership, and professionalism and reflects a military approach.

Cal Maritime considers the campus a "workplace," so cadets wear uniforms during the class day. All cadets are required to live on campus, and study abroad is also required for all majors. All Cal Maritime cadets in the Marine Transportation program and all three Engineering programs become members of the crew of the 500-foot Training Ship *Golden Bear* on at least one sixty-day journey visiting a number of ports around the Pacific Rim (CAL Maritime).

Fig. 0-14. Marine Transportation Major Hands-on learning at Cal State University Maritime Academy

Highlights of the 23 CSU Campuses

Fig. 0-15. SDSU Division of Student Affairs Facebook page.

San Diego State University

Admission: All undergraduate programs Impacted. Highly Competitive.

Environment: Beach City, Sunny and warm, Exciting, Students Love it Here. Big campus, with a large student population with lots of student clubs and activities, and always something to do on campus.

Popular majors: Business Administration, Kinesiology, Psychology, Biology

Interesting, lesser-known majors: Zoology, Environmental Engineering, Geological Sciences, Hospitality & Tourism, Recreation Management, International Business with regional emphasis, International Security, Public Administration, Urban Studies, Fully Online Business Degree

Fig. 0-16. CSU San Marcos Office of the President: Student life

CSU San Marcos

Admission: Some Majors Impacted. Competitive.

Environment: North of San Diego, suburban area, new facilities, medium size, commuter campus, sunny, calm, friendly, beautiful views, easy to stay focused on one's studies, plenty of clubs and campus activities

Popular majors: Social Science, Business Administration, Health, Psychology

Interesting, lesser-known majors: Pre-Med, Pre-Dental, Applied Physics, Electrical Engineering, Biotechnology, Music, Bus Admin Global Chain Management, Human Development, Teacher Education

Fig. 0-17. CSU Fullerton, Titan Student Union (Source: Architect Magazine, Steinberg Hart architect).

CSU Fullerton

Admission: All undergraduate programs Impacted. Highly Competitive.

Environment: Located in Orange County, suburban area, commuter campus, medium size, new facilities, sunny, calm, easy to stay focused on one's studies, plenty of clubs and campus activities

Popular majors: Business Administration, Health, Communication, Psychology, Social Sciences, Visual & Performing Arts, Kinesiology

Interesting, lesser-known majors: Art: Glass, Bus Admin: Legal studies, Bus Admin: Finance & Accounting, Bus Admin: Risk Management & Insurance, Dance, Earth Science, Architectural Engineering, Human Services

Fig. 0-18. CSULB Go Beach sign (Source: U.S. News, Sean Dufrene, CSULB Photographer)

CSU Long Beach

Admission: All undergraduate programs Impacted. Highly Competitive.

Environment: Beach City, Sunny and warm, Exciting, Students Love it here.Big campus, modern, lots of student clubs and activities, Big campus with a large student population

Popular majors: Business Administration and Management, Psychology, Computer Science, Nursing, Biological Sciences, Kinesiology.

Interesting, lesser-known majors: Film and Electronics Arts, Design, Education and Counseling, Electrical Engineering, Criminology and Criminal Justice, Health Science, Physical Therapy, Social Work, Public Policy and Administration, Recreation and Leisure Studies, Military Science, Journalism and Public Relations, Ocean Studies.

Fig. 0-19. CSU Dominguez Hills Campus Life

CSU Dominguez Hills

Admission: Non-Impacted campus.

Environment: A commuter campus, newer facilities, urban surroundings, affordable, sunny, and warm. Lots of student clubs and activities.

Popular majors: Business Administration, Kinesiology, Psychology, Sociology, Criminal Justice, Early Childhood Education, Nursing, Human Development.

Interesting, lesser-known majors: Advertising and Public Relations, Audio Engineering, Design, Journalism, Music, Business Admin-Information Security Systems, Business Admin-Sports, Entertainment and Hospitality, Information Technology, Radiologic Technology, and Pre-Physical Therapy.

Fig. 0-20. Cal State LA Dean's Welcome

CSU Los Angeles

Admission: All undergraduate programs Impacted. Highly Competitive.

Environment: A commuter campus near downtown LA, affordable, sunny, and warm. Lots of clubs and student activities.

Popular majors: Business Administration, Sociology, Psychology, Criminal Justice, Social Work, Speech Communication, Public Health, Computer Science, Nursing.

Interesting, lesser-known majors: Fire Protection Administration and Technology, Kinesiology, Nutritional Science, TV, Film, & Media Studies, Theatre, Urban Learning, Engineering Technology, Communicative Disorders, Communication, and Aviation Administration.

Fig. 0-21. CSUN Today Campus (photo by Lee Choo)

CSU Northridge

Admission: Some Majors Impacted. Competitive.

Environment: Suburban/Urban area. Sunny and warm, Safe environment, Commuter campus, Diverse Student Body, and several on-campus Events. Near Film Industry, Burbank lots.

Popular majors: Business Administration, Psychology, Cinema & Television Arts, Criminology & Justice.

Interesting, lesser-known majors: Radiologic Sciences, Central American Studies, Public Sector Management, Screenwriting, Music, Journalism, Athletic Training, Construction Management Technology, Biotechnology, Business Admin: Real Estate, Environmental and Occupational Health, Urban Studies and Planning, Geology, Radio Production.

Fig. 0-22. Cal Poly Pomona Overview

Cal Poly Pomona

Admission: Some Majors Impacted. Competitive.

Environment: 40 acres, farming landscape. Sunny and Warm. Campus town with many students living on or near campus. Safe environment. Diverse student population.

Popular majors: Engineering, Business Administration, Computer Science, Biological Sciences, Psychology, Communication.

Interesting, lesser-known majors: Animal Science, Architecture, Biotechnology, Aerospace Engineering, Agricultural Science, Apparel Merchandising and Management, Accounting, E-Business, Chemical Engineering, Journalism, Public Relations, Construction Engineering, Food and Nutrition, Graphic Design, Landscape Architecture, Theatre, Urban and Regional Planning.

Fig. 0-24. CSUSB Santos Manuel Student Union North

CSU San Bernadino

Admission: Some Majors Impacted. Competitive

Environment: Located between a mountain range and a suburban area. Commuter campus. New facilities, large campus. Safe, sunny, warm climate.

Popular majors: Business Administration, Psychology, Criminal Justice, Sociology, Nursing, Liberal Arts, Communication, Health, Computer Science.

Interesting, lesser-known majors: Art History, Design Studies, Information Systems and Technology, Bioinformatics, Public History, Social Work, Public Administration, Career and Technical Studies, Geology, Nutritional Sciences and Dietetics, Environmental Health Science.

Fig. 0-25. CSUCI News Campus Aerial View.

CSU Channel Islands

Admission: Non-Impacted campus.

Environment: Beach City, Sunny and warm, Exciting, Students Love it here. Big campus, modern, with a large student population and lots of student clubs and activities.

Popular majors: Business Administration, Kinesiology, Psychology, Biology.

Interesting, lesser-known majors: Health Science, Environmental Science & Resource Management, Art History, Early Child Studies, Organizational Communication, Managerial Economics, Marine and Coastal Systems, Information Technology, Performing Arts, and Mechatronics Engineering.

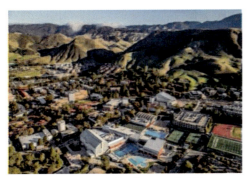
Fig. 0-26. About Cal Poly San Luis Obispo

Cal Poly San Luis Obispo

Admission: All undergraduate programs Impacted. Highly Competitive.

Environment: Beach City, Sunny and warm, Exciting, Students Love it here. Big campus, modern, with a large student population and lots of student clubs and activities.

Popular majors: Engineering, Business Administration, Computer Science, Hospitality Administration, Biological Sciences, Sociology.

Interesting, lesser-known majors: City and Regional Planning, Construction Management, Architecture, Art and Design, Animal Science, Agricultural Business, Biomedical Engineering, Environmental Management Protection, Forest and Fire Sciences, Food Science, Graphic Communication, Landscape Architecture, Marine Science, Manufacturing Engineering, Electrical Engineering, Industrial Engineering, Wine and Viticulture, Recreation, Parks and Tourism Administration.

Fig. 0-27. CSU Bakersfield: A University on the Rise

CSU Bakersfield

Admission: Non-Impacted campus.

Environment: Commuter campus. Rural area. Sunny and warm. Affordable surrounding area. New facilities, big campus.

Popular majors: Business Administration, Psychology, Criminal Justice, Biological Sciences, Liberal Studies.

Interesting, lesser-known majors: Accounting, Human Resources Management, Child and Adolescent Family Studies, Supply Chain Logistics, Public Policy and Administration, and Small Business Management.

Fig. 0-28. Fresno State Campus

CSU Fresno

Admission: All undergraduate programs Impacted. Highly Competitive.

Environment: Rural area, affordable. Sunny. Commuter campus. Big campus, with lots of campus activities.

Popular majors: Business Administration, Psychology, Criminology, Health Sciences, Liberal Arts

Interesting, lesser-known majors: Animal Sciences, Architectural Studies, Bus. Admin. - Sports Marketing, Communication-Speech Language Pathology, Deaf Studies, Fashion Merchandising, Industrial Technology, Kinesiology Sports Administration, Digital Journalism, Advertising and Public Relations, Recreation Administration, Social Work.

Fig. 0-29.CSU Stanislaus: Students outside Bizzini Hall.

CSU Stanislaus

Admission: Non-Impacted campus.

Environment: Rural area, Calm and quiet campus, College town, Affordable, strong Greek Life, Diverse, Safe surroundings. Sunny.

Popular majors: Criminal Justice, Business, Psychology, Liberal Studies, Sociology, Biology

Interesting, lesser-known majors: Accounting, Criminal Justice-Law Enforcement and Corrections Concentration, Health Leadership and Administration, Leadership Studies, Communication Studies-Relational, and Organization track.

Fig. 0-30. CSU Monterey Bay Campus Life Tradition.

CSU Monterey Bay

Admission: Non-Impacted campus.

Environment: Beach Town surrounded by rural area. Sunny, Colder. An affluent area and most students live on campus. Calm, relaxed campus.

Popular majors: Business Administration, Computer Science, Health Sciences, Human Services, Liberal Studies, Biological Sciences, Humanities.

Interesting, lesser-known majors: Cinematic Arts and Technology, Communication Design, Human Development and Family Science, Marine Science, Visual and Public Art, and Sustainable Hospitality Management.

Fig. 0-31. SJSU Campus Life

San José State University

Admission: All undergraduate programs Impacted. Highly Competitive.

Environment: Silicon Valley, Large Campus, Urban Area, Large campus, lots of student activities, clubs, and sports, Affluent surrounding area, Big student population.

Popular majors: Business Administration, Psychology Engineering, Computer Science, Child and Adolescent Development, Administration of Justice.

Interesting, lesser-known majors: Industrial Design, Aviation, Animation, Design Studies, Business Admin-Business Analytics, Accounting, Forensic Science, Journalism, Meteorology, Nutritional Science, Public Health, Social Work, Television, Radio, Film, and Theater Arts.

Fig. 0-32. CSU East Bay Student Life University Facts.

CSU East Bay

Admission: Non-Impacted campus.

Environment: Smaller campus, on a hill, scenic location. On-campus housing and commuter campus. Affordable surrounding area. Sunny. Urban area.

Popular majors: Business Administration, Psychology, Health Sciences, Human Development, Sociology, Criminal Justice, Computer Science.

Interesting, lesser-known majors: Bus. Admin. Information Technology, Theatre Performance, Hospitality and Tourism, Speech Pathology and Audiology, Recreation Therapy, Art-Animation, Art-Game Design, Construction Management, Political Science-Pre-Law, and Statistics.

Fig. 0-33. SFSU Students Get Involved

San Francisco State University

Admission: Non-Impacted campus.

Environment: Located in San Francisco, near the Beach, Beautiful setting. Big campus, vibrant student life. Urban area. Affluent surroundings. Largely a commuter campus.

Popular majors: Business Administration, Psychology, Biological Sciences, Engineering Communication, Early Childhood Education, Computer Science.

Interesting, lesser-known majors: Ethnic Studies, Apparel Design & Merchandising, Biotechnology, Health Education, Creative Writing, Dance, Data Science, Theater Arts-Design/Technical Production, Industrial Design, International Business, Journalism, Marine Science, Photojournalism, Public Health, Social Work, Visual Communication Design, Urban Studies & Planning.

Fig. 0-34. Cal Maritime Campus

CSU Maritime

Admission: Non-Impacted campus.

Environment: Small Campus, located on the waterfront. Housing on campus is required. International travel is required. Urban surroundings.

Popular majors: Business Administration, Global Studies and Maritime Affairs, Marine Science, Mechanical Engineering.

Interesting, lesser-known majors: Marine Transportation, Facilities Engineering Technology, Marine Engineering Technology, Oceanography, and Naval Science.

Fig. 0-35. Sonoma State University Campus

Sonoma State University

Admission: Non-Impacted campus.

Environment: Located in wine country, Sunny, Warm, Scenic area. Commuter campus that offers on-campus housing. Active Greek Life and student activities. Rural area. Safe.

Popular majors: Business Administration, Psychology, Sociology, Liberal Arts, Biological Sciences, Health, Education, Communication, Criminal Justice.

Interesting, lesser-known majors: Computer Science, Early Childhood Studies, Electrical Engineering, Environmental Science, Geography & Management, Human Development, Physical Science, Theater Arts, Statistics, Earth Sciences, and Music.

Fig. 0-36. Sacramento State Tree Campus USA (Sacramento State/Jessica Vernone)

Sacramento State University

Admission: Some Majors Impacted. Competitive.

Environment: Urban/Suburban area. Sunny, warm, and safe. Surrounding area Affordable and student housing available. Big campus.Active Greek Life and student activities.

Popular majors: Business Administration, Biological Sciences, Psychology, Criminal Justice, Kinesiology, Speech and Communication, Early Childhood Education, Computer Science, Sociology.

Interesting, lesser-known majors: Communication Disorders, Deaf Studies, Design Studies, Computer Engineering, Electrical Engineering, Film (Digital Film/Video Production), Geography (Metropolitan Area Planning), Geology, Graphic Design, Health Science, Interior Architecture, Athletic Coaching, Journalism, Music, Liberal Studies, Nutrition and Food, Public Health, Social Work, Recreation Therapy, and Theatre.

Fig. 0-37. Chico State Students Walking (Photo by Jason Halley/Chico State).

Chico State University

Admission: Non-Impacted campus.

Environment: Rural surrounding area. Sunny. Affordable area. College town. On-campus housing. Strong student life, Greek Life.

Popular majors: Business Administration, Psychology, Liberal Arts, Criminal Justice, Sociology, Kinesiology, Communication.

Interesting, lesser-known majors: Advanced Manufacturing and Applied Robotics, Animal Science, Computer Science, Construction Management, Concrete Industry Management, Computer Animation and Game Design, Communication Disorders, Electrical Engineering, Health Administration, Mechanical Engineering, Musical Theater, Social Work, and Theater Arts.

Fig. 0-38. Cal Poly Humboldt Campus.

Cal Poly Humboldt

Admission: Non-Impacted campus.

Environment: Rural area. Scenic, Beach town, affordable surrounding area. Small college town. Student housing is readily available. Large campus, new facilities, strong student life. Calm campus.

Popular majors: Psychology, Environmental Science, Business, Liberal Arts, Biology Sciences, Wildlife, and Fisheries Management.

Interesting, lesser-known majors: Cannabis Studies, Applied Fire Science and Management, Energy Systems Engineering, Data Science, Marine Biology, Software Engineering, Mechanical Engineering, Geospatial Information Science & Technology, Energy Systems Engineering, Zoology, Social Work, Rangeland Resource Science, Forestry, Recreation Administration.

Works Cited

California Community Colleges. "Associate Degree for Transfer." California Community Colleges, 2023,

icangotocollege.com/associate-degree-for-transfer#programs. Accessed 11 Mar. 2023.

California State University. *CSU Local Admissions and Service Areas*. California State University Office

of the Chancellor, www.calstate.edu/apply/freshman/Documents/CSULocalAdmission-

ServiceAreas.pdf. Accessed 23 Jan. 2023.

---. "Impacted Undergraduate Majors and Universities, 2023-24." *CSU The California State University*, California State University Office of the Chancellor, www.calstate.edu/attend/degrees-certificates-credentials/Pages/impacted-degrees.aspx. Accessed 22 Jan. 2023.

---. "Introduction." *CSU The California State University*, California State University Office of the Chancellor, www.calstate.edu/csu-system/about-the-csu/facts-about-the-csu/Pages/introduction.aspx. Accessed 21 Jan. 2023.

---. "Transfer." *CSU The California State University*, www.calstate.edu/apply/Transfer. Accessed 11 Mar. 2023

---. "Upper-Division Transfer." *CSU The California State University*, www.calstate.edu/apply/transfer/Pages/upper-division-transfer.aspx. Accessed 21 Jan. 2023.

CAL Maritime. "Why Choose Cal Maritime? Explore Us!" *CAL Maritime*, California State U Maritime Academy, 2022, www.csum.edu/about/explore.html. Accessed 11 Mar. 2023.

Lozano, Rene, and Blanca Prado. *2020-2021 CSU Impaction and Local Area*. Transfer Counselor Website, 2020. *CCC Transfer Counselor Website*, ccctransfer.org/wp-content/uploads/2021/03/2020_2021_CSU-IMPACTION-AND-LOCAL-AREA.pdf. Accessed 23 Jan. 2023. Table.

Munoz-Murillo, Nicole, compiler. *Student Admissions and Impaction Policies Report - 2021*. California State University Office of the Chancellor, 3 May 2021, www.calstate.edu/impact-of-the-csu/government/Advocacy-and-State-Relations/legislativereports1/Admissions-and-Impaction-Policies-Legislative-Report.pdf. Accessed 22 Jan. 2023. Legislative Reports.

San José City College. *Communications Studies AA-T*. San José City College, 2022,

sjcc.edu/_resources/PDF/degrees_and_certificates/2022_2023_degrees_and_certificates/ADTs/AA-

T%20Communications%20Studies.pdf. Accessed 11 Mar. 2023.

Chapter 7:
University of California (UC)

Let's turn our attention now to the Blue planet, the University of California (UC). There are technically ten UC campuses in California if we include the University of California at San Francisco (UCSF). However, UCSF is not available for undergraduate study or transfer admission. There are, in practice, nine UC campuses available for transfer admission. The following is a list of UC campuses with the corresponding map.

1. University of California at Davis (UCD)
2. University of California at Berkeley (UCB)
3. University of California at Santa Cruz (UCSC)
4. University of California at Merced (UCM)
5. University of California at Santa Barbara (UCSB)
6. University of California at Los Angeles (UCLA)
7. University of California at Riverside (UCR)
8. University of California at Irvine (UCI)
9. University of California at San Diego (UCSD)

Fig. 0-1. *University of California (UC)* Campus Map

What's required for transferring to the UC?

According to the UC transfer admissions site, the minimum eligibility requirements for transfer applicants are the following:

1. Complete the 7-Course Pattern
2. Complete 60 (semester) or 90 (quarter) transferable units to the UC
3. Apply with a 2.4 min GPA in UC-transferable courses for California resident students
4. Completion of required and recommended courses for the intended major with minimum grades met
5. Be in good academic standing at the last college attended
6. Earn a C or better in each course or a Pass (P) if Pass is equivalent to a C (2.00)

Those are the *minimum eligibility* requirements Transfer applicants must satisfy to be considered for admission. However, as you may have guessed, the entire UC system is highly competitive. Why? For one, six of the UC campuses (UCB, UCD, UCSD, UCSB, UCI, UCD) are ranked "among the top 10 public universities in the country, with all nine UC undergraduate campuses among the top 50 in the 2022 Best Colleges rankings, published today by U.S. News & World Report" (Schelenz). In other words, they are highly sought-after universities by both national and international applicants. That said, let's not forget the 1960 Master Plan for Higher Education in California, which essentially commits UC to admit *one Transfer* student for every *two Freshman* applicants, specifically California Community College (CCC) applicants that satisfy Transfer eligibility. So, let's first agree that even though the UC campuses hold great prestige and status, they are California universities with a commitment to California students, first and foremost, to CCC students. Our students, *by design*, have a place at the table for some of the most incredible public universities in the United States.

Is the UC affordable?

For many CCC students, the cost is the biggest obstacle to even considering the UC as a Transfer option. I see many students rule out the option of even considering a UC Transfer application because the assumption is that it's just too expensive. So let me say these words to those students: the Blue and Gold Opportunity Plan.

Under the UC's Blue and Gold Opportunity Plan, the UC will ensure that student tuition and fees are covered for California residents whose **total family income is less than $80,000 yearly and who qualify for financial aid.**

Blue + Gold ↓ $80k

Eligible California families with incomes below $80,000 pay no tuition under UC's Blue and Gold Opportunity Plan

Eligibility requirements for the Blue and Gold Opportunity Plan:

☐ Submit a FAFSA or California Dream Act Application and Cal Grant GPA Verification Form **by March 2nd**
☐ **California resident or have AB 540 status**
☐ Demonstrate total **family income below $80,000** and financial need, as determined for federal need-based aid programs
☐ Be in your first four years as a UC undergraduate **(the first two for transfer students)**
☐ Meet other campus **basic requirements** for UC grant aid (for example, be enrolled at least half-time during the academic year, meet campus academic progress standards, not be in default on student loans, etc.)

Note that in addition to the Blue and Gold program, students with sufficient financial need can also qualify for aid to help reduce the cost of attending, which can include the cost of housing, meals, and personal expenses. Also, students do not need to apply separately for the Blue and Gold program because by making a UC Transfer application and submitting their FAFSA or California Dream Application, students are automatically reviewed for the program, with details provided in the financial aid package after admission. So, what does this mean? Basically, while the UC system does cost more, it also provides substantially more aid to students with financial needs that can close the affordability gap. So don't be quick to rule out the UC based on the cost of attendance.

UC Comprehensive Review

Similar to the impaction at CSU, which has more qualifying student applicants that meet the basic admissions eligibility, the UCs utilize a system of Comprehensive Review to evaluate transfer applicants. In the following nine Tables, let's carefully explore each of UC Admissions' nine factors listed as comprehensive review criteria and how *you* can best prepare for those evaluation items in advance.

Table 0-1. Bullet Point One from UC Admissions' "Factors we consider" webpage.

1. "Completion of a specified pattern or the number of courses that meet breadth or general education requirements."	
Factor Explained:	**What you can do to gain competitiveness:**
The idea here is that students applying with the minimum GE coursework and those included in the Seven-Course Pattern are more competitive and more prepared to transfer. The Seven-Course Pattern is flexible and permits transfer students to apply without completing their GE pattern at their local CCC. The IGETC is the CCC GE pattern aligned to the UC requirements. By fulfilling IGETC, you satisfy the Seven-Course Pattern, can certify GEs at your local CCC, and not have to take more GE courses after transfer.	☐ **Complete the IGETC GE pattern** at your CCC before the transfer application and get certified before transferring. ☐ It's okay to have courses in progress while you apply; however, it's strongly recommended to **complete the two English courses and one transferable Math course before applying** for transfer. ☐ STEM majors can complete the partial IGETC, but check with your UC Rep. on what is recommended for your major. Some majors prefer completion of the full IGETC.

Table 0-2. Bullet Point Two from UC Admissions' "Factors we consider" webpage.

2. "Completion of a specified Pattern or the number of courses that provide continuity with upper division courses in the student's major, such as a UC Transfer Pathway, AA degree for Transfer (offered at CA community colleges only), or UC campus-specific major prerequisites."	
Factor Explained:	**What you can do to gain competitiveness:**
The focus here is that incoming transfer students arrive prepared for their chosen major. They demonstrate that status by fulfilling the Major Prep required by UC for the major listed on their website and ASSIST. Students can also utilize the UC Transfer Pathways sequence, which is recommended but not required. This tool organizes the Major Prep for the most popular 20 or more majors at the UC for Transfer and shows students where the UCs differ and where they are similar, which helps streamline the process for students as they prepare.	☐ Plan carefully with your CCC counselor to ensure you are fulfilling each of the requirements listed in your major for EACH UC Campus Transfer application, especially your top choice. ☐ Complete the UC TAP account and connect with the UC admissions representatives at each campus where you apply for assistance. Review your coursework ahead of time and ensure you have met each requirement and recommendation. ☐ Complete an ADT for your major if that's an option. Work with your Counselor and Transfer Center for guidance to ensure meeting all major requirements and recommendations before transferring.

Table 0-3. Bullet Point Three from UC Admissions' "Factors we consider" webpage.

3. "Grade point average in all transferable courses-especially in a UC Transfer Pathway or in major prerequisites."

Factor Explained:	What you can do to gain competitiveness:
The UC will evaluate your GPA carefully, including your overall GPA of transferable coursework and the GPA of your Major Prep courses – that is why they mention the UC Transfer Pathway courses, which are essentially your Major Prep sequence. This guidance is especially true for STEM majors.	☐ Complete the UC TAP account and keep your grades up to date to get the most accurate read of your UC transferable coursework GPA. ☐ Study ASSIST carefully and work with the UC Reps to make sure you understand the GPA expectation for your major coursework. ☐ Apply for Academic Renewal or retake courses needed for Transfer that carry grades of a C- or lower for UC to increase your GPA for transfer.

Table 0-4. Bullet Point Four from UC Admissions' "Factors we consider" webpage.

4. "Participation in academically selective honors courses or programs."

Factor Explained:	What you can do to gain competitiveness:
The UC reviews applicants to see not only what courses have been taken but what rigor level the student sought. Students that have taken the initiative to participate in honors courses or programs will stand out.	☐ Enroll in an honors course at your local CCC. If you have difficulty finding one, use the CCC California Virtual Campus for online options at different campuses. ☐ At San José City College, we have multiple options for honors courses; see the SJCC Honors Program coordinator to learn more.

Table 0-5. Bullet Point Four from UC Admissions' "Factors we consider" webpage.

5. "Special talents, achievements and awards in a particular field, such as visual and performing arts, communication or athletic endeavors; special skills, such as demonstrated written and oral proficiency in other languages; special interests, such as intensive study and exploration of other cultures; experiences that demonstrate unusual promise for leadership, such as significant community service or significant participation in student government; or other significant experiences or achievements that demonstrate the student's promise for contributing to the intellectual vitality of a campus."

Factor Explained:	What you can do to gain competitiveness:
The UC is interested in knowing what makes an applicant stand out beyond what is evident in their transcript. For example, do you have a special talent or ability, show leadership or service? What is special or unique beyond what someone can tell about the student from the application packet?	☐ Utilize the UC Insight response to highlight special talents, achievements, awards, performances, leadership, service, or unique experiences. ☐ Join organizations like your CCC's student government or clubs related to your major. Participate in community service or community activism that's meaningful to you. Participate in internships if you can; even short ones can provide a great experience. Participate in team sports or campus group performances. There's always a way to spread your wings locally.

Table 0-5. Bullet Point Six from UC Admissions' "Factors we consider" webpage.

6. "Completion of special projects undertaken in the context of the college curriculum or in conjunction with special school events, projects, or programs."	
Factor Explained:	**What you can do to gain competitiveness:**
Remember that you are applying to a competitive and rigorous university that's especially interested in knowing who you are academically. Things like how connected and engaged you are with your major, if you participated in research or have direct experience, or if you have other academic, in-class or in-school experiences that can reveal more about who you will be as a student, scholar, and engaged learner. It cannot feel like you are geeking out too much. This place is 100% where to get geeky about what excites and propels you in your field— without apology, show your passion, academic voice, the questions and inquiries you want to explore, and how early experiences connect to how you are thinking about your future at the UC.	☐ In response to one of your UC Insight questions, describe an in-class project, academic-related program or event that best addresses this area. ☐ Some general examples include research projects, research papers, participation in an academic conference, working as a lab assistant. Others include a performance you participated in related to your major or interests, or a course taken related to your major that also demonstrated your academic interests and engagement. ☐ A great example at San José City College is students participating in the *Cultivamos Excelencia* program. That program involves collaboration and mentorship with UCSC faculty and graduate students to complete a research project and then participate in a presentation of their work at a UCSC-hosted research symposium. ☐ Other examples from SJCC can include participation in a *Umoja* or *Puente* project through class, training, and work that are related to our Peer-Led Team Learning (PLTL) or Supplemental Instruction (SI) groups and special projects completed through Honors courses or the *Let Your Life Speak* series.

Table 0-6. Bullet Point Seven from UC Admissions' "Factors we consider" webpage.

7. "Academic accomplishments in light of the student's life experiences and special circumstances," including but not limited to: disabilities, low family income, status as a first-generation college student, need to work, disadvantaged social or educational environment, difficult personal and family situations or circumstances, refugee status or veteran status.

Factor Explained:	What you can do to gain competitiveness:
These criteria help UC understand and consider the challenges Transfer students often must overcome beyond completing their academic coursework for transfer. The UC seeks to understand your transcript and academic journey in the context of the added challenges you have undergone while completing your studies. For example, suppose a student has been homeless while attending school but managed to achieve a high GPA while working and managing those added stressors. That student's profile is very different from one whose GPA might be a few points higher but hasn't dealt with challenges on their path. Further, these criteria aim to help honor the journey and resilience shown by students who face such barriers.	☐ Using the Personal Insight questions and the application itself, take time to share what your challenges have been. Be specific when you write about the day-to-day ways you overcame them, and how those experiences impacted you and made you a better student. ☐ Do not shy away from sharing those challenges in your application. Applications are read privately and by a limited number of reviewers. You should feel safe about sharing difficulties that can be hard to talk about. These experiences are also used to evaluate students for scholarships and added resources. It's quite important that admissions evaluators have a true sense of who you are and your accomplishments in light of the challenges you faced. ☐ Be sure to provide enough detail so the reader can fully appreciate your circumstances and challenges. Don't assume they will just *get it* with a few sentences; make things real for them, and always include how you overcame the problems. Character shows up most in the face of adversity, so it's important you don't feel like you are writing a *sad* story or seeking *pity*. Instead, feel proud you are writing a true story that is very honest about the difficulties but also what you had to muster up within yourself to keep going and pressing towards your goals.

Table 0-7. Bullet Point Eight from UC Admissions' "Factors we consider" webpage.

8. "Location of the student's college and residence.

Factor Explained:	What you can do to gain competitiveness:
For this criteria, UC takes into account your location, access to courses required for your major, and any regional difficulties or unique factors. For example, if a student lives in the Central Valley and must drive far to attend school, or suppose their campus has limited options for their major—those are important factors the UC takes into account.	☐ Take advantage of the Personal Insight questions or the "Other Comments" section at the end of the UC application. Tell *your* story about how location impacted your studies by making it more difficult to take courses required for your major or other unique factors related to your region that impacted you. For example, the yearly California fire seasons impact students in those areas and disrupt their learning opportunities.

Table 0-8. Bullet Point Nine from UC Admissions' "Factors we consider" webpage.

9. "Completion of a UC Transfer Pathway or an AA degree for transfer offered by a California community college."	
Factor Explained:	**What you can do to gain competitiveness:**
Completion of the UC Transfer Pathway or the Associate Degree for Transfer (ADT) at your local CCC indicates to UC that you are coming in prepared. You have satisfied the Major Prep for your major and are ready to be an upper-division Transfer student at the UC.	☐ If possible, aim to complete an ADT at your CCC related to your major. Review the UC Transfer Pathway and aim to complete the recommended sequence. Work closely with your CCC Counselor and UC Admissions representative to plan for both.

What are the UC Transfer Pathways?

The UC Transfer Pathways is a UC resource for students that outlines the major requirements for the top 20 Transfer admission majors. These majors include:

1. Anthropology
2. Biochemistry
3. Biology
4. Business administration
5. Cell Biology
6. Chemistry
7. Communication
8. Computer science
9. Economics
10. Electrical engineering
11. English
12. History
13. Mathematics
14. Mechanical engineering
15. Molecular biology
16. Philosophy
17. Physics
18. Political science
19. Psychology
20. Sociology

Each of those majors includes the sequence of courses required for entry into the major that should be taken at your local CCC with your Counselor's guidance. Also included in this site is the list of names a major can go by at each campus, sometimes varying by degree type (BA versus BS) or by concentration. Each college lists this information on ASSIST in more detail, but the UC Transfer Pathways tool provides an easy-to-read overview of how to prepare for

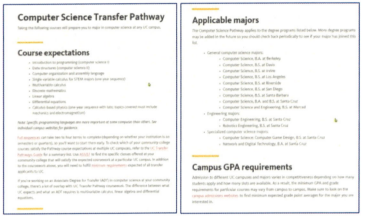

Fig. 7-2. Screenshot of "Computer Science Transfer Pathway" (University of California Admissions.

this pathway. Here's an example of the Transfer Pathway for Computer Science (**fig. 7-2**), one of the most competitive and sought-after majors at UC.

The UC Transfer Pathways also provides students with a Guide. (**fig. 7-3**). The guide allows students to enter their CCC campus and the desired major, then provides the list of the CCC courses required for that major. It will break down course trends, like whether most of the nine UC campuses require the same course and also where campuses

Fig. 0-3. Screenshot of "Transfer Pathways Guide" Search Results using San Jose City College and Computer Science (University of California Admissions).

will differ. Always do this activity with the guidance of your CCC counselor for a full picture of how to embed this plan into your Student Educational Plan (SEP).

What is the TAG?

TAG stands for "Transfer Admission Guarantee (TAG)." It is, in fact, a *guaranteed admission* for Transfer students designed specifically for CCC students. There are six UC campuses that participate in the TAG: **UC Davis, UC Irvine, UC Merced, UC Riverside, UC Santa Barbara, and UC Santa Cruz** (University of California Admissions)**.**

    The other UC campuses, UCLA, UC Berkeley, and UC San Diego, do not participate in the TAG. These campuses DO admit a high number of Transfer students. However, due to their high volume of eligible applicants, they do not have the capacity to *GUARANTEE* admission.

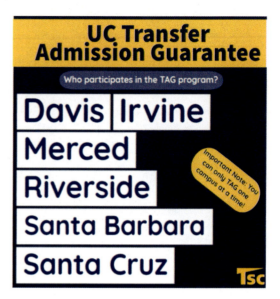

Fig. 0-4. List of the Six UC TAG Campuses, courtesy of Santiago Canyon College

How does TAG work?

Here's an overview of how TAG works for CCC transfer students (**Table 7-10**):

Table 0-9. Summary of How UC TAG Works for CCC Transfer Students.

Who can submit a TAG?	Only CCC students who apply for UC Transfer admission.
How many campuses can you TAG to?	One of the six UC campuses (UCD, UCI, UCM, UCR, UCSB, UCSC)
When do you apply for TAG?	Sept. 1st – 30th for Fall Admission May 1st – 30th for Winter/Spring Admission *Currently, UC Merced & UC Riverside offer Winter/Spring Admission on a consistent basis*
Where do you apply for TAG?	Students apply for TAG by creating a "Transfer Admission Planner (TAP)" account (Fig. 7-5). Application for TAG is the final step of the TAP account. * *Note, do not submit the TAG application until it can be reviewed by your Transfer Center or UC admissions representative.*

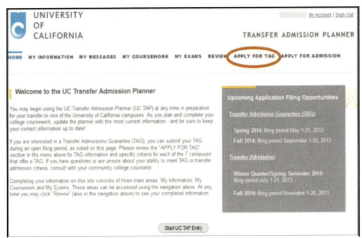

Fig. 0-5. Student UC TAP Account Welcome Page Example.

The *TAG* is optimal for transfer, but **NOT required for transfer admission** to the UC.

The **TAG is also a separate application** from the UC Admissions application. Click the circled tab (Fig. 7-5) on your UC TAP account page to access the TAG application.

TAG Eligibility Requirements Differ by Campus

It's very important that students take time to study the individual differences between each of the six campuses that offer the TAG. They will differ on important areas for qualifying, such as the student eligibility GPA, completion of the two English and one Math courses, and what majors are available for TAG. **Table 7-11** has direct links to view the specific campus TAG requirements for your major.

Table 0-10. Direct Links to UC Campus TAG Requirements.

UC Davis	UC Santa Barbara	UC Santa Cruz
TAG Requirements	TAG Requirements	TAG Requirements
UC Irvine	UC Merced	UC Riverside
TAG Requirements	TAG Requirements	TAG Requirements

Students can also view the UC TAG Matrix in the "UC Transfer Admission Guarantee" PDF (**fig. 7-6**), which summarizes basic TAG requirements for each of the six UC campuses. Students use both the individual campus sites, which will list important GPA, course, and other information about the TAG *in addition* to the UC TAG Matrix (University of California Admissions). Together with their Counselor, students can plan how to optimize their qualifications for the TAG and the UC. The goal is not only to apply to the TAG but *to apply correctly and to the campus you qualify for* so that you can reap the benefits of this program.

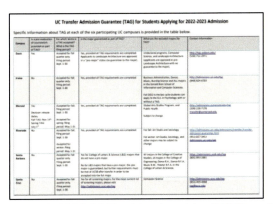

Fig. 0-6. 2022-23 Tag Matrix guide, "UC Transfer Admission Guarantee"

Is the TAG worth all the Extra Work? Absolutely!

A big factor in gaining UC admission is meeting the GPA threshold for your major. That's tricky when the line continues to move every year. A campus is popular, a major is popular, and so more students apply for that major, and the GPA bar gets raised each year.

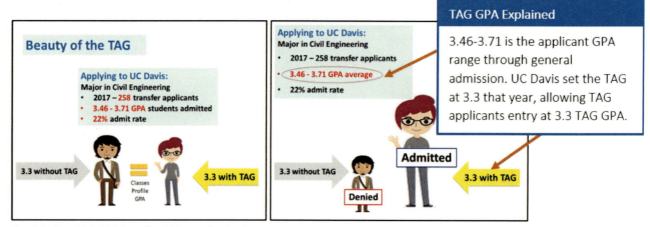

Fig. 0-7. How TAG GPA Benefits CCC Transfer Students.

What **the TAG allows transfer students to do is qualify for the TAG GPA,** which can be anywhere from one to three points different from the general requirements. As you can see above (**fig. 7-7**), the TAG GPA gives students applying *with* a TAG a very BIG advantage. But students only gain from this advantage if they **Apply** for the TAG, do it **CORRECTLY,** *and* it's a campus where they **Qualify** for Transfer admission. How do *you* do that? Work with your Transfer Center and UC Admissions Representatives to review your TAG application before submission, and start planning for TAG early with your CCC Counselor. Take time to review the individual Transfer requirements and ensure each requirement is being met by the time you expect to apply for TAG.

What's the TAP, and why do you NEED one?

The UC TAP stands for "Transfer Admission Planner." *TAP* is a Transfer tool students use throughout their planning process for UC Transfer. Students can create their accounts as soon as they begin their classes at a CCC (University of California Admissions). Using the TAP account, each semester, students will enter their courses, grades, and the majors and campuses they're interested in. This does a few things. First, TAP connects students to UC representatives that are assigned to different CCCs, who visit and meet with students, host local workshops, answer emails, or invite CCC students interested in their UC campus to visit and

Sign up for your TAP account here.

participate in a Transfer program or special transfer event. It's a win for students and a win for the UC campus that can start communicating early with prospective transfer students.

The UC TAP account is also incredibly useful for planning with your CCC Counselor and UC Admissions Representative. Using this tool, students can track their true transferable UC GPA and units. Remember that not all CCC units are UC transferable. Also, students will often enroll in more than one CCC, and this tool allows students to integrate their academic records for UC. This ability can be especially helpful for students with a mix of quarter and semester units. When you meet with a UC representative, they will often ask you to update your UC TAP account ahead of time so that they can provide accurate feedback. Here's an example of what the UC TAP report looks like:

The summary *GPA & Units section* will display the student's true UC GPA and the true unit count for UC transferable units.

The summary *Courses & Exams section* will also review if you've completed the requirements for the Seven-Course Pattern.

Under the course entry, students can view if their courses are listed as *Cert* which means it was found on ASSIST and is a UC transferable course. *Note that when entering classes be sure to use the *drop* menu instead of typing the name of the course, otherwise errors can be made that count courses as non-transferable when they are actually transferable.

Under the *UC Area* the report will list which UC GE area the course is approved for at the UC, which is important for satisfying the Seven-Course Pattern.

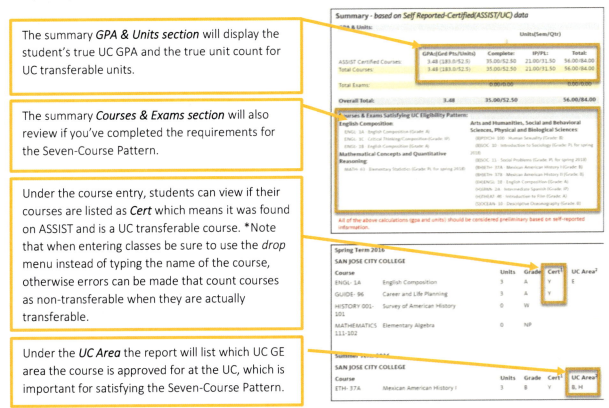

Fig. 0-8. Example of a Student UC TAP Report.

Selective Majors

Similar to Major Impaction at CSU, the UCs use the terms *Selective* or *Screening* to describe the same dynamic of popular majors that become competitive due to too many eligible applicants. There are likewise non-selective, non-screening, or alternative majors that are more open and accessible for transfer applicants. Use **Table 7-12** to view which majors at each campus fall under these categories, and visit each UC campus site to learn more.

Table 0-11 Direct Links to Selective or Screening Majors Information at Each UC Campus.

UC Berkeley High demand/Impacted Majors Alternatives to High-Demand Majors	UC Davis Selective Majors	UC Santa Cruz Screening majors & Non-Screening Majors
UCLA Highly Selective Majors & Alternative Majors	UC Irvine Major Specific Requirements	UC Merced Selective Majors
UC San Diego Capped Major	UC Santa Barbara Selective Majors	UC Riverside Selective Majors

Here are examples of how each UC campus shares information about *Selective* majors. Each campus site holds important information about the major and how to best prepare. Campuses like UCLA (**fig. 7-8**) receive a high volume of applicants for their top 10-20 majors, yet the remaining majors—nearly 100—receive relatively few, although they are in related areas of study. Others, like UC Merced (**fig. 7-9**), may specifically ask Engineering applicants to complete the full IGETC for the major.

Those like UCSB (**fig. 7-10**) may require students to receive no grade lower than a C in their Major Prep courses.

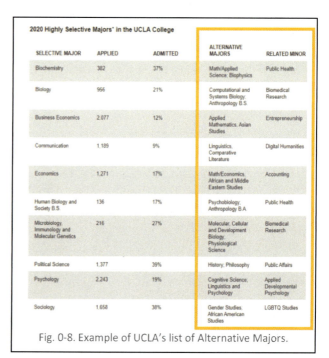

Fig. 0-8. Example of UCLA's list of Alternative Majors.

Fig. 0-9. Example of UC Merced's Recommendations for Engineering transfer student

Fig. 0-10. Example of UCSB's GPA criteria for a screening major.

The UC Data Center by Transfer Admission

The UCs provide a wonderful, public-facing tool whereby they share admissions metrics, including Transfer admission. Here are some tips for students to use the tool and get an overview of how each campus varies based on the number of applicants for a major, the GPA range for admission, and each major's admit rates (**fig. 7-11**). Students who qualify for application fee waivers for the UC (a large majority of CCC Transfer applicants) will be eligible to apply to four campuses in one application. It's important to take time and really investigate the campuses where you meet (or are close to meeting) GPA eligibility to increase your chances of admission.

Again, always do this with your CCC Counselor.

Use the CAMPUS drop down menu to search one of the nine UC campuses and then select the admissions term you want to search.

By major name | By federal CIP category | By community college

Fall term transfer applications by major

Search for major name

Campus: UCB   **Fall term:** 2021

Compare selected broad discipline across campuses (Ignores college/school)

Broad discipline: All

Compare selection to campus overall

Admit rate	19%
Overall campus admit rate	19%
Yield rate	62%
Overall campus yield rate	62%

Mouse over "Broad discipline" or "College/School", then click the minus or plus to collapse or expand. Click on a category to select it.
The GPA range represents the middle half of admits and enrollees (the 25th to 75th percentile).

Totals may not add up because majors with fewer than 5 applicants or fewer than 3 admits or enrollees are masked (not shown).

Campus	Applicants	Admits	Enrolls	Admit GPA range	Enroll GPA range	Admit rate	Yield rate
UCB	22,182	4,303	2,648	3.65 - 3.97	3.62 - 3.95	19%	62%
UCD	18,765	9,454	2,817	3.47 - 3.88	3.37 - 3.80	50%	30%
UCI	25,857	9,674	2,863	3.62 - 3.93	3.53 - 3.87	37%	30%
UCLA	28,464	5,435	3,434	3.80 - 4.00	3.78 - 4.00	19%	63%
UCM	4,962	3,056	268	3.11 - 3.69	2.93 - 3.47	62%	9%
UCR	14,740	9,234	2,056	3.11 - 3.73	2.91 - 3.51	63%	22%
UCSD	22,492	12,175	3,594	3.48 - 3.91	3.37 - 3.84	54%	30%
UCSB	20,573	10,040	2,102	3.55 - 3.91	3.46 - 3.82	49%	21%
UCSC	13,237	7,644	1,728	3.12 - 3.76	2.96 - 3.57	58%	23%

Broad discipline	College/School	Major name	Applicants	Admits	Enrolls	Admit GPA range	Enroll GPA range	Admit rate	Yield rate
Agriculture & Natural Resources	College Of Letters & science	Environmental earth science	23	9	4	3.28 - 3.73	masked	39%	44%
		Environmental economics & policy	114	42	34	3.60 - 3.97	3.65 - 3.97	37%	81%
		Geography	70	19	12	3.65 - 3.98	3.64 - 4.00	27%	63%
	College Of Natural resources	Conservation & resource studies	48	23	18	3.38 - 3.90	3.35 - 3.81	48%	78%
		Ecosystem management and forestry - forestry	17	3	3	masked	masked	18%	100%
		Ecosystem management and forestry - natura...	24	7	4	3.39 - 3.71	masked	29%	57%
		Environmental economics & policy	76	24	21	3.66 - 3.97	3.66 - 3.97	32%	88%
		Environmental science	182	21	11	3.58 - 3.85	3.56 - 3.84	12%	52%
		Society and environment	105	35	21	3.59 - 3.94	3.59 - 3.94	33%	60%
Architecture & Environ Design	College Of Environmental design	Architecture	262	56	50	3.48 - 3.85	3.49 - 3.83	21%	89%
		Landscape architecture	43	7	7	3.55 - 3.84	3.55 - 3.84	16%	100%
		Sustainable environmental design	41	4	3	masked	masked	10%	75%
Area, Ethn, Cultur & Gender Stu	College Of Letters & science	African-american studies	32	7	3	3.16 - 3.66	masked	22%	43%
		American studies	33	19	12	3.43 - 3.90	3.44 - 3.90	58%	63%
		Chicano studies	34	9	6	3.55 - 3.91	3.67 - 3.92	26%	67%
		Ethnic studies	43	4	3	masked	masked	9%	75%
		Gender & women's studies	93	19	7	3.77 - 4.00	3.64 - 4.00	20%	37%
Biological Sciences	College Of Letters & science	Integrative biology	200	53	25	3.68 - 3.93	3.57 - 3.81	27%	47%
		Molecular & cell biology	856	221	105	3.63 - 3.94	3.59 - 3.93	26%	48%

Number of Major Applicants for the Term/Year referenced.

GPA range of admitted applicants by major.

Percentage of Major students admitted based on applications

Fig. 0-11. Example of [UC Data Center's transfer admission data dashboard](#).

Highlights of the 9 UC Campuses

Fig. 0-12. UC Davis West Campus Student Life.

University of California at Davis

Admission: Competitive. TAG campus.

Environment: Northern California. Campus town environment, most students will live on or near campus. Agricultural surroundings. Spacious, affordable, and safe. Big campus, yet it doesn't feel so crowded.

Popular majors: Several Biological Sciences Majors, Psychology, Economics, Animal Science, Computer Science, Political Science, and Communication.

Interesting, lesser-known majors: Nursing, Biomedical Engineering, Genetics, Neurobiology, Human Development, Global Disease Biology, Aerospace Science and Engineering, Agricultural and Environmental Technology or Education, Atmospheric Science, Biotechnology, Community and Regional Development, Design, Data Science, Ecological Management and Resources, Etymology, Hydrology, Food Science, Landscape Architecture, Marine and Coastal Science, Materials Science and Engineering, Pharmaceutical Chemistry, and Native American Studies.

Fig. 0-13. Unfiltered Life at UCI, Student Blog

University of California at Irvine

Admission: Competitive. TAG campus.

Environment: Southern California. Suburban area. Big, safe, sunny, and warm. Partly a commuter campus. Surrounding area expensive. Near beaches.

Popular majors: Computer Science, Biological Sciences, Business/Managerial Economics, Social Psychology, Public Health, Criminology, Psychology, Economics, Education.

Interesting, lesser-known majors: Game Design and Interactive Media, Aerospace Engineering, Business Information Management, Cognitive Sciences, Dance BFA, Data Science, Drama, Earth System Science, Film and Media Studies, Informatics, Music Theater, Pharmaceutical Sciences, Urban Studies, Chinese Studies, Japanese and Korean Literature, and Culture.

Fig. 0-14. UC Merced.

University of California at Merced

Admission: Competitive. TAG campus.

Environment: Central California. Agricultural surroundings. College town. Warm and sunny. Near Yosemite. Big, safe, affordable area. Most diverse of all the UC campuses. Semester-based campus.

Popular majors: Biological Sciences, Psychology, Business Administration and Management, Mechanical or Computer Engineering, Public Health, Sociology, Political Science

Interesting, lesser-known majors: American Studies, Civil Engineering, Environmental Engineering, Electrical Engineering, Global Arts Studies, Critical Race and Ethnic Studies, Environmental Systems Science, Cognitive Science

University of California at Santa Cruz

Fig. 0-15. UC Santa Cruz Student Life.

Admission: Competitive TAG campus.

Environment: Northern California. Woodsy campus. Surrounding area is a beach town, expensive; most students live on or near campus. A college town. Safe area. Near Silicon Valley. Big campus.

Popular majors: Psychology, Business Management, Computer Science, Biology, Sociology,

Interesting, lesser-known majors: Art & Design: Games & Playable Media, Earth Science, Legal Studies, Community Studies, Biotechnology, Linguistics, Marine Biology, Critical Race and Ethnic Studies, Argroecology, Film and Digital Media, Network and Digital Technology, and Robotics Engineering.

University of California at Santa Barbara

Fig. 0-16. Aerial View of UC Santa Barbara Campus.

Admission: Competitive TAG Campus.

Environment: Beach City, Sunny and warm, Exciting, Students Love it here. Big campus with a large student population, modern, lots of student clubs and activities,

Popular majors: Biological Sciences, Psychology, Computer Science, Engineering, Communication, and Journalism.

Interesting, lesser-known majors: Pharmacology, Ecology, Evolution and Marine Biology, Hydrologic Science, Chicano & Chicana Studies, Geography, Dance, Music, Film and Media Studies, Financial Mathematics & Statistics, Zoology, Biopsychology, Economics & Accounting, and History of Public Law & Policy.

University of California at Riverside

Fig. 0-17. UC Riverside Student Life, photo courtesy of Green River College.

Admission: Competitive TAG Campus.

Environment: Southern California. Inland area. Sunny and warm. The surrounding area is affordable, agricultural, and suburban. Commuter campus, with a large student percentage living off campus. Big campus, new facilities. Less impacted.

Popular majors: Business administration and Management, Biological Sciences, Computer Science, Political Science and Government, Sociology, Psychology, Economics, English Language and Literature.

Interesting, lesser-known majors: Art (Studio), Art History, Foreign Languages, Environmental Engineering, Accounting & Auditing, Operations & SupplyChain Management, Neuroscience, Community Leadership, Policy, & Social Justice, Computer Science & Business Applications, Data Science, Public Policy, Robotics, Geophysics, Theater, Film, and Digital Production, and Environmental Science.

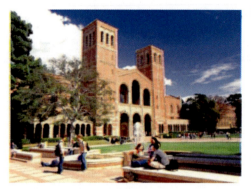

Fig. 0-18. UCLA Student Life, photo courtesy of UCLA

University of California at Los Angeles

Admission: Highly Competitive   No TAG option.

Environment: Southern California. Warm and Sunny. Near beaches. Very large campus, crowded. Feels like a small city. Surrounding area is a safe, affluent, expensive city/suburb. Tons of student activities. Half of the students live off campus. Strong campus student life.

Popular majors: Political Science, Biological Sciences, Psychology, Computer Science, Quantitative Economics, Communication, Sociology, Business Economics, Engineering.

Interesting, lesser-known majors: Nursing, Linguistics, Foreign Languages, Architectural Studies, Design & Media Studies, Dance, Music, Film & Television, Public Affairs, Theater, Education & Social Transformation, Astrophysics, Atmospheric & Oceanic Sciences, Climate Science, Earth & Environmental Science, Mathematics, Financial Actuarial, and Neuroscience.

Fig. 0-19. UC Berkely Student Life at Sather Gate, photo courtesy of Berkeley.

University of California at Berkeley

Admission: Highly Competitive   No TAG option.

Environment: Northern California. Near the water. Surrounding area is expensive, urban/suburban. Many students live on or near campus. Large campus, crowded. Feels like a small city. Strong campus student life.

Popular majors: Computer Science, Business Administration, Biological Sciences, Political Science & Government, Engineering, Cognitive Science, Environmental Studies.

Interesting, lesser-known majors: Aerospace Engineering, City Planning, Legal Studies, Social Welfare, Data Science, Earth & Planetary Sciences, Ecosystem management & Forestry, Nutritional Sciences, Film & Media, Global Poverty & Practice, Media Studies, Operations Research & Management Sciences, Rhetoric, Theater Studies & Performance, Urban Studies, Architecture, Landscape Architecture, and Sustainable Environmental Design.

Fig. 0-20. UC San Diego Aerial Campus View, courtesy of LA Times.

University of California at San Diego

Admission: Highly Competitive   No TAG option.

Environment: Southern California. Beach City. Sunny and warm. Surrounding area is suburban, Exciting. Affordable off-campus housing. Strong student life.

Popular majors: Biological Sciences, Computer Science, Global Studies, Political Science & Government, Cognitive Science, Communication, Quantitative Economics, Engineering, and Psychology.

Interesting, lesser-known majors: Pharmacological Chemistry, Critical Gender Studies, Data Science, Education Studies, Public Health, Human Developmental Sciences, International Studies, Mechanical Engineering (various specializations), Music, Dance, Oceanic and Atmospheric Sciences, Urban Planning, and Visual Arts

Works Cited

"Assist IS Here To Help." *Assist*, California Community Colleges / California State U / U of California,

2022, www.assist.org/. Accessed 26 Feb. 2023.

Schelenz, Robyn. "UC Campuses Earn Top Spots in U.S. News and World Report's 2022 Best Colleges

Rankings." *University of California*, Regents of the U of California, 13 Sept. 2021,

www.universityofcalifornia.edu/news/uc-campuses-earn-top-spots-us-news-world-reports-

2022-best-colleges-rankings. Accessed 12 Mar. 2023.

University of California. "Transfer Pathways Guide." *University of California*, Regents of the U of

California, pathwaysguide.universityofcalifornia.edu/college-pathways/0/0. Accessed 12 Mar.

2023.

---. "Transfer Pathways Guide: San José City College, Computer Science." *University of California*,

Regents of the U of California, pathwaysguide.universityofcalifornia.edu/college-

pathways/San%20Jose%20City%20College/Computer-Science. Accessed 25 Jan. 2023.

---. "Transfers by Major." *University of California*, Regents of the U of California, 9 Feb. 2023,

www.universityofcalifornia.edu/about-us/information-center/transfers-major. Accessed 12

Feb. 2023.

University of California Admissions. "Basic Requirements." *University of California Admissions*, Regents

of the U of California, admission.universityofcalifornia.edu/admission-requirements/transfer-

requirements/preparing-to-transfer/basic-requirements.html. Accessed 12 Mar. 2023.

---. "Blue and Gold Opportunity Plan." *University of California Admissions*, Regents of the U of

California, admission.universityofcalifornia.edu/tuition-financial-aid/types-of-aid/blue-and-

gold-opportunity-plan.html. Accessed 12 Mar. 2023.

---. "Computer Science Transfer Pathway." *University of California Admissions*, Regents of the U of

California, admission.universityofcalifornia.edu/admission-requirements/transfer-

requirements/uc-transfer-programs/transfer-pathways/computer-science.html. Accessed 25

Jan. 2023.

---. "Transfer Admission Guarantee (TAG)." *University of California Admissions*, Regents of the U Of

California, admission.universityofcalifornia.edu/admission-requirements/transfer-

requirements/uc-transfer-programs/transfer-admission-guarantee-tag.html. Accessed 25 Jan.

2023.

---. "Transfer Admission Planner." *University of California Admissions*, Regents of the U of California,

uctap.universityofcalifornia.edu/students/. Accessed 25 Jan. 2023.

---. "Transfer Comprehensive Review." *University of California Admissions, Counselors*, Regents of the

U of California, admission.universityofcalifornia.edu/counselors/preparing-transfer-

students/comprehensive-review.html. Accessed 25 Jan. 2023.

---. "Transfer Pathways." *University of California Admissions*, Regents of the U of California,

admission.universityofcalifornia.edu/admission-requirements/transfer-requirements/uc-

transfer-programs/transfer-pathways/. Accessed 25 Jan. 2023.

---. *UC Transfer Admission Guarantee (TAG) for Students Applying for 2023-2024 Admission*. Regents

of the U of California, 2022. *University of California Admissions*, admission.universityofcalifornia.edu/counselors/_files/documents/tag-matrix.pdf. Accessed

25 Jan. 2023.

Chapter 8: CA Private Colleges (AICCU)

Let's start by discussing what a private college is and how that differs from the UC and the CSU systems that are predominantly used in this guide and when planning for transfer as a whole within the California Community College system (CCC)

Public vs. Private Colleges

There are three kinds of colleges and universities in California that are partly based on how their campuses are funded. Public universities and colleges are largely government funded. So for example, in California, there are three kinds of public colleges:

California Community College (CCC) system of which includes	California State University (CSU) system of which includes	University of California (UC) system of which includes
116 individual colleges	23 individual colleges	9 individual colleges

Each type of public college represents a *system* of colleges that are government funded and regulated by the California legislature. Ideally, they are aligned in their missions and designed to play unique roles in fulfilling the California mandate for higher education and, ultimately, the economic demands for skilled labor.

Two key factors distinguish private colleges and universities: first, they are *individual* colleges and not *systems* of colleges, and second, they are privately funded. Because they are privately funded, they have much more autonomy in setting individual campus policies like admissions requirements, financial aid costs, articulation, and credit policies—all of which impact our Transfer students.

Non-Profit vs. For-Profit Colleges

Private colleges are also separated by their *non-profit* or *for-profit* status. What's the difference? The *for-profit* colleges are set up like a business; their goal is to make money for their investors and owners and to profit from their student enrollment—YOU. In contrast, *non-profit* or *not-for-profit* private colleges are not designed using a business model but structured and regulated as non-profit organizations designed to reinvest their earnings back into their college and towards their mission. *When discussing private colleges throughout this guide, we will refer exclusively to non-profit private colleges.*

For-Profit Colleges: Be Careful!

In this guide, we will not discuss for-profit colleges. In my experience, there are many reasons for students to be highly cautious when dealing with *for-profit* colleges. For example, in early 2022, after becoming concerned about performance and fraud and abuse risks, the **CCCs Chancellor ended CCC's transfer agreement with a for-profit university system ([Smith](#)).**

Ruby Maldando, a medical assistant student, reading a note explaining the closing of Everest College in Industry, Calif., in April. Al Seib/Los Angeles Times, via Getty Images

[NY Times Article on fraud investigations of For-Profit Colleges (Cohen).](#)

Fig. 0-1. Example of For-Profit Fraud Investigations

Let me give you an example of how this can play out. Years ago, I had a student—I'll call him Fabian. Fabian had completed a program in Medical Coding at a for-profit college in California. Fabian was a single dad raising his daughter and had been diagnosed with Multiple Sclerosis (MS) a few years before I met him. He had been working in medical coding at a local hospital for a few years, paying off his student loans for his medical coding degree. That degree cost him $40,000, which our community college offered essentially for free—as he qualified for tuition-waived student aid known as the BOG in each CCC.

About five years after graduating, Fabian got word that his for-profit college had lost its accreditation. *Accreditation* is a process of evaluation that each college and university must satisfy in order to retain their status as an institution of higher education that can confer degrees to students. In Fabian's case, when his for-profit college lost accreditation, his degree lost its value, and he lost his job. He ended up coming to Skyline College—where I met him—to re-enroll in the same medical coding courses he had already taken and was still paying off. For-profit colleges will often advertise on TV; they're

— Harold Poling, left, and Ted Weisenberger check the doors to the ITT Technical Institute after ITT Educational Services announced that the school had ceased operating in Rancho Cordova, Calif., on Sept. 6, 2016. Rich Pedroncelli / AP File

[NBC News article on loan relief for students of for-profit colleges (Associated Press)](#)

Fig. 0-2. Example of efforts to help fraud victims.

often located in malls or easy-to-access areas and will often—much like in car sales—get people in quickly, offer them instant admission, and sign them up for student loans that can be easier to access than credit cards and carry a higher load of student debt. It's been reported that for-profit colleges often target poor and vulnerable communities by design. Additionally, many colleges, like the **Corinthian Colleges**, which in California included *Everest, Heald,* and *WyoTech,* have shut down due to investigation or bankruptcy ([Cohen](#)).

While there may be some reputable for-profits in operation—my overall guidance to students is to "**do your research and be very cautious**." In most cases, they can attain the same degree being offered at a lower cost, if not free, by attending a local CCC. I realize we do not always make it easy for students to get started or register. Sometimes, our process can seem confusing, impersonal, or feel burdensome. That's a fair criticism. But do you know what else is incredibly burdensome? Student Loans. Big student loans follow you whether or not the for-profit college program is completed. So please, be careful there.

Non-Profit, Private Colleges in California

The first point of reference for reviewing your options for transfer to an accredited private college in California that is not-for-profit is the Association of Independent California Colleges and Universities (AICCU). The AICCU offers several resources for transfer students to research each of the 85 private college and university options for transfer.

Fig. 0-4. The AICCU site is an important transfer resource.

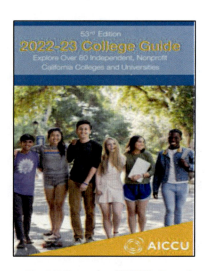

Fig. 0-5. Example of AICCU's Annual College Guide.

Fig. 0-3. Example of an individual campus information page from the AICCU Annual College Guide

AICCU
INDEPENDENT COLLEGES & UNIVERSITIES MAIN CAMPUSES BY REGION

Northern California

Simpson University	Redding
William Jessup University	Rocklin

San Francisco Bay Area

California College of the Arts	San Francisco
California Institute of Integral Studies	San Francisco
Dominican University of California	San Rafael
Golden Gate University	San Francisco
Holy Names University	Oakland
Menlo College	Atherton
Minerva University	San Francisco
Notre Dame de Namur University	Belmont
Pacific Union College	Napa
Palo Alto University	Palo Alto
Saint Mary's College of California	Moraga
Samuel Merritt University	Oakland
San Francisco Bay University	Fremont
San Francisco Conservatory of Music	San Francisco
Santa Clara University	Santa Clara
Saybrook University	Oakland
Stanford University	Stanford
Touro University California	Vallejo
University of San Francisco	San Francisco
Zaytuna College	Berkeley

Central Valley

Fresno Pacific University	Fresno
Humphreys University	Stockton
University of the Pacific	Stockton

Central Coast

California Lutheran University	Thousand Oaks
Fielding Graduate University	Santa Barbara
The Colleges of Law	Santa Barbara
Thomas Aquinas College	Santa Paula
Westmont College	Santa Barbara

Los Angeles

American Jewish University	Bel Air
Antioch University Los Angeles	Los Angeles
ArtCenter	Pasadena
Azusa Pacific University	Azusa
Biola University	La Mirada
California Institute of Technology	Pasadena
California Institute of the Arts	Valencia
Charles R. Drew University of Medicine and Science	Los Angeles
Chicago School of Professional Psychology, The	Los Angeles
Claremont Graduate University	Claremont
Claremont McKenna College	Claremont

Los Angeles (continued)

Columbia College Hollywood	Tarzana
Harvey Mudd College	Claremont
Hope International University	Fullerton
Keck Graduate Institute	Claremont
Life Pacific University	San Dimas
Los Angeles Pacific University	San Dimas
Loyola Marymount University	Los Angeles
Master's University, The	Santa Clarita
Mount Saint Mary's University	Los Angeles
Occidental College	Los Angeles
Otis College of Art and Design	Los Angeles
Pacific Oaks College	Pasadena
Pepperdine University	Malibu
Providence Christian College	Pasadena
Pitzer College	Claremont
Pomona College	Claremont
Scripps College	Claremont
Southern California Institute of Architecture	Los Angeles
Southern California University of Health Sciences	Whittier
Touro University Worldwide	Los Alamitos
University of La Verne	La Verne
University of Southern California	Los Angeles
University of the West	Rosemead
Western University of Health Sciences	Pomona
Whittier College	Whittier
Woodbury University	Burbank

Orange

Chapman University	Orange
Concordia University Irvine	Irvine
Laguna College of Art & Design	Laguna Beach
Soka University	Aliso Viejo
University of Massachusetts Global	Irvine
Vanguard University	Costa Mesa

Riverside / San Bernardino

California Baptist University	Riverside
La Sierra University	Riverside
Loma Linda University	Loma Linda
University of Redlands	Redlands

San Diego

California Institute for Human Science	Encinitas
John Paul the Great Catholic University	Escondido
National University	La Jolla
Point Loma Nazarene University	San Diego
San Diego Christian College	El Cajon
University of Saint Katherine	San Marcos
University of San Diego	San Diego

Fig. 0-6. Example of AICCU's Regional List of Independent Colleges and Universities from the 2022-23 College Guide

How does transfer differ for CA private colleges?

Let's review some ways that the transfer admissions process will change for students applying to CA private colleges and universities.

1. Minimum Units for Transfer Admission

Transfer admissions to a private college in California will include the student's GPA and, in most cases, a minimum number of college credits or units to qualify for transfer admission. Campuses will vary widely on the minimum number of units required for Transfer students to apply. Some campuses, like Stanford, will define this as any college credits completed after high school graduation that count towards an Associate or Bachelor's degree. Others, such as St. Mary's College of California, will indicate 23 semester-based units completed. These numbers vary but generally lay between 15-30 units. What does this mean? It means one big benefit of applying to a Private college, in general, is that you can apply for transfer much sooner.

2. Competitive GPA for Transfer Admission

Another focus of eligibility for transfer admission is the student's GPA. At some campuses, like Santa Clara University, that GPA might be based on the student's major, so an applicant applying into Engineering should satisfy the 3.5 GPA to be competitive for admission versus the student applying into a major like Communication which would require a 3.3 GPA. Campuses will vary widely in terms of GPA competitiveness and in **how openly they share this information openly with prospective students.**

For example, buried in the USC Transfer Planning brochure is the updated recommendation of a 3.8 GPA for Transfer admission, which has increased from a 3.7 GPA in recent years. This information is not listed on the main Transfer website but inside a brochure that students need to know about and review. Other campuses will list on their

Here's a list of questions to consider asking representatives at Private Colleges:

> What is the Competitive GPA for Transfer Admission based on the prior admissions cycle?

> What is the minimum number of units I need to complete in order to apply for transfer admission?

> Which of my courses will transfer to your college and what will they count towards (general ed, major, graduation requirements, etc.?)

> Do you accept the ADT or the IGETC?

> Does your college have a Transfer Admissions Agreement (TAA) with my college?

> What was the transfer admissions rate at your college based on the last application cycle?

> What is the ratio of CCC transfer students at your campus versus freshman admit students?

> What is the average student loan amount that your students graduate with, for students with high financial need?

> What is the graduation rate at your college for CCC Transfer students?

public site the minimum GPA, such as a 2.0 or 2.2, yet in practice, the competitive GPA for admission can be much higher. Unfortunately, universities will vary as to how transparent they are in sharing this data, which leaves students blind in the process both when applying and paying for applications.

3. SAT/ACT Test Scores

Most private colleges in California will not ask Transfer students to submit their SAT / ACT test scores. One exception is Stanford University and other *Ivy League* universities. Be sure to research the average test score for admitted students, as this will also impact how competitive your application is viewed.

4. Exams for Transfer Credit

Like most universities, Private colleges will allow students to transfer AP and IB exam scores. Often those units are welcomed with great flexibility, allowing students to count them towards a core requirement, for example. But every campus is different, so always check with the admissions office. In addition, some Private colleges will allow students to use Transfer credits for CLEP exams and coursework completed in another country. This flexibility can benefit students greatly, of course, as it can shorten their timeline toward graduation.

5. Articulation and Transfer Agreements

Articulation is how colleges evaluate coursework you have completed at one college and how it will count at their college. For example, let's say you took a Biology course in forensic science at your local CCC. That course counted towards your IGETC, so you might assume it will count at any private college you apply to—not necessarily. Private colleges might differ in how they define their version of GEs. They might want all students to complete a lab-based Biology course, either in Cell or Anatomy. In that case, you might receive credit for the units, but the course would not *articulate* the same GE requirement.

To assist with the articulation process and create pathways for transfer students to private colleges, many private colleges in California have established Transfer Admissions Agreements (TAA) with individual CA community colleges. The TAAs help students understand upfront which courses at their local community college will articulate towards the private college and satisfy the college's local core requirements. They are contractual agreements and will vary widely in terms of the set policies and deadlines they include. They usually offer some form of guaranteed admission for students that complete these requirements and also meet the overall transfer admissions requirements like GPA and minimum units.

Here's an example of a TAA between Santa Clara University and San José City College.

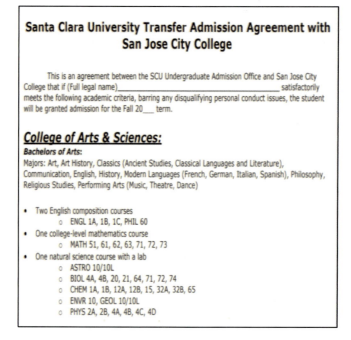

Fig. 0-7. Excerpt from Transfer Agreement between Santa Clara University and San José City College outlining the SJCC courses that meet SCU's core requirements.

6. Transferology instead of ASSIST

Another important tool for transfer students that will aid in the articulation process and overall planning is called Transferology. Figure 8-X shows an example of directions from Whittier College in Southern California, directing Transfer students to review their coursework using Transferology. Transferology is a platform similar to ASSIST that will help students to search if their courses count and for what purpose at the private college. Many private colleges increasingly use this tool; however, many do not. Others, like **University of Southern California (USC),** house their own articulation sites that list the courses they accept from each CCC and how they will count them.

Fig. 0-8. Example of Transferology directions for transfer students from Whittier College.

7. Focus on Graduation Requirements

Most private colleges in California will admit students with anywhere from 15-30 units minimum. This changes the focus for students in a fundamental way. Rather than seeking to meet major requirements, the focus leans more towards meeting the overall graduation requirements. Some major preparation courses might be included, but overall, the admissions review is looking to see if students have satisfied the college's version of GEs or the core requirements that are necessary to graduate as a whole. The upside of this is that if you start early and work closely with the private college's admissions representative, you really can transfer early and be on track to graduate as well. It does simplify the process because instead of transferring as an upper-division student, you are transferring as a lower-division student and can take the major-specific coursework once you are admitted. Now, can that be costly if you're paying a lot more for college? Yes. Definitely. That's an important piece to consider.

8. ADTs for Private Colleges

As recently as 2018, the **AICCU and our CCC Chancellor's Office signed a memo** agreeing that several of the 86 Private Colleges and Universities in California would agree to honor the Associate Degree for Transfer (ADT) for CCC students (Jimenez). To date, 36 campuses have agreed to accept the ADT for transfer admission. This has some important benefits for students. It allows them to save time and money towards completing their degree at a Private college because more coursework coming in is accepted. It also provides a way of guaranteed admission—even for campuses with no TAAs in place. The policies around these admissions practices are still early, and they will vary from campus to campus. It is emphasized that students applying must still meet that college's Transfer admissions requirements. For example, if there's a GPA requirement that must be satisfied for the ADT to count. Also, each college might have different majors and count each ADT differently. Still, it's an important win for transfer students that will widen their options at application time. **Table 8-1** lists California's private colleges that accept the ADT for CCC transfer students based on the 2018 CCC press release. However, view AICCU's <u>matrix of ADT Participating Institutions and majors</u> for a detailed and current list of participating colleges and universities.

Table 0-1. California Private Colleges and Universities accepting the (ADT) for CCC Transfer Students

1. Azusa Pacific University	**16. Mount Saint Mary's University**	**31. Point Loma Nazarene University**
2. Univ. of Massachusetts Global (formerly Brandman University)	17. National University	32. Saint Mary's College of California
3. California Baptist University	18. Pacific Oaks College	33. University of the West
4. California Baptist University Online	19. Pacific Union College	34. Westmont College
5. California Institute of Integral Studies	20. Palo Alto University	35. William Jessup University
6. California Lutheran University	21. Pepperdine University	36. John Paul the Great Catholic University
7. The Chicago School of Professional Psychology	22. San Diego Christian College	
8. Concordia University Irvine	23. Simpson University	

9. Fresno Pacific University	24. University of La Verne	
10. Golden Gate University	25. University of Redlands	
11. Holy Names University	26. University of Saint Katherine	
12. Humphreys University	27. University of San Francisco	
13. La Sierra University	28. Whittier College	
14. Los Angeles Pacific University	29. Marymount California University	
15. Mills College	30. Notre Dame de Namur University	
Source: Jimenez		

9. Application Waivers and Deadlines

Private colleges will often offer students with financial need application waivers so that the cost of applying does not pose a challenge to students. To learn more about this, reach out to the admissions office and also speak with your Career Transfer Center for help.

In terms of deadlines, each Private college could not operate more differently. Some colleges will only open transfer admissions for the Fall cycle. Others will include a Fall and Spring or a Fall and Winter cycle. Many will offer what's called *Rolling Admissions*, meaning students can apply and be admitted at any time throughout the year. Some, like Holy Names University, will offer transfer students *on-the-spot* admissions decisions, meaning if you go to their admissions office to apply, they will make the decision for admission during your visit. In many ways, this is how colleges and universities seek to recruit students—to make the process of applying that much easier. Overall, that's a good thing for students; just remember to always work with your CCC Counselor and take a step back to make sure you know all your options. It's easy to get caught up in a moment of excitement, be sure you are clear about what you're signing up for before attending.

Top 10 Most Expensive Private Colleges in California	Undergraduate Tuition Only / Per Year
Stanford University	$77,034
University of Southern California	$63,468
Harvey Mudd College	$62,516
Pepperdine University	$62,390
Claremont McKenna College	$60,715
Chapman University	$60,290
Occidental College	$59,970
California Institute of Technology	$58,479
Scripps College	$56,970
California Institute of the Arts	$52,850

Fig. 0-9. Forbes Magazine's 2022 list of 10 Most Expensive Private Colleges in California.

10. Financial aid & Affordability

For the large majority of our CA Private Colleges, the issue at hand for transfer students is not so much whether or not you will 'get in'—but instead, **how you will pay for it**. The price tag across Private Colleges really does vary, but most are, on average two-three times the cost of a UC on annual tuition of **$13,104** and still much more compared with the CSU's annual tuition rate of **$5,742**. What's tricky about this is that scholarships and grants will be factored in to lower the costs. For example, a student attending Pepperdine University might receive a $20,000 university scholarship and a $10,000 Cal Grant as part of their financial aid offer letter—and yet, still owe $32,390 in tuition alone for one academic year.

Table 0-2. Comparison of Private Colleges in the California Bay Area region using 2021-22 data.

CAMPUS	TRANSFER ADMIT RATE	TRANSFER ADMIT GPA	UNDERGRAD TUITION	2021 TRANSFER ADMIT DEADLINES	MIN UNITS TRANSFER	ACCEPTS CCC ADT	ADMIT POLS & REQS
STANFORD	1-4%	4.0	$77,034	March 15th	Graduated High School and completed any college credits toward Associate or Bachelor's program	NO ADT	SAT or ACT Test
SANTA CLARA	45%	3.3 - 3.5 required	$56,880	**Fall Admission** January 7th - April 15th **Winter Admission** October 1st	30 semester-based units min recommended	NO ADT Does offer Transfer Admission Agreements (TAA) for CC's	2nd language requirement for some majors
HOLY NAMES	89%	2.2 min	$41,579 OR **Adult Degree Completion** $495/unit **($14,850 / 30 sem. units or 1 yr full-time)**	Rolling Admissions All Year	24 semester units minimum; 30 semester units required at HNU to earn BA	Accepts ADT	Offers on-The-spot admissions decisions
ST. MARY'S COLLEGE OF CA	71%	2.0 min	$50,460	**Priority Fall** March 1st **Fall** June 1st **Spring** December 1st	23 semester units minimum	Accepts ADT	--

At heart, I hope you can see that Private Colleges will differ widely. We're so lucky in California to have so many options for students and that more and more private colleges are accepting the IGETC and Associate Degree for Transfer. These are big wins for our students; those will shorten student graduation paths and save both money and time. My biggest advice for those interested in a private college is "do your homework early." Start talking with admissions representatives and planning for the financial costs. Keep your GPA high and start researching outside scholarships as well that can help you to graduate with as little debt as possible. Table 8-X shows how widely private colleges can vary as to admission rates, costs, admission GPA, deadlines, and specific campus policies. There are some colleges with programs, like Holy Names University's Adult Completion Program, which offer overall great deals for students—especially working adults through their cohort-based model. Work with your Counselor and Transfer Center to learn about local options or partner campuses which may be a great fit for you.

Top 50 California Private Colleges and Universities

Based on the CCC Transfer Counselor listing of the top 50 California Private Colleges & Universities (Reference).

National University (685)
Transfer Information

West Coast University Los Angeles (640)
Transfer Information
West Coast University Transfer Equivalency System (TES)
Phone: 866-508-2684

The University of Arizona Global Campus (Ashford University) (612)
Transfer Information
Phone: 866-711-1700

UMass Global (Brandman University) (364)
Transfer Information
Transfer Your College Credit
Phone: 800-746-0082

Fresno Pacific University (301)
Transfer Information
Phone: 559-453-2039
Toll-free: 800-660-6089
Email: ugadmis@fresno.edu

University of Southern California (289)
Transfer Information
Articulation Agreements
Interactive Planning Guide
Transfer Planning Worksheet
Find Your Admissions Counselor

California Baptist University (265)
Transfer Information
Transferology
Transfer Agreements
Phone: 877-228-3615

University of La Verne (236)
Transfer Information
LaVerne General Education
LVGE General Education
Conversion Chart
Phone: 909-593-3511
Los Angeles Pacific University (198)
Transfer Information
Phone: 855-527-2768
Email: admissions@lapu.edu

Azusa Pacific University (187)
Transfer Information
Transferology
Transfer to APU
Phone: 626-812-3016
Email: admissions@apu.edu
Devry University California (154)
Transfer Information
CCC Transfer Guides
Phone: 866-338-7934

Point Loma Nazarene University (127)
Transfer Information
Transfer Credit
Transfer Evaluation System (TES)

University of San Francisco (117)
Transfer Information
Phone: 415-422-6563
Email: transfer@usfca.edu

California Lutheran University (92)
Transfer Information
Articulation Agreements
Phone: 805-492-2411

University of the Pacific (92)
Transfer Information
Transfer Guide
Phone: 209-946-2211
Email: admission@pacific.edu

Transfer Information
Phone: 626-529-8061
Toll-Free: 800-201-2296
Email: admissions@pacificoaks.edu

University of San Diego (90)
Transfer Information
Transfer Roadmap
Phone: 619-260-4506
Phone: 619-260-6836
Email: admissions@sandiego.edu

Chapman University (85)
Transfer Information
Transferring to Chapman University
Phone: 714-997-6711
Email: transfers@chapman.edu

Academy of Art University (80)
Transfer Information
Transfer Students
Phone: 415-274-2222

Loyola Marymount University (77)
Transfer Information
Transfer Requirements
Contact
Phone: 310-338-5913

Biola University (75)
Transfer Information
Transfer Pathways
Transfer Evaluation System (TES)
Phone: 1-800-OK-BIOLA
Email: transfer.admissions@biola.edu

Mount St. Mary's University (75)
Transfer Information
Eric Danielson
Director of Admissions
Email: danielson@msmary.edu
Phone: 301-447-5214

Simpson University (72)
Transfer Information
Transfer Evaluation System (TES)
Phone: 888-974-6776
Email: admissions@simpsonu.edu

Samuel Merritt University (71)
Admission
Phone: 800-607-6377
Email: admission@samuelmerritt.edu
University of Redlands (70)
Transfer Information
Phone: 909-793-2121

William Jessup University (53)
Transfer Guidelines for California
Community Colleges
Phone: 916-577-2298
Email: advising@jessup.edu

Golden Gate University, San
Francisco (51)
Undergraduate Transfers
Phone: 415-442-7000
Email: info@ggu.edu

Pepperdine University (47)
Transfer Information
Phone: 310-506-4000

Vanguard University of Southern
California (47)
Transfer Information
Transfer Policy
 -6279

Saint Mary's College of California
(45)
Transfer Information
Articulation Agreements
Phone: 925-631-4244
Email: smcadmit@stmarys-ca.edu

Santa Clara University (43)
Transfer Information
Transferring Credits
Transfer Admission Agreements
Phone: 408-554-4700
Email: admission@scu.edu

Woodbury University (41)
Transfer Information
Transfer Evaluation System (TES)
Los Angeles Phone: 818-252-5221
San Diego Phone: 619-235-2900
Email: info@woodbury.edu

Antioch University - Los Angeles
(39)
Transfer Information
Articulation Agreements
Contact Antioch University

Notre Dame de Namur University
(36)
Admissions
Phone: 650-508-3600

The Master's College and Seminary
(32)
Transfer Information
Phone: 705-749-0725
Email: info@mcs.edu

Concordia University-Irvine (29)
Transfer Information
Articulation Agreements
Tamara Oseguera
Transfer and Readmits
Phone: 949-214-3032
Email: tamara.oseguera@cui.edu

Mills College (28)
Transfer Information
Connect With a Counselor
Email: admission@mills.edu

Stanford University (27)
Transfer Information
Email: transferadmission@stanford.edu

Art Center College of Design (25)
Transfer Information
Phone: 626-396-2373
Email: admissions@artcenter.edu

California Institute of Integral
Studies (25)
Admissions and Financial Aid
Admissions Team

Holy Names University (24)
Transfer Information
Transfer Credits
Articulation Agreements / Course
Equivalencies
Phone: 510-7819379
Email: admissions@hnu.edu

Musicians Institute (23)
Admissions
Phone: 323-462-1384
Email: admissions@mi.edu

Hope International University (23)
Transfer for Undergraduate on Campus
Transfer for Undergraduate Online
GE Transfer Forms
Phone: 888-352-HOPE
Email: hiuadmissions@hiu.edu

Trident University International (22)
Transfer Information
Contact

California College of the Arts (21)
Transfer Information
Articulation Agreements
Phone: 415-529-4802
Email: transfer@cca.edu

Westmont College (21)
Transfer Information
Transfer Credit / Transfer Agreements
Connect with Your Admissions Counselor

New School of Architecture and Design (20)
Transfer Information
Transferring College Credits
Phone: 619-684-8766
Email: enrollment@newschoolarch.edu

San Diego Christian University (20)
Transfer Information
Articulation Agreements
Email: admissions@sdcc.edu

Menlo College (19)
Transfer Information / Transfer Agreements
Phone: 650-5433753
Email: transfer@menlo.edu

University of Silicon Valley (Cogswell College) (17)
Transfer Information
Connect with the USV Community

Works Cited

Associated Press. "Biden Administration Grants Loan Relief to Former For-Profit College

    Students." *NBC News*, NBC Universal, 16 June 2021, www.nbcnews.com/politics/politics-

    news/biden-administration-grants-loan-relief-former-profit-college-students-n1270985.

    Accessed 12 Mar. 2023.

Cohen, Patricia. "For-Profit Colleges Accused of Fraud Still Receive U.S. Funds." *The New York*

    Times, New York Times Company, 12 Oct. 2015, www.nytimes.com/2015/10/13/business/for-

    profit-colleges-accused-of-fraud-still-receive-us-funds.html. Accessed 24 Jan. 2023.

DePietro, Andrew. "The Most Expensive Colleges in California." *Forbes*, Forbes Media, 2 Dec.

    2022, www.forbes.com/sites/andrewdepietro/2022/12/02/the-most-expensive-colleges-

    in-california/?sh=35a2a62d5d91. Accessed 13 Mar. 2023.

Jimenez, Christina. "New California Community Colleges Agreement with Private Colleges and

    Universities Marks Major Expansion of Associate Degree for Transfer Program." *California*

    Community Colleges, California Community Colleges Chancellor's Office, 25 July 2018,

    www.cccco.edu/About-Us/News-and-Media/Press-Releases/ADT-Expansion-2018.

    Accessed 24 Jan. 2023.

Smith, Ashley A. "Community Colleges Chancellor Announces End to For-profit Transfer

    Agreement." *EdSurge*, 24 Jan. 2022, edsource.org/updates/community-colleges-

    chancellor-announces-end-to-for-profit-transfer-agreement. Accessed 24 Jan. 2023.

University of Southern California. *Transferring to USC*. U of Southern California, 2023. *ISSUU*,

issuu.com/esdwebm/docs/transferring_issuu_?fr=sMGU5ZTE3OTIyODA. Accessed 12

Mar. 2023.

Chapter 9: Out-of-State Colleges

There are countless options available for students interested in studying outside of California. One great tool available for students to perform this search is with the College Board, called Big Future.

Perhaps the biggest obstacle students will face when seeking to study out-of-state is the non-resident tuition fee structure, meaning it will cost two to three times more to attend than the in-state student.

There is, however, something known as the WUE, which will allow students in **participating states**, like California, to study in another state that's part of this 'exchange' agreement for a reduced cost.

The Western Undergraduate Exchange (WUE)

The Western Undergraduate Exchange (WUE) is an agreement among WICHE's 16 members, through which 160+ participating public colleges and universities provide steep non-resident tuition savings for Western students. (See the illustration of states to the right.)

Through WUE, eligible students can choose from hundreds of undergraduate programs outside their home state and pay no more than 150 percent of that institution's resident tuition rate.

Since full non-resident college tuition rates may exceed 300 percent of resident rates, WUE increases affordable higher-education choices for students and minimizes the adverse impacts of student loan debt. To search for WUE, visit the WUE savings finder tool and follow the steps below.

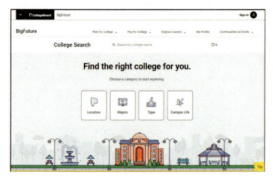

Fig. 0-1. BIG FUTURE search for colleges across the US.

Fig. 0-2. Member States of the Western Undergraduate Exchange.

WUE is 150% of the enrolling INSTITUTION'S resident tuition (sometimes less!)

For Example*:

Resident = $6,990

WUE = $10,485
(resident x 1.5)

Nonresident = $22,041

Tuition Savings = **$11,556!!**
($22,041 - $10,485)

Fig. 0-3. Example of how the WUE tuition savings works for out-of-state colleges.

Saving through WUE is simple.

1 Check your eligibility

2 Check schools and degrees

3 Meet your school's WUE requirements

4 Apply directly to the school

Fig. 0-4. Steps to apply for the WUE.

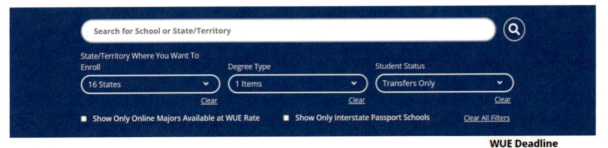

Welcome to Your WUE Savings Finder.

Search among hundreds of undergraduate degrees offered at the WUE rate of 150% of resident tuition (or less) by 160+ public colleges and universities across the West. Find the school and program that fits your geographic and educational goals.

Start here to save an average of $9,000 a year!

Search for School or State/Territory				

State/Territory Where You Want To Enroll	Degree Type	Student Status
16 States	1 Items	Transfers Only
Clear	Clear	Clear

■ Show Only Online Majors Available at WUE Rate ■ Show Only Interstate Passport Schools   Clear All Filters

School ▲	Location ▲	Program/Major	WUE Tuition	WUE Deadline for Fall Admission
University of Alaska Anchorage	Anchorage, AK	See Programs ⌄	$10,530	7/15/22
University of Alaska Fairbanks	Fairbanks, AK	See Programs ⌄	$10,530	6/15/21
University of Alaska Southeast	Juneau, AK	See Programs ⌄	$10,530	Contact School
Northern Arizona University	Flagstaff, AZ	See Programs ⌄	$15,975	Contact School
Arizona State University / Polytechnic Campus	Mesa, AZ	See Programs ⌄	$14,460	Contact School
Arizona State University / Downtown	Phoenix, AZ	See Programs ⌄	$16,065	Contact School
Arizona State University / West Campus	Phoenix, AZ	See Programs ⌄	$14,460	Contact School
University of Arizona Sierra Vista	Sierra Vista, AZ	See Programs ⌄	$13,839	Contact School

Fig. 0-5. WUE Savings Finder Dashboard.

HBCU Transfer Guarantee Pathway

In addition to the WUE, our California Community College CCC) students can benefit from the **Historically Black Colleges and Universities (HBCU)** Transfer Guarantee Pathway. There are just over 100 HBCUs recognized by the US Dept. of Education, including public, private, denominational, liberal arts, land-grant, independent university systems, single-gender serving, researched-based that award Bachelor's Degrees, Graduate / Masters / Professional Degrees, and Doctoral Degrees offering competitive tuition rates.

The majority of classes at HBCUs are smaller and are taught by professors rather than teaching assistants in a nurturing and supportive environment.

HBCUs were established primarily to serve the higher education needs of the Black community; however, they are open to students of all ethnicities. Most HBCUs are located in the South and on the East Coast. They award bachelor's degrees in many fields, and many award master's and doctorate degrees.

Thanks to an agreement signed on March 17, 2015, between the CCC and select HBCUs, CCC students who complete certain academic requirements are guaranteed to transfer to a participating HBCU.

To learn more about the HBCU Transfer Guarantee Pathway, click here.

Transfer Advantages:
- Acceptance of completed transfer-level community college courses
- A free single application for up to four participating partner HBCU institutions
- A simplified transfer process
- Priority consideration for housing when application submitted by the posted deadline
- Consideration for transfer scholarships if you have a 3.2 or higher grade point average (based on funding availability)
- Pre-admission advisement

Click here to view the list of participating HBCU's.

Fig. 0-6. Historically Black Colleges Transfer Guarantee Pathway.

Student Qualification Requirements for the HBCU Transfer Guarantee Program

Any CCC student with a **GPA of 2.0** or higher (NOTE: certain partner HBCUs will require a higher GPA) is guaranteed admission to all partner HBCU institutions using either of the following two options while at a CCC:

1. Complete an **Associate degree (ADT)** using the Intersegmental General Education Transfer Curriculum (IGETC) or the California State University General Education Breadth pattern

   or

2. Complete a minimum of **30 UC or CSU units**.

Those students completing an Associate Degree (Non-ADT) are welcome to apply to all partner institutions. However, the benefit of guaranteed admissions is not offered, and all degree-applicable units are subject to transcript evaluation.

Part III: Transfer Application Overview

This section is intended to provide an overview of how the application process generally works for students applying to UC and CSU. Always work with your Counselor, Transfer Center, and Admissions representatives for individualized assistance. In addition, there are many places in which I refer you to recorded workshops, CSU or UC-designed guides, or websites that have the most up-to-date instructions. The purpose of this section is not to recreate instructions for applying to the CSU or UC but instead to provide students with a preview of the overall process when applying and hands-on resources for additional support and guidance. Please also note that each California Community College (CCC) Transfer Center provides students with the most up-to-date information, workshops, and support during the process.

Chapter 10: Applying to the CSU

Step 1	**Step 2**	**Step 3**	**Step 4**	**Step 5**
Submit CSU Application	Submit Supplemental Application	Submit SIR & Pay Deposit	Submit Official Transcripts, AP/IB Scores	Sign up for Orientation & Classes

Application Phase — *Acceptance Phase*

Fig. 0-1. The CSU Application Process in Five Steps

There are two phases when applying to the CSU: the *Application Phase* and *Acceptance Phase*. Students must complete Steps 1 through 5 of both phases successfully to complete the entire application process. Not doing so can result in denial of admission or revoking of admission.

Step 1. CSU Application – *Application Phase*

The first step is to submit the CSU Application for **Upper Division** Transfer Admission. Students apply using one application website available on CalState.edu/Apply. There are 23 CSU campuses for transfer admission through this site.

Fig. 0-2. The CSU Application Website.

The CSU Application takes about 1-2 hours to complete. Students can work through sections of the application and save their work as they go. Students preparing to apply should have copies available of their unofficial or official transcripts, AP or IB scores, and if possible, a copy of their high school transcripts is helpful but not required. In addition, they should have their social security number, green card, or student visa information. However, students without a social security number can apply to the CSU without an SSN. This applies to undocumented students, with or without DACA. Students should also have their parent(s) financial information, their own financial information, or both ready as a reference.

Fig. 0-3. California State University, "Transfer Student Application Checklist."

Where to find help completing the CSU Application

Look for your Transfer Center's CSU Application Workshops

The best support for students applying to the CSU for transfer admissions is to attend a CSU Application workshop provided by your campus Transfer Center. **In addition, students should have their application reviewed by their Counselor, Transfer Center, or CSU Admissions representative** to ensure it is completed correctly *before* **submitting their application.** Applications may be denied due to entry errors, incomplete information, or submitting the wrong set of final courses required for admission. These are all areas your CCC Counselor and Transfer Center staff are trained to review.

In addition to those workshops, there are several online resources to aid you while completing the CSU Application, and we'll review a few. These supports help save time and make sure you understand the information you are being asked to enter, so take your time and review the resources discussed.

The CSU Transfer Application Guide

California State University's CAL STATE APPLY: Transfer Application Guide is the most reliable and up-to-date resource available to help transfer students walk through much of the CSU Application for Transfer process.

This guide is updated each year by the CSU—so be *sure to utilize the current guide that corresponds to the year you are applying for transfer when completing your application materials.* Here's a preview of some pages from this guide.

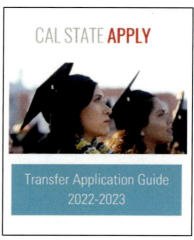

Fig. 0-4. Cal State Apply Transfer Application Guide.

Fig. 0-5. Page 21, Cal State Apply Transfer Application Guide.

Fig. 0-6. Page 25, Cal State Apply Transfer Application Guide.

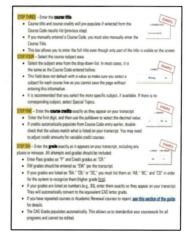

Fig. 0-7. Page 26, Cal State Apply Transfer Application Guide.

Online CSU Application Videos Available

The pandemic caused everyone in education to rethink online instruction and content. One silver lining of the pandemic is that there is now a wide variety of transfer admissions workshops, fairs, tours, panels, and other online resources available to assist. I want to highlight a few related to the CSU Application that are especially great options for students because they walk us through the process.

1. CCC Transfer Counselor Videos

The CCC Transfer Counselor Website offers an excellent series (Fig. 10-8) that walks through the CSU Application entry process for any CCC Transfer student. These are generously put together by **Butte College's Transfer Center Counselor/Coordinator Steve St. Cin**. Big shout out to him for these videos and all his work on the CCC Transfer Counselor Website.

Fig. 0-8. CCC Transfer Counselor Video Playlist.

2. CCC Transfer Center Videos

Many CCC Transfer Centers have also put together online application videos for students to access remotely and to aid them in the application process. However, Cypress College's Transfer Center has a really exceptional video series (Fig. 10-9). It's comprehensive, professional, and also lends a lot of great advice from a counselor's perspective. Although these videos are customized with Cypress College examples, they are ones any CCC student can utilize—much like this guide!

Fig. 0-9. Cypress Transfer Center video channel.

3. CSU Transfer Application Videos

All CSUs have a kind of outreach team focused on getting transfer students information about their college and aiding them in applying. Additionally, many CSUs have put together some great online content to help students walk through the CSU Application and Transfer process. For example, CSU East Bay's Outreach Team does a great job of introducing the campus and team while also walking students through the 2022 CSU transfer application (**fig. 10-10**).

Fig. 0-10. CSUEB Outreach video

CSU Transfer Application Dashboard

The 1st quadrant: Personal Information

This quad asks students to enter their personal, biographic, and financial information.

The 2nd quadrant: Academic History

This quad asks students to enter their full academic records. Utilize the CSU Transfer Application guide and attend a CSU Application workshop for special guidance.

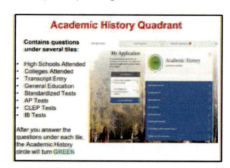

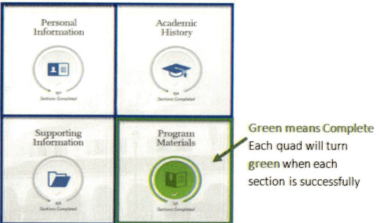

Green means Complete Each quad will turn green when each section is successfully

Fig. 0-11. Overview of CSU Transfer Application Dashboard.

The 3rd quadrant: Supporting Information

This quad includes the CSU EOP Application for transfer students. The applications is a drop down menu and will include short paragraph responses and recommender's contact info. This is the only opportunity to apply for EOP at most CSU's, it's highly recommended you do so if you have financial need.

The 4th quadrant: Campus Specific Questions

This quad will differ from campus to campus and also based on your major. Some campuses or major programs may ask additional questions or require additional materials for evaluating applications, for example nursing majors are asked to submit nursing related tests scores and many CSU's will ask students to upload a copy of their unofficial transcripts.

The CSU Application – A Bird's Eye View

As I've explained, great workshops, videos, and guides are already available to help complete the CSU Application for Transfer Admission. So, let's spend time taking a bird's eye view of the application and highlight each section's common questions that come up or frequent pitfalls where things can go wrong.

Fig. 0-12. Quadrant 1: Personal Information, Cal State Apply Quadrants.

Quadrant 1: Personal Information

Since the first quadrant is not always discussed in greater detail in the CSU Application guide, let's take a moment to understand what each section means and how to complete it.

Release Statement
This statement asks students to declare that all the information submitted in their application is accurate and for permission to share the applicant's data with individual CSU campuses that may then contact the applicant. It also allows the applicant's CCC, its counseling office, or both to verify records like transcripts or ADTs to the CSU, which is really important for admission.

Biographic Information
These are the biographic items requested from Transfer applicants, including Name, Alternate Name, Gender, Date of Birth, Location of Birth, foster care status, ward of the state information, or housing status.

Some important pitfalls to avoid here are issues with name differences across student records. For example, if a student lists one version of their name on the CSU application that does not match their college transcripts, it could create issues for the student later when verifying their coursework and degree completion. Please note that this information is kept confidential and protected under FERPA for student privacy. Sharing this kind of sensitive data will not impact the evaluation of your admission. It will allow the college to identify students in need of additional resources and support, which is overall a good thing for any student,

Contact Information

The requested contact information includes four items: Current Address, Permanent Address, Email, and Phone. Note that if you have one mailing address, you can list that for both options. *Current Address* refers to students that might live away from home during the school year and then, for example, move back to their parent's home afterward. In that example, their parent's home is their *permanent address*.

Citizenship Information

This section asks applicants to identify their citizenship status, which has several categories. The types identified are *US Citizen* (must give social security number), *Permanent Resident,* or *Green Card Holder* (must give permanent resident number). Applicants with other visa types include J-1, F-1, and U (must give visa information). Undocumented student applicants can enter 'None' under citizenship and then 'USA' under residency. Questions about California Residency follow this section. Note, for undocumented students, California residency is established by the amount of time you have lived in California and is not related to citizenship status. Please note that students sharing their undocumented status is protected under FERPA student privacy. Even under the most difficult political circumstances, California has stood strong in protecting this data and thereby protecting our Dreamer student's pathway to higher education.

Race & Ethnicity

This section will ask students to identify which Ethnicity and Race best apply to them. I want to emphasize how important these questions are to answer as they relate to schools and colleges. Special funding—such as funding for Hispanic Serving Institutions (HIS)—is often secured based on this data. I've seen students often enough skip these questions or decline to answer, which is their choice, of course. However, I want students to be aware that their responses have consequences and particularly for students of diverse backgrounds. When colleges have this data, it allows them to either qualify for additional state or federal funding or to argue for expanded services to meet the needs of all students in an equitable manner. It's a powerful tool you have to help expand students' access to resources and services.

Other Information

This section will ask applicants to include information about a number of miscellaneous items: social security number, California (CA) statewide ID, language proficiency, military status, military application questions, military dependent questions, academic standing, academic infractions and conduct, teacher credential interest, CalFresh, CA Promise, RN License, and "how did you hear about us."

- Note for Social Security Number - Undocumented students can click 'NO" under the social security number question and check the box that reads "I acknowledge that I do not have a US social security number."

- The *CA statewide ID* is the 10-digit number listed in your high school transcript for students that attended a public high school. If you did not attend a public high school or simply do not know this number, you can leave it blank—it is not required.

- Military status and application questions will connect students with on-campus veteran centers and services and help each campus to identify applicants seeking to utilize those benefits.

- Academic standing, in part, means that students who are applying acknowledge they have, at minimum, a 2.0 GPA or above; it also includes acknowledging that there are no issues of student misconduct related to the applicant at their current college.

- Teacher credential refers to students interested in pursuing their teaching credentials as part of their study. This category can include students with majors in Child Development or Liberal Studies, which are common for achieving a multiple-subject teaching credential, or subjects like a specific foreign language, English, History, and Math that are common for pursuing a single-subject teaching credential.

- *Cal Fresh* is a food-buying program that allows low-income households to receive electronic benefits such as the EBT card, which is like a debit card and can be used to purchase groceries.

- *CA Promise* is an incentive program for students transferring into the CSU with an Associates Degree for Transfer (AA-T or AS-T). This program provides additional benefits, such as priority registration or 2-year degree plans with full-time registration, to aid transfer students in graduating with their Bachelor's Degree in two years.

- RN License is simply asking students if they currently have a Registered Nurse license or expect to achieve one.

- "How did you hear about us" is simply asking how you became aware of the CSU, your transfer options, and the application.

Financial and Parental Info

This portion of the application will determine if you qualify for the application fee waiver; it is not the FAFSA or the California Dream Application. Students that qualify based on their financial need will receive a fee waiver to apply to four CSU campuses at no cost. This qualification status is determined at the end of the application but prior to submission. If you did not receive the fee waiver but believe you would qualify as a student with financial need, check in with your Transfer Center to verify if you completed this section correctly. A common error I have seen is students entering their parent's "gross income" twice—in two separate fields—due to confusion. Take your time and work with your Transfer Center for help on this section.

Fig. 0-13. Visit the Federal Student Aid "Dependency Status" Webpage.

One aspect of the financial aid application process that can be confusing is whether you, as a student, are considered Dependent or Independent. Whether you qualify for financial aid or, in this case, qualify for the application fee waiver—will be determined based on your parents' income or your own. That decision is made based on federal guidelines questions given in **Figure 10-14**. The decision *is not based on whether or not your parents list you as a "Dependent" on their taxes, if you do or do not live at home, or whether your parents actually assist you financially.* If you are **under 24 years old** and answer **"NO" to each question below**, you are considered Dependent and should list your parent's financial information. If you answer **"YES"** to any of the questions below and are **24 years old** or older, then you are considered **Independent** and should use your financial information ("Dependency Status"). Please note undocumented students that will apply for financial aid using the California Dream Act Application (CADA) will utilize the same criteria for determining independent vs. dependent status (**fig. 10-14**)

Dependency Status Questions on the 2023–24 FAFSA® Form

	Yes	No
Were you born before Jan. 1, 2000?	Yes	No
As of today, are you married? (Also answer "Yes" if you are separated but not divorced.)	Yes	No
At the beginning of the 2023–24 school year, will you be working on a master's or doctorate program (such as an M.A, MBA, M.D., J.D., Ph.D., Ed.D., graduate certificate, etc.)?	Yes	No
Are you currently serving on active duty in the U.S. armed forces for purposes other than training? (If you are a National Guard or Reserves enlistee, are you on active duty for other than state or training purposes?)	Yes	No
Are you a veteran of the U.S. armed forces?⁺	Yes	No
Do you now have—or will you have—children who will receive more than half of their support from you between July 1, 2023, and June 30, 2024 (during the award year)?	Yes	No
Do you have dependents (other than your children or spouse) who live with you and who receive more than half of their support from you, now and through June 30, 2024?	Yes	No
At any time since you turned age 13, were both your parents deceased, were you in foster care, or were you a dependent or ward of the court?	Yes	No
Has it been determined by a court in your state of legal residence that you are an emancipated minor or that someone other than your parent or stepparent has legal guardianship of you? (You also should answer "Yes" if you are now an adult but were in legal guardianship or were an emancipated minor immediately before you reached the age of being an adult in your state. Answer "No" if the court papers say "custody" rather than "guardianship.")	Yes	No
At any time on or after July 1, 2022, were you determined to be an unaccompanied youth who was homeless or were self-supporting and at risk of being homeless, as determined by (a) your high school or district homeless liaison, (b) the director of an emergency shelter or transitional housing program funded by the U.S. Department of Housing and Urban Development, or (c) the director of a runaway or homeless youth basic center or transitional living program?⁺⁺	Yes	No

Fig. 0-14. Questions that determine your dependency status for completing the FAFSA form ("Dependency Status").

Quadrant 2: Academic History

When completing the Academic History quadrant, it's important to **enter *everything***. Enter every college attended, every course registered for, and every grade or mark received. Ideally, when you are finished, your entries should read line by line, semester by semester, as they do on your transcript.

So, where do things get tricky? When entering F grades, D grades, or courses marked "Repeated," "Academic Renewal," or "Academic Forgiveness," things get tricky. When entering a course that was retaken at a different college, things get tricky. Let's use the example from earlier:

Table 0-1. Common CSU Application Entry Error for Academic Renewal.

				Incorrect	Correct
1st attempt	SPANISH 1A	5 units	Grade	F	AR
2nd attempt	SPANISH 1A	5 units	Grade	B	B
				1.5 GPA	3.0 GPA

In Table 10-1, the student attempted the same class twice; they received an F grade the first time and the second time a B grade. If the student enters the F *and* the B grade, then the student's GPA will be off and read much lower than it actually is. As shown in Table 10-2, this situation gets more complicated when students enter courses from different colleges that were taken to replace the first grade.

Table 0-2. Common CSU Application Entry Error for Academic Renewal from Different Colleges.

Transcript 1 **Mission College** **(first attempt)**	SPANISH 101	4 units	Grade	F

Transcript 2 **San José City College** **(Second attempt)**	SPANISH 1A	5 units	Grade	B

In this case, it's more confusing because *the course names do not match*, the units differ, and you'd have to know how to read the transcript to understand that the Mission College grade was actually an AR for Academic Renewal.

What is Academic Renewal, and why do you need it?

Academic renewal on a transcript indicates that the original grade received in the course is no longer factored into the GPA. Although the transcript will show the course was taken and the original grade, the grade is not factored into the GPA. **There are two ways to qualify for Academic Renewal,** one is to retake the course and replace the grade, and the other—which many students are *not* aware of—is to **submit an application for Academic Renewal through your Counselor for a course or set of courses with D or F grades, which can run across different semesters (or quarters) based on that college's policies and limitations for doing so**. This strategy is important to use when applying for Transfer. As a Transfer Counselor, I work carefully with students to help rebuild their GPA using tools like this at the right time. That is another reason students are advised to review their applications with a Counselor.

The Academic History section of the CSU Application is usually the hardest part for many students to complete, and the reason is twofold:

1. It is very common that students have **retaken a course** at some point, so you have to know how to enter those courses properly.

2. It is very common that students have **attended multiple community colleges** and will need to enter each transcript correctly.

If either of those reasons is true for you, be sure to **work with your Counselor and Transfer Center to verify that everything is entered correctly on your application.**

Tips for working with your Counselor and reviewing your application materials:

□ Get up to date copies of your transcripts from each college you have attended prior to meeting with your Counselor. Unofficial is okay, official is better.

□ Start drafting your application entry early! In the Fall the application opens Oct. 1st, take time that week to get started. Use the videos, guides, and workshops available to you to get started with your transfer application materials. **Just do not submit anything until it is reviewed.**

□ Make an appointment with your Counselor, particularly a Transfer Counselor if available. Try not to lean on drop in times, these are rushed slots and not enough time to fully review your application.

□ Ask your Counselor about academic renewal options at your college or other colleges if needed. Many colleges will process these requests in 2 -3 weeks giving students enough time to boost their GPA and chances for admission.

□ Confirm with your Counselor which courses you'll need to register for in the following semester or quarter to complete your transfer requirements. It's important that your unit count, GE requirements, and major prep courses are fulfilled to increase your eligibility for transfer.

□ **After submitting your application, don't disappear!** Set follow up appointments to ensure you are completing each next step with the support you need.

Fig. 0-15. Tips for working with your Counselor to review application materials.

Quadrant 3: The CSU EOP Program & Application

First, what is EOP?

The CSUs Educational Opportunity Program (EOP) provides admission, academic, and financial support services to historically underserved students throughout California. It is designed to offer specialized services and supports for low-income, first-generation college students.

The history of EOP is quite special and grew out of the Civil Rights movement. I encourage all students to learn more about EOP through videos like the 50th Anniversary video of EOP and by visiting the individual EOP sites of the CSUs where they want to apply.

Fig. 0-16." EOP 50th Anniversary Video." YouTube, uploaded by CSU EOP, 19 Sep. 2019, www.youtube.com/watch?v=f-OB1ZCf-Ho.

How can EOP help transfer students?

EOP will differ at each campus but will often include access to individual advising, priority registration, a specialized summer orientation to college, summer bridge programs, college mentors, career guidance, access to academic tutoring, and attending special conferences or workshops geared to empower first-generation college students. It can also include additional financial aid grants or scholarships, an EOP graduation ceremony, and an EOP center that provides a home base on campus and a greater sense of community.

So should Transfer students—especially those that qualify for financial aid at their local CCC—apply for EOP at the CSU?

YES.

Y-E-S!

YES. YES. YES.

Visit the "Campus EOP Contacts" webpage to click the button or red dots or button and visit each CSU EOP location.

Fig. 0-17. The CSU "Campus EOP Contacts" webpage.

How and when do you apply for EOP?

Transfer students have basically one opportunity to apply for EOP, and that is when they apply for admission to the CSU campus using the 3rd Quadrant. In most cases, you cannot apply for EOP *after* the Transfer.

Unfortunately, EOP is also not open each application cycle at each campus—typically, it's open at each campus for Fall admission. So, for example, one possibility is that students applying for Spring admission will not be able to apply for EOP at a CSU campus even though they would qualify for the program. In truth, there are more qualified students for EOP at each CSU than there is funding for them, so application into the program is limited to when students apply for admission.

The CSU EOP Application Process

First, like everything else—there's a guide for that. The CSU offers an EOP application worksheet to assist students in understanding how to apply for EOP (**fig 10-18**). Second, check in with your

Transfer Center since there are usually EOP application workshops offered there as well.

The EOP application has four sections:

1. General questions

2. Parent/Guardian Information and Financial Status

3. EOP Biographical questions

4. Two Recommenders

Because each EOP program seeks to assist the most vulnerable students, the application will include very specific questions about financial need and whether the student, their family, or both, have participated in public assistance programs. In my experience, students are often unfamiliar with the official names of programs they may have received help from throughout the years, or it is something their parents may know instead. **Table 10-3** is a list of common public assistance programs at the federal and state level to assist students. Students should take time to

Fig. 0-18. Cover of 2022-23 CSU EOP Applicant Preparation Worksheet.

identify the programs they or their families have participated in throughout their lives and be sure to discuss these in the biographical questions portion.

Table 0-3. Federal and State Public Assistance Programs.

PUBLIC ASSISTANCE PROGRAMS	
CALFRESH	California program that grants cash aid through the EBT card, used in participating grocery stores.
CALWORKS	California welfare program that grants cash aid to families in need.
AFDC	Aid to Families with Dependent Children *cash welfare as part of parental support for a parent that was absent from the home
TANF	Temporary Assistance for Needy Families *cash aid for eligible families/children in need
SOCIAL SECURITY	Grants cash aid to disabled adults/children in need
SSDI	Social Security Disability Insurance *monthly payments to people with disabilities
SSI	Supplemental Security Income *monthly payments to people with disabilities or people over 65 with limited income
SECTION 8	California program that assists low-income families with 70% assistance on rent.
FREE AND REDUCED LUNCH PROGRAMS	Provides children with free lunch or reduced costs of lunch at school
MEDI-CAL	California's health program to pay for medical services for children/adults in need
GA/GR	General Assistance or General Relief to provide assistance for adults in need that do not qualify for other forms of assistance or public funds
CAPI	Cash Assistance Program for Immigrants Provides cash assistance for elder or disabled non-citizens ineligible for SSI

Writing the EOP Biographical Response

The biographical questions do not require an essay response, and *what* a student writes is not connected to *how* their application is evaluated for admission. It's a space for students to be very honest about their lives, their family's experiences, and any financial struggles they've experienced. It is also a place to share any academic challenges they have experienced. Students should write these in a specific way and really take the time to truly tell their story. Again, this information is protected under student privacy and is meant to help colleges identify students in need.

Two Recommenders

Students must provide the full name and contact emails of two recommenders. These recommenders will be contacted after they submit the EOP application. Recommenders will be asked to complete a similar online form and answer specific questions about the applicant.

Here are some tips for students:

☐ Choose recommenders you have a relationship with and with whom you trust to share your story.

☐ At least one recommender should be from a teacher or counselor that can speak to your academic preparation for college.

☐ Be sure to ask the recommender for permission before entering their name on the form so that they can confirm if this is a commitment they can complete.

☐ Provide your recommender with a biography or resume or even portions of your EOP biographical responses—if you are comfortable—so that they can provide detailed support for your application.

EOP Deadlines Will Vary

To apply for EOP, students can submit that application at the same time they submit their CSU Application for admission for a Fall cycle, which means by November 30th. I highly recommend submitting EOP at the same time as submitting CSU because otherwise, it's easy to forget and lose track of deadlines.

Students also have the option to submit the EOP application separately and follow the individual campus deadline set by each CSU. To do that, choose "Yes, will return later to complete the EOP questions" when starting the EOP application (**fig. 10-19**).

Recommendations deadlines will vary. Most CSUs will list January 31st for Fall applications, but some colleges will opt for different dates—earlier or much later. Check the CSU EOP Deadlines to be sure (**fig. 10-20**).

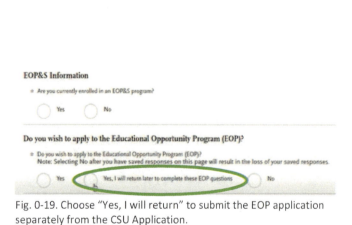

Fig. 0-19. Choose "Yes, I will return" to submit the EOP application separately from the CSU Application.

CSU EOP Deadlines Fall 2023

Campus	EOP Application Deadline	Documents Deadline
Bakersfield	January 15, 2023	January31, 2023
Channel Islands*	Not Accepting Applications	
Chico	December 15, 2022	January31, 2023
Dominguez Hills*	Not Accepting Applications	
East Bay*	January 15, 2023	January31, 2023
Fresno	November 30, 2022	December 15, 2022
Fullerton	December 16, 2022	January6, 2023
Humboldt	January 15, 2023	January 31, 2023
Long Beach*	January 15, 2023	January31, 2023
Los Angeles	January 15, 2023	January 31, 2023
Maritime	July 1, 2023	July1, 2023
Monterey Bay	January 15, 2023	January 31, 2023
Northridge*	January 15, 2023	January31, 2023
Pomona	January 15, 2023	January 31, 2023
Sacramento	December 15, 2022	January31, 2023
San Bernardino*	January 15, 2023	January 31, 2023
San Diego	January 15, 2023	January31, 2023
San Francisco	January 15, 2023	January 31, 2023
San Jose*	January 15, 2023	January31, 2023
San Luis Obispo	January 15, 2023	January 31, 2023
San Marcos	January 15, 2023	January31, 2023
Sonoma	January 15, 2023	January 31, 2023
Stanislaus	January 15, 2023	January 31, 2023

Fig. 0-20. Individual **CSU Campus EOP Deadlines**.
Note: The Recommendations Deadline appear in the yellow box area, third column.

Step 2. CSU Supplemental Application – *Application Phase*

What happens after you submit your CSU transfer application? First, you sleep. Then, make sure to focus on finishing the Fall term with strong grades. Why do that, you ask?

Because after you apply, the next step will be to complete something called the **CSU Supplemental Application** or PART II of the CSU Application. Much like most sequels, it's often forgotten, which is a problem. This example is one I hope will help you remember – you are not done with the CSU Application process until both Grease 1 and Grease 2 are complete.

Now that you know to think of the CSU Application in two parts, let's rewind to which next steps to do first after submitting your Part I application on November 30th.

CSU Application Part I is like Grease 1—everyone knows about it.

During the Fall Season students have one big CSU deadline for transfer: Nov. 30th when the CSU Application aka Part I is due.

Fig. 0-21. CSU Application Part I is like Grease 1..

CSU Supplemental Application aka the Part II is like Grease 2—no one knows about it and so it's easy to miss this deadline. Don't!!

Missing this deadline is an automatic denial. Yikes! Time to learn about the details!

Fig. 0-22. CSU Application Part II is like Grease 2.

Log into your Student Portal (obsessively is okay). The first thing that happens after submitting your CSU Application (Part I) is that each CSU you applied to will email you and ask you **to log into your student portal** for their CSU campus. So, if you applied to FOUR campuses, look for FOUR emails with instructions to log into each portal. If you do not receive a message like that from each CSU campus, be sure to check your Junk folders and follow up with the admissions office.

Your student portal is how each campus will communicate with you. Once you are logged onto your portal, you will need to log in regularly and check two areas especially: the **Inbox for messages** and **Student To Do List**. Those two portal areas are the primary spots where the next steps for each campus will appear, including the deadline for that campus's supplemental application, how they want you to submit the information, and any special instructions. It's also where offices like Financial Aid may request that you complete a form and, ultimately, how they will notify you about admissions status.

Here's some basics about the **CSU Supplemental App**:

1. It's due in January.
2. Every CSU picks a different deadline, check your portals to find out when. If you applied to four campuses, that's four deadlines you need to meet.
3. Every CSU asks students to submit in a different manner. Some will have their own site (like SJSU, CSULB, and SDSU), many now ask you to log back into your CSU Apply application (Part I) and add in your Fall grades and Spring course updates.
4. It's pretty short and easy to complete.
5. You are asked to report Fall grades & Spring courses.
6. Applications are not reviewed by admissions until *after* the CSU Supplemental Applications are submitted. So relax and enjoy the Winter break, just remember after New Year's Day… look for those instructions in your portal about completing the CSU Supplemental Application.

Fig. 0-23. CSU Supplemental Basic Facts.

The Waiting Period
After submitting the CSU Supplemental application, the next phase in the process is waiting to hear back from colleges. **All CSUs must notify students before May since the deadline to accept an offer of admission is May 1ˢᵗ. Students can accept an offer of admission to only *ONE CSU campus*.** When you are in the waiting period, it can cause the most anxiety. During this time, take care of yourself, continue to focus on earning strong grades in your final classes, check your CSU portals for notifications, and reach out to the CSU admissions representatives or your Transfer Center with any questions.

Overview of Next Steps After Applying

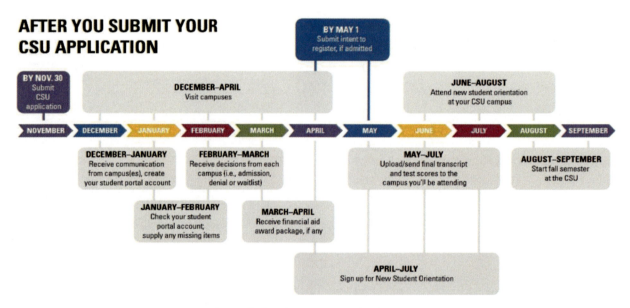

Fig. 0-24. CSU Next steps: <u>You've Applied to the CSU: Now What?</u>

The Big News

The admissions decision will be listed in your student portal. Figure 10-25 is an example of a CSU student portal using a CSU Channel Islands example:

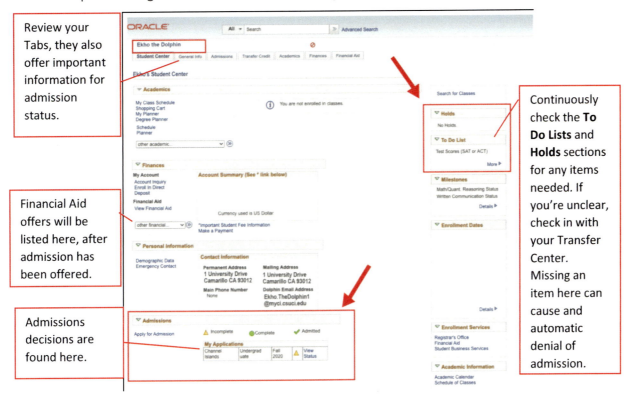

Review your Tabs, they also offer important information for admission status.

Financial Aid offers will be listed here, after admission has been offered.

Admissions decisions are found here.

Continuously check the **To Do Lists** and **Holds** sections for any items needed. If you're unclear, check in with your Transfer Center. Missing an item here can cause and automatic denial of admission.

Fig. 0-25. Student Portal Example Screenshot from CSU Channel Islands.

Step 3. Submit SIR and Deposit – *Admissions Phase*

There are three outcomes for any application for admission. One, you are offered admission to the college. Two, you are offered a spot on the waitlist for admission. Three, you are denied admission to the college. Let's walk through the next steps for each scenario.

Scenario 1. Offer of Admission
First, of course, you celebrate—this is a big deal and a reflection of all your hard work. (YAYYY!)
Next, you take time to **read through the fine print**.
Most campuses will have a set of *next steps* students need to follow to secure their admission. If you notice,

Fig. 0-26. CSU Channel Islands Provisional Offer of Admission Example.

the message in **Figure 10-26** says the student's admission is *provisional*. **That means it's pending**. Pending until the student completes the outlined steps. Pending until the student passes their current classes and fulfills their admissions requirements. The *Next Steps* for CSU admission are typically the following,

Accept the offer of admission by May 1 Also known as SIR which is to submit your "Statement of Intent to Register"	→	Pay a Deposit	→	Register for a Mandatory Transfer Admission Orientation

- The deadline to accept an offer to the CSU is May 1st for all campuses.
- Students can accept admission to one campus.
- The UC deadline for accepting admission is June 1st which presents a difficulty when students are still waiting to hear back from the UC and having to pay a deposit to hold their spot at the CSU. This is a real issue of equity for our

- Each campus will require a different option for deposit amount, for example SJSU asks for a $250 deposit. To learn more about each CSU's process and prepare ahead of time visit the CSU's SIR site.
- Some campuses will allow students apply for **a deposit waiver** through EOP or other means. Check in with your Transfer Center for assistance.

- Each campus will seek for incoming students to attend a MANDATORY transfer orientation, in the summer for Fall transfers.
- During orientation students will receive their student ID card, register for classes, learn about supports and clubs, and get set up for the start of classes.
- **Do not miss your summer orientation** date, doing so can risk you offer of admission.
- Students admitted to EOP will be asked to attend an EOP sponsored orientation, often longer than day

Statement of Intent to Register

Statement of Intent to Register (SIR) or Admission Acceptance or Enrollment Confirmation procedures have been instituted by CSU campuses and monetary deposits may be required. Applicants who have been offered admission should notify the campus of their acceptance and if required, make a deposit by the specified campus deadline.

The enrollment deposit is applied as payment against the tuition fee payable at the time of registration for students who matriculate. An enrollment deposit may be forfeited for a student who does not enroll.

Students eligible for need-based financial aid and/or fee waivers may or may not be required to pay the deposit.

Deadlines and deposit fees are subject to change without prior notice. Students should check with the specific CSU campus where they are admitted for up-to-date information.

Select a Campus
Bakersfield
Channel Islands
Chico
Dominguez Hills
East Bay
Fresno
Fullerton
Humboldt
Long Beach
Los Angeles
Maritime Academy
Monterey Bay
Northridge
Pomona
Sacramento
San Bernardino
San Diego

To learn more about the SIR process for each CSU campus, visit the CSU Statement of Intent to Register. Click on the drop down menu for each CSU campus and look for next steps after transfer admission. Campuses will list the deposit amounts required, the orientation process, and other important

Fig. 0-27. California State University. "Statement of Intent to Register."

Reasons for Denial of Admission

Let's face it, getting a denial or rejection letter for admission feels awful. It feels personal. I get that feeling, but I'd like to take time to really unpack why students are typically denied admission, what they can do about those decisions, and why it's not the end of the world and also—not at all personal. In fact, often, if you correct the issue(s) for denial, you can, in many cases, reapply and be admitted.

First, the reasons. There are really two kinds of denials: one based on **ineligibility** and one based on an **incomplete** application.

Ineligibility

Ineligibility means that the student did not meet the requirements for admission or for the major. This can indicate that the GPA was too low for this major or for CSU, that a required course was missing from either the Major Prep or the Golden Four, that the student's units were under 60 transferable units, or that a requirement for a competitive major—like completion of the ADT—had not been completed. In this case, the student would work with their counselor to identify the issue and can take additional coursework to remedy the area and then reapply for the CSU campus or identify other campuses that might be a better fit. The bottom line here, **you can still transfer successfully**—so don't lose hope, and don't disappear. Work with your counselor, regroup, and you'll see how quickly you can take a turn for the better if you are patient and diligent.

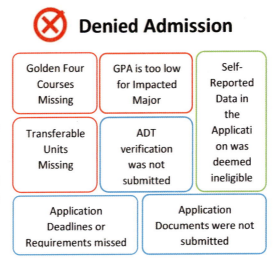

Fig. 0-28. Common Reasons for Ineligibility Denials.

Incomplete Application

Incomplete applications are ones where a deadline was missed, and documents like the student's transcripts, ADT verification, or AP/IB test scores were not submitted. In this case, students often have the **option to "Appeal" the decision** and request a chance to remedy the issue. Students usually have **15 days after notification to submit an appeal** to the CSU. Every campus is very different, often based on impaction. Impacted campuses that have an abundance of qualified student applicants may not be as flexible as non-impacted campuses or majors might be. The best thing to do is to try and appeal the decision, work with your Transfer center to review your appeal prior to submission, and see how it goes. If it is approved, then you can submit an incomplete and keep moving forward; if not, you can decide if you'd like to reapply for the next cycle. The fact that you're reading this guide goes a long way in helping you avoid this scenario.

Fig. 0-29. San José State University. "Admissions Appeal Request" webpage.

Self-Reported Data

Another common issue is that students enter the wrong information in their application when listing their courses and grades (remember the example above). In this case, students may have a good chance to appeal the decision if they can demonstrate the correct information using their transcripts.

Step 4. Submit Official Transcripts & Exam Scores Admit Phase

An important next step towards admission is to submit copies of your Official Transcripts for each college attended. Since many students attend multiple California community colleges (CCC), even if it is for just one course or credit, it's important that students understand they *must submit an official transcript for EACH college attended*. This is part of the academic integrity clause signed within each application.

Order Official Transcripts

Requests are usually made through the college's Office of Admissions and Records. Most colleges now allow students to order transcripts ONLINE, which is a great option for convenience and expediency. I also recommend always keeping sealed extra copies of your transcripts from each campus just in case any issues arise, you have copies on hand to provide to your college. Note, official copies must be sealed or unopened to remain official.

Multiple Colleges Attended,

Most CCCs are linked to a 'sister' college. To view the list of CCC Districts and which you have attended visit this site.

For example, our college—San José City College's sister college is Evergreen Valley College (EVC). This means, if a course offered at SJCC is full then students can opt to take the equivalent course at our sister college—EVC without having to take extra steps like applying separately to that college. None of this is an issue. The problem arises when students submit their transcripts for admissions. Students must remember to submit their official transcript to BOTH SJCC and EVC if they took courses at our sister college. Not doing so is an automatic denial of admission because the application would be incomplete. To avoid this, **always order transcripts separately for each college attended, including sister colleges within the same district.** For example, if I took even one course at each of the college below, then I would need to place four separate orders for each college (color) listed.

Student transcripts are usually ordered through the Office of Admissions and Records

Fig. 0-30. Screenshot of San José City College, "Transcript Information Request. sjcc.edu/admissions-records/transcripts.aspx

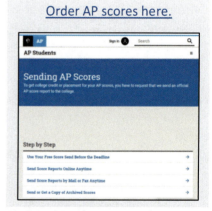

Order AP scores here.

Fig. 0-31. AP webpage screenshot.

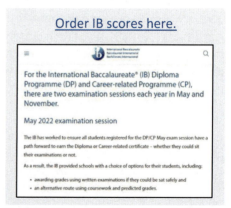

Order IB scores here.

Fig. 0-32. International Baccalaureate (IB) website screenshot.

Fig. 0-33. Example of CCC Sister College System.

Step 5. Sign up and complete the student Orientation – *Admissions Phase*

The final step of the Admissions Phase is registering for the new student orientation and completing the orientation steps designated by each campus. Again, not doing so could compromise your admission to the college. For most students that apply for Fall admission, these orientations will occur during the summer months. Most orientations happen over a full day, and some will offer specialized orientations, as with EOP, which usually includes multiple days of engagement with students.

What happens during Orientation?
The fun stuff, really. This event is when, most importantly, you schedule courses for your first semester. It's when you'll receive your student ID card and gain access to the library and important campus resources. You can learn about support services and clubs and register online for any added features or secure items like a parking pass to get started for school. Often family members can join you and, in some cases, are invited to special events.

The main takeaway is ***Do not miss your Orientation!!***

Here are some fun examples from San José State University.

Fig. 0-34. Example of San José State University Student Orientation event.

Works Cited

California State University. *Cal State Apply: Transfer Application Guide*. California State University

    Office of the Chancellor, 2021, www.calstate.edu/apply/transfer/Documents/transfer-

    application-guide-23-24.pdf. Accessed 27 Jan. 2023.

---. "EOP Admission by Term." *CSU The California State University*, California State University

    Office of the Chancellor, www.calstate.edu/attend/student-services/eop/Pages/eop-

    campus-status.aspx. Accessed 29 Jan. 2023

---. "Statement of Intent to Register." *CSU The California State University*, California State

    University Office of the Chancellor, www.calstate.edu/attend/student-

    services/casper/Pages/statement-of-intent-to-register.aspx. Accessed 29 Jan. 2023.

---. *Transfer Student Application Checklist*. California State University Office of the Chancellor,

    www.calstate.edu/apply/transfer/Documents/application-checklist-transfer.pdf.

    Accessed 28 Jan. 2023.

San José City College. "Transcript: Information." *San José City College*, San José Evergreen

    Community College District, 2021, sjcc.edu/admissions-records/transcripts.aspx.

    Accessed 29 Jan. 2023.

U.S. Department of Education, Federal Student Aid. "Dependency Status." *Federal Student Aid*,

    studentaid.gov/apply-for-aid/fafsa/filling-out/dependency. Accessed 28 Jan. 2023.

Chapter 11: Applying to the UC

Step 1	Step 2	Step 3	Step 4	Step 5	Step 6
Submit UC Tag (optional)	Submit UC Application	Submit Transfer Academic Update (TAU)	Submit SIR & Pay Deposit	Submit Official Transcripts, AP/IB Scores	Sign up for Orientation & Classes

Application Phase   *Acceptance Phase*

Fig. 0-1. Two Phases, Six Steps for Applying to UC.

UC TAP
Transfer Admission Planner

Want to transfer to the UC, start here!
Create your UC TAP account today.

Applying to UC. Where to start?

Fig. 0-2. UC Transfer Admission Planner Home Page.

Start with the UC **Transfer Admission Planner (TAP)** Account. If you are interested in applying to a UC campus, creating a UC TAP account is the best place to start. You can start your UC TAP account anytime, even if it is your first semester/quarter attending a CCC. You can also complete the UC TAP account even if you are not sure you will apply to a UC. Here are some great reasons to use the UC TAP account.

First, it's a place for students to **add all their coursework and AP or IB exams.** It's especially helpful for students that have attended multiple colleges and are unsure about their true transferable coursework credit for the UC. The UC TAP calculates your **true UC transferable unit count and true UC GPA**.

Second, it is how students can begin working with the **UC Admissions representatives**. However, the representatives do not have access to student transcripts or academic records as CCC counselors do, so it is hard for UC representatives to answer admissions questions accurately without a clear picture of the student's coursework, GPA, and unit count. So, UC TAP helps them to do just that. As long as you keep your UC TAP account up-to-date and accurate, it will be a great tool to connect you with UC representatives and ensure you are on track for admission.

Third, when it comes time to apply for the **UC TAG—Transfer Admissions Guarantee**—this is where you do that. In fact, applying for TAG is pretty easy and quick if your UC TAP account is up-to-date. It is mostly just a matter of selecting the campus you want to TAG to and ensuring you meet that campus's TAG criteria. Finally, when it comes time to complete your **UC Transfer Admissions application**, you can import the data from your UC TAP account into your application, saving you a good deal of time in completing your UC application. So, keeping your UC TAP account accurate and up-to-date is key to success here!

Phase I: Application

Step 1. Apply for the UC TAG (Application Phase)

First, what is the UC TAG? The UC TAG stands for Transfer Admissions Guarantee. It is, in fact, a guarantee of admission to **ONE of the six participating UC campuses (UC Davis, Irvine, Merced, Riverside, Santa Barbara, or Santa Cruz)** so long as students meet that campus's TAG criteria. So, where does one find those criteria? Use the UC TAG Matrix, which is updated each year by the UC, usually in the summer (**fig. 11-3**).

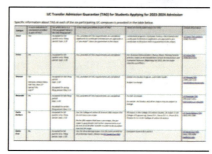

When to apply for the UC TAG?

The application for the UC TAG occurs during the entire month of **September** for Fall admissions cycle applicants. Some campuses, like UC Merced and UC Riverside, are also open for Spring admission. Their UC TAG Spring cycle is during the month of May.

Fig. 0-3. UC TAG Matrix 2023-24 example.

What kind of criteria does the UC TAG include?

In order to qualify for the UC TAG, each campus will indicate the specific campus criteria they will vet before approving the student UC TAG application. Some criteria include,

- Student GPA required for their major
- Majors available for the TAG—Note: not all majors are available for the UC TAG. Highly selective majors are often not available for TAG.
- When students should have completed their two transferable English and one transferable Math course
- Completion of a minimum of 30 semester/45 quarter transferable units
- Demonstrated coursework to complete the major preparation requirements.

Fig. 0-4. Example of the UC TAG application.

Is the UC TAG required?

No, applying for the UC TAG is *not required* to attend a UC campus. Also, a student who applied for the UC TAG but was turned down may still be admitted to a UC campus. It is not an admission requirement. As previously noted, the TAG is especially helpful for students applying with slightly lower GPAs for their major.

Does a student have to attend their TAG campus?

No, it is not required to attend the TAG campus. For example, if a student applied for TAG to UC Davis and was admitted to UC San Diego, their first choice campus. That student can attend UC San Diego.

Is the TAG for everyone?

No. The TAG is a specific benefit offered to CCC upper-division transfer students. It offers strong benefits, especially when applying to more competitive majors with higher GPAs. It can be a great tool for securing your admission by allowing students to utilize the UC TAG GPA criteria. Some campuses, like UC Davis or UC Merced currently, will also offer to review student applications early and offer early admissions decisions. This review can offer wonderful relief to students throughout the Transfer Application process. I cannot overstate how

Who cannot apply for the UC TAG?

☐ Students with a Bachelor's degree, graduate degree, or professional degree.

☐ Students that have previously attended a UC.

☐ High school students participating in dual enrollment courses at the time of application

☐ Students transferring from Non-CCC colleges.

much it helps students to relieve their anxiety and stay motivated throughout the year when they hear back early about the admission guarantee—*big shout out to UC Davis & Merced for continuing to offer early admissions notification for the TAG!*

Step 2. Complete the UC Transfer Admissions Application (Application Phase)

When to Apply?

Most UC campuses and majors are open for Fall Admission only. For **Fall Admission**, the **UC Application** *opens* as early as **August 1st.** However, the application is not open for submission until October 1st. The **deadline to apply** is November 30th.

How to Apply?

To begin your UC Application, go to the UC Application website to create your login and begin your application. Each year the UC creates a guide for transfer applicants to walk students through the application (**fig. 11-5**). This guide is a wonderful resource for help as you complete the application.

Fig. 0-5. View the UC Admissions application guide for Transfer Applicants – 2022.

In addition, look out for UC application workshops provided by your Transfer Center or check with your local UC representative for workshops they are hosting for transfer students. Many of these application workshops are posted online as an additional resource. **Figure 11-6** shows a great example from UC Davis, as part of their TOP program—which San José City College students qualify for ☺

Where to apply? Apply here:
UC Application Website.

Fig. 0-6. UC Davis Application Video Workshop.

The UC Application allows students to complete ONE application that can then be used to apply to any of the nine campus options.

UC TAP to APP

The application will take about 2 hours to complete. Students can complete it in sections and save their work as they go. It will also require that students self-report their entire coursework—which simply means entering every course, grade, and unit completed at the college level listed in your transcript. Also, it's a big help if you keep your UC TAP account up to date because that lets you import the academic history from your UC TAP account into your UC Application (**fig. 11-7**). That will save you a good deal of time,

Fig. 0-7. Page 21 of the UC Admissions Application Guide explains how Students import their UC TAP account Academic History into the UC Application.

although you must comb through the data carefully to ensure everything was imported correctly!

Remember—and I can't say this enough— *always* make sure your Counselor, Transfer Center, or UC admissions representative has **reviewed your UC application BEFORE you submit your application**. It is easy to make simple errors that compromise your application.

Let's talk about the UC Insight Questions

The UC Application for Transfer Admission requires students to provide answers to **four questions**. These questions are designed to act as short interview questions, like ones you would answer in a personal interview. They are not meant to be formal or academic but intended to allow students to describe themselves, their achievements, their goals, and also their resilience in overcoming unique challenges. The idea is to help the UC to understand you—your coursework— within the context of your life. To *humanize your transcript* in a sense by taking time to fully make the UC aware of you in all your colors.

Fig. 0-8. UC Insight Questions Video.

The first Personal Insight Question—is required of all transfer applicants. From there, students can select the second, third, and fourth questions out of seven potential options. Let's take a look at the questions and recommendations on how to approach these questions provided by the UC.

Question REQUIRED BY ALL APPLICANTS:
*Please describe **how you have prepared for your intended major**, including your readiness to succeed in your upper-division courses once you enroll at the university.*

Things to consider:
- ☐ How did your interest in your major develop?
- ☐ Do you have any experience related to your major outside the classroom — such as volunteer work, internships, employment, or participation in student organizations and activities?
- ☐ If you haven't had experience in the field, consider including experience in the classroom. This experience may include working with faculty or doing research projects.
- ☐ If you're applying to multiple campuses with a different major at each campus, think about approaching the topic from a broader perspective, or find a common thread among the majors you've chosen.

Optional Question 1: *Describe an **example of your leadership experience** in which you have positively influenced others, helped resolve disputes, or contributed to group efforts over time.*

> **Things to consider:**
> - A leadership role can mean more than just a title. It can mean being a mentor to others, acting as the person in charge of a specific task, or taking the lead role in organizing an event or project.
> - Think about your accomplishments and what you learned from the experience.
> - What were your responsibilities?
> - Did you lead a team? How did your experience change your perspective on leading others?
> - Did you help to resolve an important dispute at your school, a church in your community, or an organization?
> - Your leadership role doesn't necessarily have to be limited to school activities. For example, do you help out or take care of your family?

Optional Question 2: *Every person has a creative side, and it can be expressed in many ways: problem solving, original and innovative thinking, and artistically, to name a few. **Describe how you express your creative side**.*

> **Things to consider:**
> - What does creativity mean to you? Do you have a creative skill that is important to you?
> - What have you been able to do with that skill?
> - If you used creativity to solve a problem, what was your solution?
> - What are the steps you took to solve the problem?
> - How does your creativity influence your decisions inside or outside the classroom?
> - Does your creativity relate to your major or a future career?

Optional Question 3: What would you say is **your greatest talent or skill**? (AND) **How have you developed and demonstrated** that talent over time?

> **Things to consider:**
> - If you are proud of a talent or skill, this is the time to share it.
> - You don't necessarily have to be recognized or have received awards for your talent (although if you did and you want to talk about it, feel free to do so).
> - Why is this talent or skill meaningful to you?
> - Does the talent come naturally, or have you worked hard to develop this skill or talent?
> - Does your talent or skill allow you opportunities in or outside the classroom? If so, what are they, and how do they fit into your schedule?

Optional Question 4: Describe how you have taken advantage of a **significant educational opportunity or worked to overcome an educational barrier** you have faced.

Things to consider:

- An educational opportunity can be anything that has added value to your educational experience and better prepared you for college.
- For example, participation in an honors or academic enrichment program, enrollment in an academy that's geared toward an occupation or a major, or taking advanced courses that interest you — to name a few.
- If you choose to write about educational barriers you've faced, how did you overcome or strive to overcome them?
- What personal characteristics or skills did you call on to overcome this challenge?
- How did overcoming this barrier help shape who you are today?

Optional Question 5: Describe the **most significant challenge** you have faced and the steps you have taken to overcome this challenge. How has this challenge affected your academic achievement?

Things to consider:

- A challenge could be personal or something you have faced in your community or school.
- Why was the challenge significant to you?
- This question is a good opportunity to talk about any obstacles you've faced and what you've learned from the experience. Did you have support from someone else, or did you handle it alone?
- If you're currently working your way through a challenge, what are you doing now, and does that affect different aspects of your life? For example, ask yourself, "How has my life changed at home, at my school, with my friends, or with my family?"

Optional Question 6: What have you done to make your **school or your community a better place**?

Things to consider:

- Think of community as a term that can encompass a group, team, or a place – like your high school, hometown, or home.
- You can define community as you see fit; just make sure you talk about your role in that community.
- Was there a problem that you wanted to fix in your community?
- Why were you inspired to act?
- What did you learn from your effort?
- How did your actions benefit others, the wider community, or both?
- Did you work alone or with others to initiate change in your community?

Optional Question 7: Beyond what has already been shared in your application, **what do you believe makes you a strong candidate** for admissions to the University of California?

Things to consider:

☐ If there's anything you want us to know about you but didn't find a question or place in the application to tell us, now's your chance.

☐ What have you not shared with us that will highlight a skill, talent, challenge or opportunity that you think will help us know you better?

☐ From your point of view, what do you feel makes you an excellent choice for UC? Don't be afraid to brag a little.

Figure 11-9 shares some wonderful tips offered by UC Merced's Undergraduate Admissions, Division of Student Affairs for writing your UC Insight Questions:

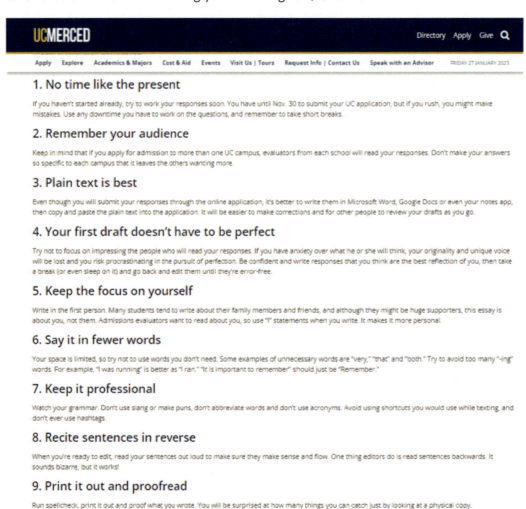

Fig. 0-9. UC Merced's Tips for Writing Your UC Insight Questions.

Step 3. Submit the Transfer Academic Update (Application Phase)

After the UC application is submitted, the next step in the application process is to complete the Transfer Academic Update (TAU) for the UC, which is **due January 31st** and can be found by logging back into the UC application.

Fig. 0-10. Recorded workshop on the TAU provided by UCSB.

The purpose of the TAU is to gather the student's grades from the Fall semester/quarter, confirm the coursework planned for the Spring / Winter, and ensure that the information originally provided—such as the Associates Degree for Transfer—is still correct. The UC does not actually begin evaluating student applications until AFTER the TAU is provided. That's why it remains part of the application process. It's a big help for transfer students, as students have one final chance to continue increasing their GPA through their performance Fall semester. Be sure to finish strong!

What happens if you miss the TAU?
It could compromise your UC application. So, check in with your UC representative and Transfer Center for assistance.

What happens after the TAU?
Campuses begin to review your application materials after the TAU is submitted. Students will begin to hear back from campuses usually between March through May.

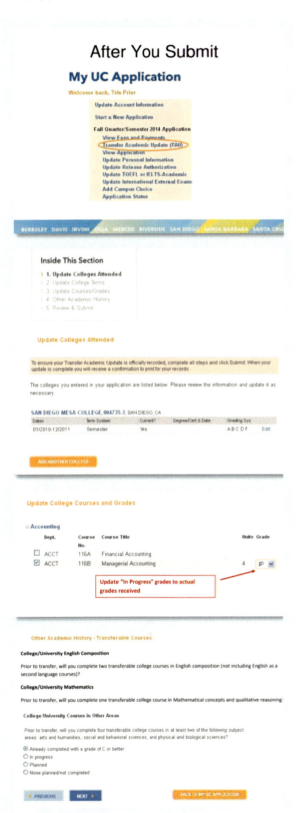

Fig. 0-11. San Diego Mesa College TAU Handout Pages.

Phase II: Acceptance

Step 4. Submit your SIR and Deposit (Acceptance Phase)

By January, after the submission of your application, each UC campus will send students an email inviting them to create their portal. It is through that portal that the notification of admissions decisions will be received.

Generally speaking, the UCs will notify students as early as March and as late as May.

Students can only accept an offer of admission to one UC campus. To accept the offer of admission, students must submit their 'Statement of Intent to Register' otherwise known as their SIR. They will also be asked to submit a deposit, currently $250.00.

Students will also be directed to complete campus-based decisions such as which 'college' to belong to or housing accommodations. Often each UC campus will host some form of a 'Next steps' workshop for admitted students to attend and receive assistance with this process. Each UC will list its own set of Next Steps after application.

The **deadline to submit SIR** to the UC—*to accept the offer of admission*—is **June 1st**.

Waitlist
Students have the option—if offered—to waitlist for another UC campus. For example, if a student was admitted to UC Irvine and waitlisted to UC Berkeley. That student could accept the offer of admission to UCI while accepting the offer to waitlist for UCB. Students can accept offers to waitlist at multiple colleges but only accept admission to one campus.

Housing
Often one of the first steps after accepting admission to the UC will be to solidify housing plans. Each UC will offer some form of on campus housing options. Some UCs will even guarantee on campus housing for transfer students.

UC Transfer Centers
Another incredible feature of the UC is that each campus now includes a Transfer Student Center. These centers help to create a hub on campus designed for transfer students to receive the unique supports they need and meet other transfer students on campus.

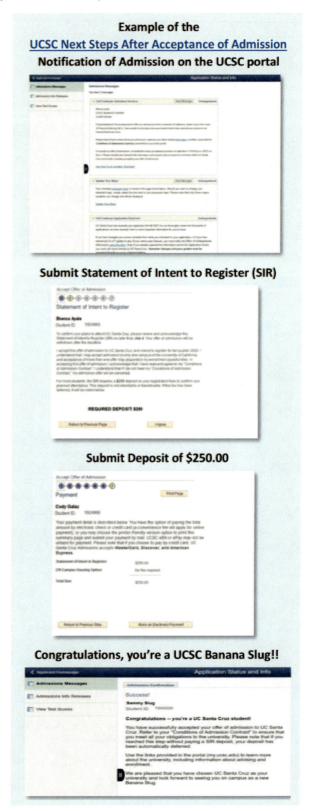

Example of the
UCSC Next Steps After Acceptance of Admission
Notification of Admission on the UCSC portal

Submit Statement of Intent to Register (SIR)

Submit Deposit of $250.00

Congratulations, you're a UCSC Banana Slug!!

Denied Admission

Example from UC Berkeley of Admissions FAQ for transfer admissions, including the process of Appeal.

Example of UC Irvine's Selection Appeal

Transfer Selection Appeal

Upload the following items **by May 15** and include student name and Application ID number on each sheet of materials submitted:

1. Letter of appeal clearly stating new and compelling information for appeal consideration, written and signed by the applicant
2. College transcript through most recent term for college(s) currently attending; updated list of courses in progress for the current term, if applicable
3. Applicable documentation: please note that the Office of Undergraduate Admissions may request additional documentation from an applicant, as needed (Letters of recommendation will not be considered as part of your appeal)

Example of UC Irvine's Appeal for Late Application

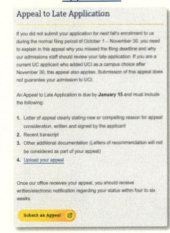

Appeal to Late Application

If you did not submit your application for next fall's enrollment to us during the normal filing period of October 1 – November 30, you need to explain in this appeal why you missed the filing deadline and why our admissions staff should review your late application. If you are a current UC applicant who added UCI as a campus choice after November 30, this appeal also applies. Submission of this appeal does not guarantee your admission to UCI.

An Appeal to Late Application is due by **January 15** and must include the following:

1. Letter of appeal clearly stating new or compelling reason for appeal consideration, written and signed by the applicant
2. Recent transcript
3. Other additional documentation (Letters of recommendation will not be considered as part of your appeal)
4. Upload your appeal

Once our office receives your appeal, you should receive written/electronic notification regarding your status within four to six weeks.

Submit an Appeal

Appealing Admissions Decisions

The UC will allow applicants to submit an appeal to admissions decisions for students that received a denial notification. Most campuses will list **May 15th** as the deadline for these appeals to be submitted.

There are two main reasons to submit an Appeal:

1. To provide **new and compelling information.**

2. If the application materials were **submitted late.**

Appeal Due to Selection

Students denied admission due to 'selection' criteria, means that the student did not meet a required criteria for the major or the university. Some common examples include,

☐ Not completing major preparation requirements
☐ Not meeting the GPA required for the major or university
☐ Not completing the IGETC GE pattern, sometimes required by the university
☐ Not demonstrating completion of 60 transferable units
☐ Not successfully passing a core requirement such as the two transferable English course or a transferable Math course

In this case, an appeal would need to demonstrate that 'new and compelling information' to the university, asking them to re-evaluate the applicants materials and supporting evidence that this criteria was indeed met.

Appeal Due to Late Application

Students denied admission due to 'late application' can include students that,

☐ Did not submit their UC Application in time
☐ Did not submit the TAU in time
☐ Did not submit their official transcripts or AP/IB exams in time or submitted these documents incomplete
☐ Did not submit their SIR or Deposit in time

Here's what you need to keep in mind if you receive a denial notice. First, if there is an option to appeal, work quickly and connect with your Transfer Center and admissions representative. Particularly in cases of late application materials, there may be a chance the appeal will be accepted. Second, if after appealing admission is not granted, it's okay. Meet with your Counselor and make a plan. There may be options to re-apply to a campus once the selection criteria is resolved or you may find other great campuses that have been overlooked. There is always a way!

It may feel like a time to disengage, but it's actually the exact opposite. It's a time to double down and finish strong. You are closer than you realize and with good guidance you can reach your goals and transfer somewhere you are genuinely excited to attend. As they say, every setback is a setup for a comeback!

Step 5. Submit Official Transcripts and Exam Scores (Acceptance Phase)

An important next step towards admission is to submit copies of your Official Transcripts for each college attended. Since many students attend multiple CCCs, even if it is for just one course or credit, it's important that students understand they *must submit an official transcript for EACH college attended*. This is part of the academic integrity clause signed within each application.

Order Student transcripts through the Admissions and Records Office

Visit SJCC's Transcript Request site.

Order Official Transcripts

Requests are usually made through the college's Office of Admissions and Records. Most colleges now allow students to order transcripts ONLINE, which is a great option for convenience and expediency. I also recommend always keeping sealed extra copies of your transcripts from each campus, just in case. If any issues arise, you'll have copies on hand to provide to your college. Note: official copies must be sealed or unopened to remain official.

Multiple Colleges Attended

Most CCCs are linked to a 'sister' college. To view the list of the CCC Districts you have attended, visit the District webpage. For example, our college—San José City College's sister college is Evergreen Valley College (EVC). This means if a course offered at SJCC is full, then students can opt to take the equivalent course at our sister college—EVC, without having to take extra steps like applying separately to that college. None of this is an issue. The problem arises when students submit their transcripts for admission Students must remember to submit their official transcript to BOTH SJCC and EVC if they've taken courses at our sister college; not doing so is an automatic denial of admission because the application would be incomplete. This is a common error, unfortunately. To avoid this, **always order transcripts separately for each college attended,** **including sister colleges within the same district.** For example, if I took even one course at each of the colleges below, then I would need to place four separate orders for each college (color) listed.

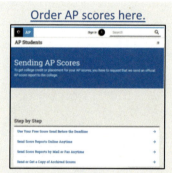

Order AP scores here.

Order IB scores here.

Step 6. Summer Orientation and Summer Transfer Programs (Acceptance Phase)

Each UC will differ in terms of their *next steps* after admission that are either required or recommended for transfer admit students. Use the UC Next Steps from Admissions guide, provided each year, for an overview of how widely **Next Steps** can differ at each UC campus. Let's take a look at two that will differ widely across campuses.

Fig. 0-12. Example of UC Next Steps

Student Orientations

Some campuses like UC Berkeley, UC Davis, UC Merced, UC San Diego, and UC Santa Barbara will hold their own mandatory Summer Orientation Program. These orientations may be one day and will often include getting set up for classes, getting an overview of how the UC campus operates and tips to get started, engaging with other students, and meeting faculty and advisers from your major. It can also include a barrage of checklists—forms to submit, housing requirements to complete, student ID, student email, parking passes—and many other important steps to get you started for classes. Be sure you find out whether the summer orientation is mandatory or recommended.

Fig. 0-13. UCB Summer Orientation

Summer Transfer Programs

In addition to the summer orientation, each UC offers some form of a summer program for transfer students. Many times, these are opportunities for students to take a summer course, experience living on campus, make friends and create community, and get a head start adapting to their new campus. Some programs can be one week long, while others may be six weeks long. Often, there is access to financial aid to assist students in participating in these options. Also, programs like EOP often offer their own version of these summer programs specifically designed for first-generation transfer students. If you have an opportunity to participate in these programs, my advice is simple: Do it!! You will not regret that early start. Often the hardest part of attending a UC is adapting to the quarter system for students that have attended a semester-based community college. This is such a great way to make any 'early' mistakes that will not hurt you but help you learn how to succeed early in your first official quarter.

Fig. 0-14. UCSB Summer Transfer Edge

Works Cited

"TOP Thursday: UC Application and PIQ Workshop." *YouTube*, uploaded by UC Davis TOP, 3 Aug.

2022, www.youtube.com/watch?v=gZboxEayltc. Accessed 15 Mar. 2022.

UC Merced, Undergraduate Admissions. "Tips from an Editor on Answering the UC Personal

Insight Questions." *UC Merced*, U of California, Merced,

admissions.ucmerced.edu/learn/uc-personal-insight-questions. Accessed 27 Jan. 2023.

University or California. "Nine Campuses. One Application." University of California, Regents of

the U Of California, apply.universityofcalifornia.edu/my-application/login. Accessed 15

Mar. 2022.

University of California Admissions. "Transfer Admission Guarantee (TAG)." *University of*

California Admissions, Regents of the U Of California,

admission.universityofcalifornia.edu/admission-requirements/transfer-requirements/uc-

transfer-programs/transfer-admission-guarantee-tag.html. Accessed 25 Jan. 2023.

---. *Transfer Admission Guarantee (TAG) Matrix 2022-2023*. Regents of the U of California, 2022,

admission.universityofcalifornia.edu/counselors/_files/documents/tag-matrix.pdf.

Accessed 13 Jan. 2023.

---. "Transfer Admission Planner." *University of California Admissions*, Regents of the U of

California, uctap.universityofcalifornia.edu/students/. Accessed 25 Jan. 2023.

---. *Undergraduate Admissions Application Guide: A User Guide for Transfer Applicants*. Regents

of the U of California. *University of California Admissions*,

admission.universityofcalifornia.edu/_assets/files/how-to-apply/application-guide-

transfer-applicants.pdf. Accessed 15 Mar. 2023.

Part IV: Financial Aid for Transfer

Chapter 12: Understanding Financial Aid

Four factors will impact the financial costs, aid options, and debt associated with paying for college. They are **Costs, Inside Aid, Outside Aid, and Debt**. Each factor will vary by institution type—UC, CSU, Private College, or Out-of-State options. They will also vary based on whether the cost of living is affordable in the surrounding area and any unique challenges or opportunities that arise based on the location.

That said, let's begin unpacking the four factors. What are they exactly?

Factor I. Costs

The first question in this math equation is, what are the costs associated with the college? Essentially, two kinds of costs are associated with paying for college: *direct costs* and *indirect costs*.

Direct Costs

Basically, any costs that will be billed to your university billing statement are called **Direct Costs**. This may include:

- The cost of annual tuition
- The cost of health insurance
- The cost of student activity fees
- The cost of health center fees
- The cost of housing for students choosing to live on campus.
- The cost of an on-campus meal plan for students that choose this option.

Fig. 0-1. Get Schooled's Tutorial webpage.

Other unique costs may be associated with an individual college or university. Still, generally speaking, these are the kinds of fees that you can expect to find on your student fee bill once you register for classes. Read "How to Read Your College Bill" from Get Schooled University (**fig. 12-1**)and watch their videos to learn more about reading and understanding a college bill.

The good news is that when it comes to Direct Costs, they tend to be *fixed* costs, meaning they are costs that do not change dramatically from year to year. If you are looking to estimate the costs associated with a campus for two to three years, you can generally estimate the fixed costs. Also, these fees tend to be publicly available information. So you truly can plan ahead for these costs and know what you're signing up for before taking the plunge into college.

Indirect Costs

Costs related to attending college but *not* included in your university fee bill are called **Indirect Costs**. These can include:

- The costs of books and supplies (laptop, printer, materials for class, etc.)
- Transportation costs (gas, parking permit, train or bus tickets, etc.)
- The costs of a cell phone device
- The costs of personal necessity items (clothes, medications, household items, etc.)
- The costs of utilities (Wi-Fi service, electricity, water, trash, etc.)
- The costs of rent if living off-campus
- The costs of groceries or meals if living off campus
- The costs of entertainment (travel, movies, concerts, etc.)

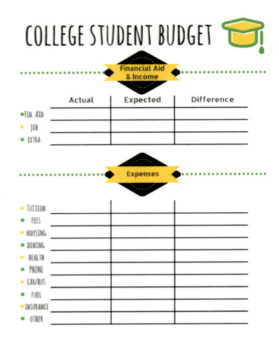

Fig. 0-2. Image of Chase the Write Dream's College Student Budget for managing Indirect Costs.

Unlike direct costs associated with college, indirect costs can vary widely and shift from semester to semester. For example, you may begin one year living off campus and paying $400 / month rent outside of UC Merced, where the off-campus rental prices are low. But then, the following year, you lose your housing lease and have to find a more costly place to rent at $600 / month. Still, it's a more affordable option compared with other cities, yet that $200 leap in costs can shift your entire annual student budget. Other examples of increases that may fluctuate:

- when a roommate moves, and you have to pay higher rent
- class material costs that one semester are twice as high compared to the previous semester
- a health accident that takes you by surprise and leaves you unable to work for a month
- your car breaking down and the added costs of maintenance
- An emergency trip home that gets placed on a credit card

There are endless examples of times indirect costs will sharply rise, and students will need to absorb those changes while still managing their course load. Students with family, parents, or spouses have some form of a safety net during these times to better weather these financial hits without necessarily disrupting their studies. However, so many of our students attending California Community Colleges (CCCs) are much more vulnerable to these incidents. Frequently, it's the reason many CCC students opt to attend a University local to them, so as not to lose that family support or job that offers the flexibility to go to school. That makes 100% sense. It's so important to always stay grounded in the financial responsibilities you are signing up for when you decide on a college. Too often, when students lack a safety net like their family or a job, these unforeseen costs are absorbed through additional student loans. Review **Table 12-1** to see

Chapter 12: Understanding Financial Aid | 205

how Direct and Indirect costs will vary when living on campus, with parents, or off-campus between a CSU and UC campus.

Table 0-1. Direct and Indirect Cost Examples

Direct Costs	SJSU Living On Campus	SJSU Living Off-Campus	SJSU Living With Parental Help	UC Merced Living On Campus	UC Merced Living Off-Campus
Tuition	$7,899 / year	$7,899 / year	$7,899 / year	$14,272 / year	$14,272 / year
Health Insurance	$190 /year	$190 / year	$190 / year	$2,210 / year	$2,210 / year
Student Fees	$1,674 /year	$1,674 / year	$1,674 / year	--	--
Health Center Fee	$72 /year	$72 / year	$72 / year	--	--
Living On-Campus	$14,000 year Triple Rm, Cheapest Option	--	--	$11,424 / year Quad Room, Cheapest Option	--
Meal Plan	Meal Plan included w/housing	--	--	$5,000 / year Meal Plan average costs	--
Total Direct Costs	$23,835 year *10 months (Sept – June)*	$9,835 / year *10 months (Sept – June)*	$9,835 / year *10 months (Sept – June)*	$32,906 / year *10 months (Sept – June)*	$16, 482 / year *10 months (Sept – June)*
Indirect Cost *Estimates*	SJSU Living On Campus	SJSU Living Off-Campus	SJSU Living With Parental Help	UC Merced Living On Campus	UC Merced Living Off-Campus
Books & Supplies	$100 / month	$100 /month	$100 / month	$100/month	$100 / month
Transportation	$40 / month	$300 / month	$300 / month	$30/month	$200 / month
Cell Phone Device	$60 / month	$60 / month	$60 / month	$60/month	$60 / month
Personal Necessity	$200 / month	$200 / month	$200 / month	$200/month	$200 / month
Utilities	-	$200 / month	-	--	$100 / month
Rent	-	$1200 / month	-	--	$600/month
Groceries	-	$400 / month	-	--	$400 / month
Entertainment	$150 / month	$150 / month	$150 / month	$150/month	$150 / month
Total Indirect Costs	$550 month *$5,500 10 months*	$2,610 month *$26,100 year 10 months*	$810 month *$8,100 year 10 months*	$540/month *$5,400 year 10 months*	$1,810/month *$18,100 10 months*
Total Combined Costs	$29,335 yr.	$35,935 yr.	$17,935 yr.	$33,446 yr.	$34,582 yr.

From the example above, I hope you can see how direct and indirect costs will vary based on the location of the college you are attending. For example, campuses like San José State University might be more affordable than a campus like UC Merced if we compare tuition alone. However, be sure to factor in the living expenses in the surrounding area of the college. For example, if renting a room nearby is expensive, you may need to pay inflated prices for gas, parking, or other transportation costs. Also, when the overall costs of living are higher—such as groceries or incidentals—those will affect the ultimate costs of attendance. On the same note, campuses like UC Merced, UC Riverside, CSU Chico, or CSU Stanislaus might easily fall under the radar for students because they are located inland. Yet these campuses offer a tremendous bargain for the pocketbook if you check for the combined direct and indirect costs based on the affordability of their locations.

If you'd like to better understand the fee structure of each college, visit their Bursar Office website. Admissions sites are not always inclined to provide detailed fee structures for students. Admissions offices are always in the business of sales and marketing in some form. Their goal is to get you to apply to their college. The Bursar's Office, however, is the place that essentially handles setting fees, setting deadlines for payment, and ensuring payment is received. These offices will usually disclose the direct costs associated with a bachelor's program in great detail. It's *that detail* you need to develop a solid budget to project costs and make good choices about which college is the most affordable option. For example, **Figure 12-3** shows SJSU's mandatory fee charts provided by their Bursar's Office for Fall 2022 and Spring 2022.

Fall 2022: Basic Registration Fees

Undergraduate

Mandatory Registration Fees	Part-Time Rate 1.0 - 6.0 Units	Full-Time Rate 6.1 or More Units
Tuition Fee	$1,665	$2,871
Student Association Fee	$100.50	$100.50
Student Union Fee	$391.50	$391.50
Health Ctr Facility Fee	$36	$36
Document Fee	$17	$17
Student Success Excel Tech Fee	$343.50	$343.50
Student Health Fee	$190	$190
Totals	$2,743.50	$3,949.50

Spring 2022: Basic Registration Fees

Undergrad

Mandatory Registration Fees	Part-Time Rate 1.0 - 6.0 Units	Full-Time Rate 6.1 or More Units
Tuition Fee	$1,665	$2,871
Student Association Fee	$98	$98
Student Union Fee	$381	$381
Health Ctr Facility Fee	$35	$35
Document Fee	$16.50	$16.50
Student Success Excel Tech	$334.50	$334.50
Health Ctr Ops Fee	$190	$190
Totals	$2,720	$3,926

Fig. 0-3. Screenshots of SJSU's mandatory fee charts for Undergraduates.

Students can usually find on-campus housing and meal plan rates through the Housing Office for each campus. Here are examples from SJSU On-Campus Housing Rates (**fig. 12-4**) and UC Merced's Housing and Meal Plan Pricing (**fig. 12-5**).

Fig. 0-4. SJSU Triple Occupancy Room Rate chart from University Housing Services.

Fig. 0-5. UC Merced Housing and Meal Plan Pricing from Housing & Residence Education.

Factor II. Inside Aid

The next factor in our equation is the one most students are familiar with, financial aid. I call this *inside aid* because it can include federal, state, and university forms of financial aid—all of which are distributed *inside* your financial aid package.

Let's review the kinds of *inside aid* offered to CCC Transfer students.

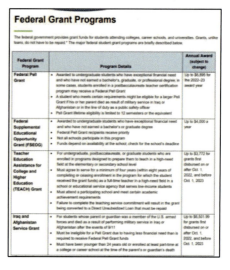

Federal Aid

Federal aid refers to a form of funding sourced from the United States Federal Government. This can include grants, loans, and work-study (**fig. 12-6**).

Fig. 0-6. Types of Federal Grant Programs from U.S Department of Education, Federal Student Aid

Federal Pell Grants usually are awarded only to undergraduate students who display exceptional financial need and have not earned a bachelor's, graduate, or professional degree (**fig. 12-7**). **Grants** are similar to scholarships in that they are *funds that will not need to be repaid*. They are usually based on financial need, student GPA, or specific forms of merit, such as students seeking to become teachers or students that have completed military service.

Fig. 0-7. Pell Grant Payment Schedule @FAFSA Tweet.

How Work-Study Works

Work-study is considered a form of financial aid, even though it usually takes the form of an on-campus job. That can sound confusing, so here is how it works. Within your student financial aid package, if *work-study* is listed, there will be an amount that can range anywhere from $1,000 to $3,000. That means whether employed on campus or for an approved organization (some non-profit or government organizations may also be approved), part of your pay as a *work-study* student comes from the U.S. Federal Government. For example, supposing you earn $15.00 per hour working at the Library's front desk, then $7.50 of that goes to your employer from the US Federal Government as part of your financial aid (**fig. 12-8**). That income is intended to help students cover indirect costs,

Fig. 0-8. Breakdown of Work Study Hourly Pay.

such as books, materials, transportation, or other forms of personal necessities. Note, often, work-study positions can pay too little compared with off-campus options. It is not required to use your work-study benefit; it is an option that is budgeted into your offer of financial aid. There are many great reasons on-campus jobs can help students, such as offering flexible schedules, professional entry experience, and also building a sense of on-campus community. Yet, students should know if work-study is offered, it is not required.

Federal Student Loans

The US Federal Government is the primary source of student loan funding. Unlike private lenders, Federal student loans offer lower interest payments, much more flexibility at the time of repayment, and options for student loan forgiveness.

There are two kinds of student loans that undergraduate students will usually be offered within their aid package: **subsidized loans** and **unsubsidized loans (fig. 12-9)**. A *subsidized loan* is a loan for which the U.S. Federal Government will pay for the interest of the loan while you attend college. This loan type is sometimes nicknamed the *good loan* for that reason. It's also the loan that financial aid offices will offer students first. The **unsubsidized loan**, in contrast, will begin to accrue interest as soon as it is used ("U.S. Department of Education Offers"). To learn more about U.S. Federal Loans, visit the Sallie Mae loans for college site.

Let's pause to talk about student loans. On the one hand, when used cautiously, student loans can be a helpful and necessary tool in filling the gaps to pay for college. But on the other hand, our country is facing a crisis in student debt, where 1 in 5 families in the U.S. have student debt, where the families that are the poorest borrow the most (DeMarco), and communities of color often borrow at higher rates (Hanson).

First Generation students, especially, must remember that taking out a student loan is a long-term commitment, so take time to think about your long-term goals when making these decisions. Are you seeking to attend graduate school? Do you know the costs of graduate school? The fact is this, the largest base of aid—free money in the form of grants—is available to students pursuing

First-Year Undergraduate Annual Loan Limit	$5,500-No more than $3,500 of this amount may be in subsidized loans	$9,500-No more than $3,500 of this amount may be in subsidized loans
Second-Year Undergraduate Annual Loan Limit	$6,500-No more than $4,500 of this amount may be in subsidized loans	$10,500-No more than $4,500 of this amount may be in subsidized loans
Third Year and Beyond Undergraduate Annual Loan Limit	$7,500 per year-No more than $5,500 of this amount may be in subsidized loans	$12,500-No more than $5,500 of this amount may be in subsidized loans
Graduate or Professional Student Annual Loan Limit	Not Applicable (all graduate and professional degree students are considered independent)	$20,500 (unsubsidized only)
Subsidized and Unsubsidized Aggregate Loan Limit	$31,000-No more than $23,000 of this amount may be in subsidized loans	$57,500 for undergraduates-No more than $23,000 of this amount may be in subsidized loans
		$138,500 for graduate or professional students-No more than $65,500 of this amount may be in subsidized loans. The graduate aggregate limit includes all federal loans received for undergraduate study

Fig. 0-9. Limits for Subsidized and Unsubsidized Loans. "U.S Department of Education Offers"

Debt type	Average debt
Bachelor's degree debt	$28,950
Graduate school loan debt	$71,000
Parent PLUS loan debt	$28,778
Law school debt	$145,500
MBA student debt	$66,300
Medical school debt	$201,490
Dental school debt	$292,169
Pharmacy school loan debt	$179,514
Nursing school student debt	$19,928: Associate Degree Nursing (ADN) $23,711: Bachelor of Science in Nursing (BSN) $47,321: Master of Science in Nursing (MSN)
Veterinary school debt	$183,302

Fig. 0-10. Average Student Loan Debt by Type. Table from Helhoski et al.

undergraduate degrees. That means a **bachelor's degree is the one degree that should cost you** *the least – so why overpay for a bachelor's degree?* The fact that you have completed your first two years of undergraduate education at a CCC is already a huge win. You have saved thousands of dollars!

When considering student loans and your budget, imagine buying yourself a car after graduation. What can you afford? Aim to graduate with a *manageable payment*—no more that the cost of a Honda Civic (fig. 12-11, about $18,000 currently). **Can you pay for a Honda Civic after graduation?** Yes. In five years, that's a payment of about $300 per month—and that is if you do not add extra payments to pay the loan off at an earlier date. **Watch yourself with loans the size of a Tesla, a Land Rover, or a Porsche.** Those are payments of **$400, $500, $600, $700, or more** per month and can range well beyond a five-year payment period.

    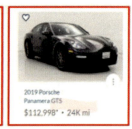

Fig. 0-11. Car Prices resulting from Carmax Comparison Tool.

Certainly, if you know you'll need to attend graduate school to reach your career goals— aim to graduate with the least amount of student loans possible. **Graduate school is primarily funded through student loans and savings.** Be strategic about student debt. Think long-term when making money decisions. Do the work of researching and applying for scholarships. Talk to your financial aid office if you are struggling; they often have options to assist you.

California Grants

The California Student Aid Commission (CSAC) oversees California Grant funding programs. They fund three Cal Grants: A, B, and C. A student's eligibility for a grant is based on their FAFSA or CA Dream Act Application responses, verified Cal Grant GPA, and the type of California colleges (**fig. 12-12**). CSAC now has several excellent online workshops and student-led panels to learn more about California-based aid and the application process.

Visit the CSAC Channel to learn more about Cal Grant and other California Aid options.

Fig. 0-12. Visit the CSAC YouTube Channel to learn more about Cal Grant and other California Aid options.

Cal Grant A

Cal Grant A will help pay for tuition and fees at **four-year colleges and has a GPA Requirement.** Award amounts vary based on the cost of tuition for the college. For example, in 2022-23, Cal Grants awarded $12,570 at a University of California campus, up to $5,742 at a California State University campus, and up to $9,538 at private non-profits (**fig 12-13**). If you are applying using your high school GPA, you must have at least a 3.0 GPA; if applying using your college GPA, you must have **at least a 2.4 GPA**. The Cal Grant also requires that your course of study leads directly to an associate or bachelor's degree or qualifies you for transfer from a community college to a bachelor's degree program.

Cal Grant B

Cal Grant B provides **a living allowance of up to $1,648** in addition to tuition and fee assistance after the first year at a two- or four-year college. Cal Grant B pays most first-year students a living allowance only, which may be used to pay living expenses, books, supplies, transportation, tuition, and fees. When renewed or awarded beyond the first year, students receive the living allowance plus a tuition and fee award that is up to $12,570 at a UC campus, up to $5,742 at a CSU campus, and up to $9,358 at private non-profits for 2022-2023 (Fig. 12-13). Cal Grant B **requires at least a 2.0 GPA**.

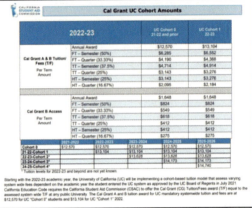

Fig. 0-13. Tables showing 2022-23 Cal Grant Amounts from California Student Aid Commission, "Cal Grant Awards. . ."

Cal Grant C

Cal Grant C is designed to assist with technical or career education costs and provides up to $1,094 for books, tools, and equipment (Fig. 12-13). The Cal Grant C is available for **up to two years** and is typically available to our CCC students pursuing a Workforce Degree program such as *Medical Assisting, Dental Assisting, Construction, Network Technology, or Cosmetology.*

University Grants

Another form of grant aid available to transfer students is known as a **University Grant**. This grant is a form of free money—usually based on the student's financial need and merit qualifications. University Grants are determined differently at each individual campus and based on a combination of factors such as their institutional endowments, campus policies for awarding aid, targeted fundraising efforts, and the discretion of the administrative leadership as to how funding is directed. Often, universities will use University Grants to supplement any gaps in aid to allow students to better afford attending their college. In addition, University Grants are often used as a recruitment tool for high-performing students, student-athletes, and students with special skills or talents the university will showcase. Importantly, those grants are also used as a tool for helping the most vulnerable populations—such as DREAM students who do not qualify for Federal Aid but through University Grants that supplement those gaps can make attending the University of California a viable option. **Figure 12-14** shows how a University Grant might appear on an offer of financial aid.

Award Description	Category	Offered	Accepted
Conditional Cal Grant A	Grant	13,104.00	0.00
University Grant	Grant	6,668.00	0.00
UC Health InsGrant	Grant	3,021.00	0.00
Federal Pell Grant	Grant	6,895.00	6,895.00
Federal Sub Student Loan	Loan	5,500.00	0.00
Federal Unsub Student Loan	Loan	2,000.00	0.00
Budget Gap or Parent Loan	Loan	2,100.00	0.00
Aid Year Totals		39,288.00	6,895.00

Fig. 0-14. Example of a 2022 student offer of financial aid from UC Santa Cruz.

While University Grants are overall a good thing for students, the one area to **be careful of when it comes to University Grants**—particularly at Private Colleges and Universities—is a process known as **frontloading aid**. Universities can use University Grants to allure students to attend their college by providing a very generous package for the first year of attendance. Still, that **aid is *not guaranteed from year to year***. Unlike the Cal Grant and the Federal Grant programs, **University Grant programs are not in fixed amounts—that is, the amounts will vary from year to year. Also, the amounts are not guaranteed for each year of attendance, AND they usually tend to decrease from year to year, sometime substantially so**. Therefore, it is possible that within the first year of attendance, a student gets generously funded with University Grants, but in the following years, University Grant funds dwindle, and students are left to increase their student loans to remain in school and reach graduation.

How do I know this? For one, these practices have become enough of an issue across the United States that Congress seeks to study the pervasive issue to design policies that would curb the practices (Hager). Secondly, this is what happened to me as an undergraduate attending USC. I had no idea at the time that this was an approach Universities took, in part, to recruit students. In my senior year of high school, I had many University options and qualified for the maximum amount of financial aid. When I compared financial aid statements, they each looked alike. I began my studies at USC with what looked like a *full ride*. I didn't know then that the ***University Grant*** in my first-year package would increasingly be traded for student loans from year to year. I didn't know I was signing up to pay for a TESLA when I accepted admission. As an undergraduate student, I carried a lot of shame because I didn't understand financial aid, and I kept losing funds rather than gaining them even though I did well in my studies and kept my GPA high. I blamed myself for not knowing better and not knowing how to better advocate for myself. That shame kept me from asking for help when I needed it most.

This matter isn't something I talk about lightly, but I do so for two reasons. One, I don't want this to happen to our students—I want you to know better and do better. I want you to ask for help if you need it. I want you to know that if this happens to you, it's not your fault, and you do have other options. The second reason I talk about this is, in all the dozens of workshops on financial aid I've attended, no one has ever spoken about the practice of frontloading aid. Often financial aid workshops are fairly basic and focused on what aid is and how to apply it. Still, our students need to know exactly what areas can trip them up as first-generation students and how to avoid them. Financial aid is a confusing and technical process, but here's the thing—you can learn it, you can research it, you can ask questions, and you can say NO when a college begins to cost too much. There are and will always be other options to help you finish your degree. There are more tools today to help you than ever before. There are videos and workshops on YouTube;

there are social media and blogs; there are reports and research that's accessible to the public about each campus and the rate at which their graduates leave with student debt.

It is important when you're at the stage of applying for college and deciding on offers for college admission that you also keep your feet grounded. It can get quite emotional when the admission letters arrive—especially for first-gen college students. When my students learn they got into UC Berkeley, UCLA, USC, Santa Clara University, or Columbia University—it's like winning the lotto. It can feel like the world looks at you differently just because of that one admissions letter. It's emotional, and sometimes it can be the hardest time to make a good sound choice. You're not just making a

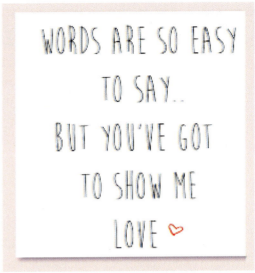

Fig. 0-15. Image source: P.S. by Macaron Hoarder

choice about college; you are making a choice about money. I sometimes think the Transfer Admissions process is so much like dating. It's easy to fall for the campus with all the bells and whistles. The one everyone gets excited about. But do your research and make sure that the campus is not in the practice of frontloading their aid or graduating their students in your major with a world of student debt. In many ways, financial aid packages are how colleges *show you their love*. Be sure the college you are considering is affordable and is showing you *the love* in the form of **funding**.

Factor III. Outside Aid

Another source of funding is one that I will call *outside aid* simply because it is outside of a student's financial aid package and includes several forms of funding options that students and families have long used to help pay for college. Let's take a look at some.

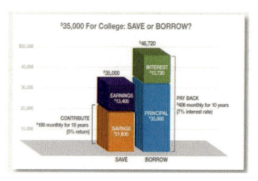

Fig. 0-16. The difference between using a 529 savings account versus using a student loan with additional interest costs (Ascensus Broker).

College Savings and the 529 Account

Something most middle and upper-class families are keenly aware of is the power of compound interest. This method is, in fact, how most wealthy individuals create and perpetuate generational wealth. Unfortunately, it is also—for the most part— something poor and low-income families either know very little about or a process that may seem out of reach when you are trying to make ends meet. And yet, there's a powerful tool available to ALL families, at every income level, that can play an important tool in leveling the playing field for higher education, and that is the 529 savings account (**fig. 12-16**). These are savings accounts that accrue compound interest— which means that both your savings amount AND the interest of that amount build additional interest together or when compounded. The result is an accelerated form of savings, which works best for long-term savings goals like college or retirement planning. Compound interest is, in fact, the basic building block for any 401K retirement account (**fig. 12-17**). The 529 account offers a similar structure and benefit—only instead of saving for your later years, you can begin in your child's earliest years to save for college and school expenses.

Fig. 0-18. Example of compound interest savings using monthly contributions to a 529 pre-taxed savings account (Bright Start).

Fig. 0-18. Screenshot of the California ScholarShare 529 website.

In California, families can utilize the ScholarShare 529 site (**fig. 12-18**) to create an account and begin saving for college. If I had one piece of advice to any new parent, it is "do not wait—begin putting away even $50-100/month towards your child's college using a 529 account." You will see how, over time, the combination of compound interest rate of return and the structure of the 529 accounts as pre-taxed income will help reduce the student loan debt for your family. This is, in fact, how most middle to upper-income families prepare to pay for college, as they will likely not qualify for most forms of grant aid.

Employers That Pay For College

Another practical way to help pay for college is to research and seek out employers that help to pay for college. Even a basic online search of *Employers that pay for college* will point to some great options for students. Let's look at a few top employers using a recent article by Jessica Bryant titled "36 Companies that Pay for College with Tuition Reimbursement." Be sure to read the article for the full listing of all 36 companies.

Allstate: After at least one year of employment, Allstate employees pursuing certain undergraduate, graduate, IT certification, or insurance designations related to an Allstate career path are eligible to receive 100% education reimbursement up to a maximum of $5,250 annually. Covered costs include tuition, books, and academic fees.

Apple: Apple offers full-time employees up to $5,250 annually in education expenses, including tuition. Employees may also attend Apple University to learn key financial, software, and business skills.

AT&T: Both management and non-management employees of AT&T are eligible for tuition assistance. The company reports that over 3,800 employees received tuition reimbursement in 2020.

Best Buy: Full-time employees of Best Buy in undergraduate or graduate programs can receive up to $3,500 or $5,250 annually in tuition reimbursement to cover tuition, books, and school fees.

Chipotle: In partnership with Guild Education, Chipotle employees have access to up to $5,250 of tuition reimbursement annually, which can be used for both undergraduate and graduate programs. In addition, some select programs may qualify for 100% tuition reimbursement. Qualified applicants in undergraduate programs also have access to an additional $5,815 in federal grants.

FedEx Ground: Eligible FedEx Ground package handlers have access to tuition reimbursement of up to $5,250 annually for college degrees, trade, vocational, or technical certificates. Employees can also receive exclusive tuition discounts at Robert Morris University.

Geico: Geico's full-time employees can receive up to $5,250 a year in tuition reimbursement for undergraduate tuition, coursework, books, and other related school fees.

Home Depot: Home Depot employees seeking an associate, bachelor's, master's, doctoral, or technical degree can receive reimbursement for up to 50% of educational costs, including tuition, books, and registration fees.

Lowe's: In partnership with Guild Education, full-time and part-time associates can access 100% debt-free academic programs to earn undergraduate certificates or degrees. Lowe's additionally provides direct payments of up to $2,500 annually in tuition assistance for more than 165 academic programs.

McDonald's: Eligible McDonald's employees can have their tuition reimbursed for approved courses at accredited institutions offering two-year and four-year degrees. In addition, some managers can have up to $5,250 reimbursed annually, while other employees can have up to $2,500 reimbursed each year.

Papa John's: Through its Dough and Degrees initiative, Papa John's offers its employees 100% free tuition for undergraduate and graduate online degree programs. Also, eligible corporate team members can enroll in any of Purdue Global's online degrees. Franchise employees can also receive tuition assistance/reductions through the program.

Starbucks: Full-time and part-time employees seeking a bachelor's degree for the first time are eligible for 100% tuition coverage for online programs at Arizona State University.

T-Mobile: Following 90 days of employment, full-time and part-time T-Mobile employees can receive annual tuition benefits. This includes up to $5,250 a year for full-time employees and up to $2,500 for part-time employees to cover tuition, books, and other academic fees.

Target: Target launched its debt-free education assistance program, offered to all full-time and part-time employees. As a result, target team members can pursue undergraduate degrees and professional certifications with no out-of-pocket costs from their first day of work at the company.

UPS: Through the company's Earn & Learn program, UPS employees can receive up to $5,250 annually in tuition assistance for a lifetime maximum of $25,000. Employees are eligible when they begin working at UPS.

Verizon: In partnership with Bellevue University, full-time Verizon employees enrolled as full-time degree-seeking students can receive up to $8,000 a year in tuition assistance. Part-time employees can also receive assistance of up to $4,000 annually.

Walmart: In August, Walmart announced that it would cover 100% of college tuition and books for employees through its Live Better U program.

Wells Fargo: Full-time and part-time employees of Wells Fargo can receive up to $5,000 in tuition reimbursement per year.

Military Educational Benefits

Another form of outside funding to pay for college is through committed service within one branch of the U.S. military, which earns educational benefits to pay for school. There are options for full-time and reserve service through the Army, the Marine Corps, the Navy, the Air Force, Space Force, and the Coast Guard. There are three methods to access the educational benefits provided by military service. *The first* is through programs like Reserved Officer Training in Corps (ROTC) in College (**fig. 12-19**), in which students complete their college studies first and then complete their military service after college. *The second* is to complete military service first and attend college afterward using educational benefits (fig. 12-20). *And third* is the option to transfer unused educational benefits to your spouse and/or children (**fig 12-21**).

Visit the U.S. Department of Defense "Ways to Serve" website **for an overview of US military service opportunities (fig. 12-22).** For an overview of the educational benefits available after serving in the military, visit the U.S. Department of Veterans Affairs "VA Education and Training Benefits" website.

Fig. 0-19. College ROTC First then Service

Fig. 0-21. Veteran's Benefits After Service

Fig. 0-21. Give Unused Benefits to Dependents

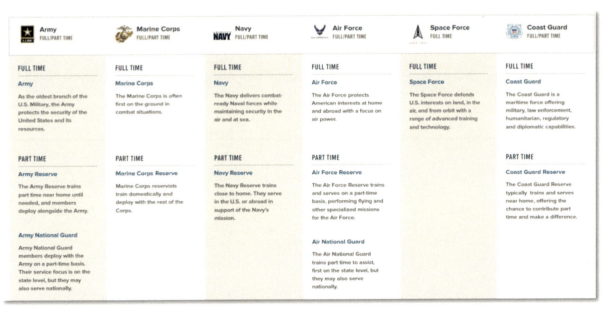

Army FULL/PART TIME	Marine Corps FULL/PART TIME	Navy FULL/PART TIME	Air Force FULL/PART TIME	Space Force FULL TIME	Coast Guard FULL/PART TIME
FULL TIME	**FULL TIME**	**FULL TIME**	**FULL TIME**	**FULL TIME**	**FULL TIME**
Army	**Marine Corps**	**Navy**	**Air Force**	**Space Force**	**Coast Guard**
As the oldest branch of the U.S. Military, the Army protects the security of the United States and its resources.	The Marine Corps is often first on the ground in combat situations.	The Navy delivers combat-ready Naval forces while maintaining security in the air and at sea.	The Air Force protects American interests at home and abroad with a focus on air power.	The Space Force defends U.S. interests on land, in the air, and from orbit with a range of advanced training and technology.	The Coast Guard is a maritime force offering military, law enforcement, humanitarian, regulatory and diplomatic capabilities.
PART TIME	**PART TIME**	**PART TIME**	**PART TIME**		**PART TIME**
Army Reserve	**Marine Corps Reserve**	**Navy Reserve**	**Air Force Reserve**		**Coast Guard Reserve**
The Army Reserve trains part time near home until needed, and members deploy alongside the Army.	Marine Corps reservists train domestically and deploy with the rest of the Corps.	The Navy Reserve trains close to home. They serve in the U.S. or abroad in support of the Navy's mission.	The Air Force Reserve trains and serves on a part-time basis, performing flying and other specialized missions for the Air Force.		The Coast Guard Reserve typically trains and serves near home, offering the chance to contribute part time and make a difference.
Army National Guard			**Air National Guard**		
Army National Guard members deploy with the Army on a part-time basis. Their service focus is on the state level, but they may also serve nationally.			The Air National Guard trains part time to assist, first on the state level, but they may also serve nationally.		

Fig. 0-22. "Military Service Branches" Table from U.S. Department of Defense, "Services Branches" webpage.

Factor IV. Debt

The final factor for consideration is how to pay for college debt. One option available students and/or their parents have the option of taking out federal student loans. These loans are managed and repaid to the Federal government. In an effort to curb the national crisis around student loans, the Obama and Biden administrations have separately made broad strokes in designing options for student loan forgiveness programs.

One program set forth by the Obama administration is a 10-year repayment program for employees of public service organizations—such as teachers, nurses, doctors, firefighters, etc.—known as the Public Service Loan Forgiveness (PSLF) program. These borrowers agree to complete 120 payments while employed in public service and, at the end of these payments, have the remaining balance on their loans forgiven (Fig. 12-23). In addition, the Biden administration has taken further strides to broaden options for student loan forgiveness, to lower the rate of student loan payments, and to provide student loan forgiveness for amounts of $10,000 - $20,000. To learn more about these programs and others, such as the Teacher Loan Forgiveness program, visit the U.S. Department of Education Federal Student Aid's "Student Loan Forgiveness" webpage.

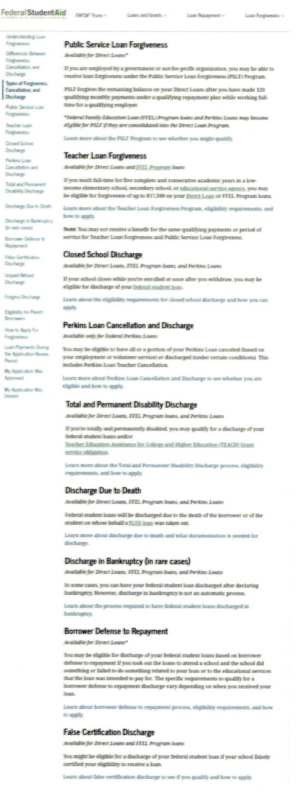

Fig. 0-23. Screenshot of "Student Loan Forgiveness" page information.

Table 0-2. Understanding Inside and Outside Aid Options.

	Funding awarded outside of College	Funding awarded within Student Financial Aid Package	
Before College	**529 Investment Savings Accounts** College savings investment account (compound interest)		
During College	**Employer Tuition Reimbursement** Some employers, like UPS or Chipotle, will reimburse employees for tuition costs (free money). **Military Education Benefits** Veteran and military service members earn educational benefits (free money).	**Work-Study**	.... On Campus Jobs (half of salary paid by Federal Aid)
		Pell Grant	.... Federal Aid (free money) (based on financial need)
		Cal Grant	.... California Aid (free money) (based on financial need)
		University Grant	.... University Aid (free money) (based on financial need)
		University Scholarship	... University Scholarship (free money) (based on merit, such as GPA, athletics)
		Outside Scholarship	... Outside Scholarship (free money) (based on financial need, merit)
		Subsidized Loan	.... Federal loan (not free, must repay) (interest paid by the Fed Government)
		Unsubsidized Loan	.... Federal loan (not free, must repay) (interest begins compounding during college)
After College	**Loan Forgiveness** Public Student Loan Forgiveness Student loans are forgiven after 10 years working for a non-profit and making 120 payments.		

FAFSA 101

What is FAFSA?

FAFSA stands for **Free Application for Student Aid**. FAFSA is an *application process* that U.S. colleges utilize to do two important things:

Fig. 0-24. FAFSA: One Student Aid Application for All Colleges.

1. **FAFSA provides an application process for all eligible U.S. students** to enter their and/or their parents' verified financial information, which will be used by colleges to determine eligibility for Federal and State financial aid at their campus.

2. **FAFSA provides students with a verified and confidential manner to provide this information to colleges**. Therefore, this information will only be sent to the colleges that the student has listed.

FAFSA alone does not determine a student's financial aid. Think of the FAFSA as an ID card used to provide permission to view your financial profile and verify for colleges that what has been entered is accurate information. Once each college receives the information, that is when each financial aid office will utilize its unique process to *package* a student. A financial aid package is a unique combination of financial aid options for which each student/family is eligible to receive, such as grants, scholarships, work-study, or loans.

When to submit FAFSA?

FAFSA is due each year by March 2nd for the following year at a 4-year campus. However, **students can complete the FAFSA as early as October 1st**—and I'd HIGHLY recommend doing so this early since missing the March 2nd deadline can compromise a student's eligibility for student aid.

Once the FAFSA application is submitted, **students can always log back in to update their FAFSA** with additional schools or a change in their financial status. For example, suppose a parent is suddenly unemployed. In that case, students should update their FAFSA and then reach out to their financial aid office to update their financial aid package—they may be eligible for additional support.

Who is eligible for the FAFSA?

U.S. citizens, permanent residents, and other eligible noncitizens can apply for the FAFSA. However, there are additional criteria to adhere to; please refer to the FAFSA website for up-to-date eligibility information.

To remain eligible for financial aid, students must maintain **a 2.0 and above cumulative GPA**. Students must also be careful not to accumulate *too many* Ws or withdraws—as this can **disqualify a student's eligibility for financial aid**.

CADAA 101

What is the California Dream Act (CADAA)?
CADAA stands for the <u>California Dream Act Application</u>. CADAA is an **application process** for California financial aid born out of the 2011 passage of the California Dream Act.

      The California Student Aid Commission "FAQs" document (**fig. 12-26**) explains how the California Dream Act made it possible for undocumented students and DACA recipients (valid or expired), among others, "to receive certain types of financial aid such as private scholarships funded through public universities, state-administered financial aid, university grants, community college fee waivers, and Cal Grants . . .[and] allows eligible students to pay in-state tuition at any public college in California. Read through the "<u>California Dream Act FAQ's for Students and Parents</u>" to learn more about the program and what makes it different from FAFSA.

Fig. 0-25. CADAA: California Dream Act Application for Financial Aid.

Fig. 0-26. Screenshot of the "California Dream ACT FAQ's" Brochure, page 1.

Who can apply for the CADAA?
"Students who live in California and meet the eligibility requirements for a *non-resident exemption*, as well as students who have a U Visa or TPS status, can use the California Dream Act application (CADAA). Similarly, students without Social Security Numbers or those who have lost DACA status (or never applied for DACA) may still be eligible. The full language of the law and eligibility requirements is stated in CA Education Code 68130.5" ("California Dream Act FAQ's"). Students can find additional help for completing the CADA Application on the California Student Aid Commission's <u>"Resources" website</u> (**fig. 12-27**).

Fig. 0-27. Screenshot of the "<u>Resources for California Dream Act Application</u>" webpage.

When to submit CADAA?
CADAA is due each year by March 2nd for the following year at a 4-year campus. However, **students can complete the CADAA as early as October 1st**—and I'd HIGHLY recommend doing that since missing the March 2nd deadline can compromise a student's eligibility for student aid.

CADAA, FERPA, and Confidentiality
Students and families should feel **secure** when submitting their information through the CA Dream Act Application (CADAA). For example, the California Student Aid Commission adheres to the **Family Educational Rights and Privacy Act (FERPA)** (20 U.S.C. §1232g; 34 CFR Part 99), a Federal law that **protects the privacy of student education records** (<u>California Student Aid Commission, "CA Dream Act"</u>).

Independent vs. Dependent

When completing the FAFSA or CADAA applications for financial aid, it's important to understand whose financial information should be reported. Are you considered "dependent" or "independent" for purposes of receiving Federal Student Aid? The best way to make an accurate determination is to answer the dependency status questions posted on the Federal Student Aid website. Figure 12-29 is a copy of those status questions taken directly from the U.S. Department of Education's Federal Student Aid "Dependency Status" webpage.

Fig. 0-29. Image from "Dependency Status" webpage.

INDEPENDENT STUDENT

If you answer **YES** to ANY of these questions, then you may be an independent student. You may not be required to provide parental information on your *Free Application for Federal Student Aid* (FAFSA®) form.

DEPENDENT STUDENT*

If you answer **NO** to ALL of these questions, then you may be considered a dependent student and may be required to provide your parents' financial information when completing the FAFSA form.

1. Yes ☐ No ☐ Will you be 24 or older by Jan. 1 of the school year for which you are applying for financial aid? For example, if you plan to start school in August 2022 for the 2022–23 school year, will you be 24 by Jan. 1, 2022 (i.e., were you born before Jan. 1, 1999)?
2. Yes ☐ No ☐ Are you married or separated but not divorced?
3. Will you be working toward a master's or doctorate degree (such as M.A., MBA, M.D., J.D., Ph.D., Ed.D., etc.)?
4. Yes ☐ No ☐ Do you have children who receive more than half of their support from you?
5. Yes ☐ No ☐ Do you have dependents (other than children or a spouse) who live with you and receive more than half of their support from you?
6. Yes ☐ No ☐ Are you currently serving on active duty in the U.S. armed forces for purposes other than training?
7. Yes ☐ No ☐ Are you a veteran of the U.S. armed forces?
8. Yes ☐ No ☐ At any time since you turned age 13, were both of your parents deceased, were you in foster care, or were you a ward or dependent of the court?
9. Yes ☐ No ☐ Are you an emancipated minor or are you in a legal guardianship as determined by a court?
10. Yes ☐ No ☐ Are you an unaccompanied youth who is homeless or self-supporting and at risk of being homeless?

*If you don't answer "yes" to any of the questions above, you're still considered a dependent student for purposes of applying for federal student aid even if you don't live with your parents, are not claimed by your parents on their tax forms, or are paying for your own bills and educational expenses. For more information, visit StudentAid.gov/dependency.

Fig. 0-28. Dependency Status Questions on the 2023–24 FAFSA® Form

Works Cited

Ascensus Broker Dealer Services. "$35,000 for College: Save or Borrow?" *College Choice 529 Direct Savings Plan*, Indiana Education Savings Authority and Ascensus Broker Dealer Services LLC., 2021, www.collegechoicedirect.com/home/planning/benefits-of-saving.html. Accessed 1 Feb. 2023. Chart.

Bright Start. "Assumed Annualized Return at 5%." *Bright Start*, 2023, www.brightstart.com/how-much-do-i-need/. Accessed 1 Feb. 2023. Chart.

Bursar's Office. "Fall Registration Fees: Fall 2022." *San Jose State University*, 7 Apr. 2022, www.sjsu.edu/bursar/fees-due-dates/tuition-other-fees/fall.php. Accessed 30 Jan. 2023.

---. "Spring Registration Fees: Spring 2022." *San Jose State University*, www.sjsu.edu/bursar/fees-due-dates/tuition-other-fees/fall.php. Accessed 30 Jan. 2023.

California Student Aid Commission. "Apply for Financial Aid." *California Student Aid Commission*, www.csac.ca.gov/. Accessed 1 Feb. 2023.

---. "CA Dream Act." *California Student Aid Commission*, dream.csac.ca.gov/landing. Accessed 2 Feb. 2023.

---. *Cal Grant Award Amounts by Segment and Term*. California Student Aid Commission, 2022, www.csac.ca.gov/sites/main/files/file-attachments/2022-23_cal_grant_award_amounts_by_segment_and_term.pdf?1663885892. Accessed 1 Feb. 2023.

---. *California Dream Act FAQ's for Students and Parents*. California Student Aid Commission,

    2021, www.csac.ca.gov/sites/main/files/file-

    attachments/california_dream_act_faq.pdf?1638916041. Accessed 1 Feb. 2023.

---. "Resources for California Dream Act Application." *California Student Aid Commission*,

    www.csac.ca.gov/post/resources-california-dream-act-application. Accessed 1 Feb. 2023.

Demarco, Jacqueline. "A Demographic Look at Who Has Student Loan Debt." Edited by Dan

    Shepherd and Xiomara Martinez-White. *LendingTree*, 14 June 2022,

    www.lendingtree.com/student/student-debt-demographics-study/. Accessed 30 Jan.

    2023.

Federal Student Aid [@FAFSA]. "Federal Pell Grant amounts for 2022–23 just dropped! Use the

    Expected Family Contribution (EFC) on your Student Aid Report (SAR) to estimate how

    much you may qualify for. https://go.usa.gov/xSu4t." *Twitter*, 15 Aug. 2022, 1:30 PM,

    twitter.com/fafsa/status/1559230974675787777.

Get Schooled. "How to Read Your College Bill or Tuition Statement." *Get Schooled*, 2023,

    getschooled.com/article/5590-how-to-read-your-college-bill/. Accessed 30 Jan. 2023.

Hager, Matt. "Congress Addresses Scholarship Displacement; Front-Loaded Financial Aid."

    Scholarship America, 2021, scholarshipamerica.org/blog/congress-addresses-scholarship-

    displacement-front-loaded-financial-aid/. Accessed 2 Feb. 2023.

Hanson, Melanie. "Student Loan Debt by Race." *Education Data Initiative*, 16 Jan. 2023,

    educationdata.org/student-loan-debt-by-race. Accessed 30 Jan. 2023.

Helhoski, Anna, et al. "Student Loan Debt Statistics: 2023." *NerdWallet*, 13 Jan. 2023,

www.nerdwallet.com/article/loans/student-loans/student-loan-debt. Accessed 30 Jan.

2023.

Housing & Residence Education. "Past Rates." *UC Merced*, housing.ucmerced.edu/past_rates.

Accessed 30 Jan. 2023.

ScholarShare 529. "ScholarShare 529: The California Way to save for College." *ScholarShare 529*,

www.scholarshare529.com/. Accessed 1 Feb. 2023.

University Housing Services. *2022-2023 Housing Rates Classics: Triple Occupancy Room*. San Jose

State University, 2022, www.sjsu.edu/housing/docs/2022-2023-ay-license-

materials/Fall_2022_Classics_Triple_v221005.pdf. Accessed 30 Jan. 2023.

University HQ. "What Are ROTC Programs and How They Work?" *University HQ*, 2023,

universityhq.org/resources/college-planning-guide/rotc-programs/. Accessed 1 Feb.

2023.

U.S. Department of Defense. "ROTC Programs." *Today's Military*, 2023,

www.todaysmilitary.com/education-training/rotc-programs. Accessed 1 Feb. 2023.

---. "Service Branches." *Today's Military*, 2023, www.todaysmilitary.com/ways-to-serve/service-

branches. Accessed 1 Feb. 2023. Table.

---. "Ways to Serve." *Today's Military*, www.todaysmilitary.com/ways-to-serve. Accessed 1 Feb.

2023.

U.S. Department of Education, Federal Student Aid. "Complete the FAFSA Form." *Federal Student

Aid*, U.S. Department of Education, studentaid.gov/h/apply-for-aid/fafsa. Accessed 1 Feb.

2023.

---. "Dependency Status." *Federal Student Aid*, studentaid.gov/apply-for-aid/fafsa/filling-

out/dependency. Accessed 28 Jan. 2023.

---. *Federal Grant Programs*. 2022, studentaid.gov/sites/default/files/federal-grant-programs.pdf.

Accessed 31 Jan. 2023.

---. "Federal Pell Grants Are Usually Awarded Only to Undergraduate Students." *Federal Student

Aid*, studentaid.gov/understand-aid/types/grants/pell. Accessed 30 Jan. 2023.

---. "Student Loan Forgiveness." *Federal Student Aid*, U.S. Department of Education,

studentaid.gov/manage-loans/forgiveness-cancellation. Accessed 1 Feb. 2023.

---. "The U.S. Department of Education Offers Low-Interest Loans. . ." *Federal Student Aid*,

studentaid.gov/understand-aid/types/loans/subsidized-unsubsidized. Accessed 30 Jan.

2023.

U.S. Department of Veterans Affairs. "GI Bill and Other Education Benefit Eligibility." *VA*, U.S.

Department of Veterans Affairs, 12 Oct. 2022, https://www.va.gov/education/eligibility/.

Accessed 1 Feb. 2023

---. "Transfer Your Post-9/11 GI Bill Benefits." *VA*, U.S. Department of Veterans Affairs, 12 Oct.

2022, www.va.gov/education/transfer-post-9-11-gi-bill-benefits/. Accessed 1 Feb. 2023.

---. "VA Education and Training Benefits." *VA*, U.S. Department of Veterans Affairs, 2 Dec. 2022,

www.va.gov/education/. Accessed 1 Feb. 2023.

Chapter 13: Scholarships

Scholarships are EVERYWHERE. If you're taking time to read this guide, then please take time to apply for at least ONE scholarship this year. Preparing to apply for one scholarship will actually prepare you to apply for MANY scholarships. Most scholarships will ask students to respond to a writing prompt, submit a letter of recommendation, and complete an application form.

Often the biggest barrier to applying for scholarships is learning *where to find them*. For this, I recommend students **ask their Counselor, Financial Aid office, and Transfer Center for local and specific recommendations**. In addition, Table 13-1 shows some sites that also list scholarships available for our CCC students.

Table 0-1. List of Scholarships Available for CCC Transfer Students.

 **CCC Transfer Counselor Website** lists several scholarship sites specifically for transfer students.

 **Silicon Valley Foundation** is an example of local or regional associations actively fundraising to offer a wide umbrella of scholarship programs that are excellent for CCC students to seek.

 **Immigrants Rising** offers a comprehensive list of scholarship opportunities for undocumented students.

 UC Santa Cruz **Karl S. Pister Leadership Opportunity Scholarship** is an example of scholarship types available at a 4-year campus specifically for transfer students. Speak with the Admissions Reps for scholarship recommendations.

 **Foundation for California Community Colleges** specifically fundraises to offer CCC students scholarships.

 **Jim McEntee Scholarship** is a regionally based scholarship for local transfer students that are excellent for our CCC students to pursue.

 **California Scholarships** is a great site to search for several excellent local scholarships.

 **AAUW Scholarship– San Jose** is a great example of local associations raising funds for a specific group, in this case, women seeking to complete their degrees.

 **SJSU external scholarship** has scholarships students can begin applying to once they accept SJSU's offer of admission. Look for other 4-year campus sites with similar offers

 **San José City College scholarships** is an example of a local community college application site offering scholarship opportunities for their students to apply.

Letters of Recommendation

Many scholarship programs will ask students to submit a letter of recommendation as part of their application. These may be written by a wide variety of people, such as mentors, community leaders, employers, etc. It is commonly requested to include a letter of recommendation from a professor, instructor, or counselor. Here are some tips for requesting a letter of recommendation:

- ☐ Ask someone you have a relationship with, someone that has gotten to know you, and you feel confident will complete this commitment.

- ☐ Ask ahead of time; 3-4 weeks is a good rule of thumb.

- ☐ Provide relevant biographic items (such as your scholarship essay) and academic information (such as a student resume) about yourself to assist the recommender in providing better context about you and a more well-rounded letter.

- ☐ Provide the recommender with information about the scholarship program, including the deadline, link to the website, the exact recommender prompt, and any specific details for submission of the letter of recommendation.

- ☐ Follow up with a sincere thank you. Letters of recommendation take time and dedication. It is important to appreciate folks that go the extra mile for you. Also—you may want to ask again for a different scholarship; it's always easiest to ask someone that has previously served as a recommender.

Fig. 0-1. Example of an email message asking a professor to write you a letter of recommendation for a scholarship application. Used by Permission.

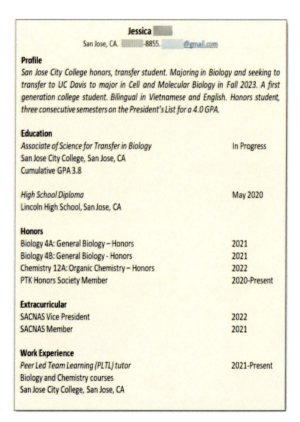

Fig. 0-2. Example of an Academic Student Resume to provide your recommender or to include in an admissions application or scholarship application. Used by Permission.

Scholarship Essay Writing

Every scholarship essay is different, yet there are usually four main goals you are seeking to achieve in your essay, and that is to share: *your personal story, your academic story, your future goals, and to connect with the overall purpose of the scholarship program.* Here are some tips on writing most scholarship application essays.

Fig. 0-3. Key Elements for Scholarship Essay writing.

1. Share Your Personal Story

Be sure to root your essay somehow in telling a story about yourself. This narrative can include sharing details about your parents and their journey, how you grew up, personal challenges you may have overcome, and personal qualities or values that have propelled you forward. In addition, if this is a scholarship based on financial need, share details about your past or current circumstances that qualify you for the scholarship.

2. Share Your Academic Story

Include your academic story. That is, who are you as a student? Are there academic challenges you have overcome? Are there academic areas you excel in or are especially proud of? When you look at your transcript, what story does it tell? Talk about your journey as a first-generation student. Talk about what has defined your experiences in school.

3. Share your Goals & Future Vision

Attending college and applying for a scholarship is innately an act of hope centered on one's future hopes, dreams, and aspirations. Be sure to let the scholarship committee know what your major, college, career, and life goals are. Also, tell them why these goals matter to you, your family, and your community. There is something about achieving your goals that is greater than yourself—what is that for you? How did your—for example—becoming the first in your family to earn a college degree impact others?

4. Connect with the Purpose of the Scholarship

Scholarships come in all shapes and sizes. Be sure to learn about the nature of the scholarship you are applying for. For example, is it for women pursuing higher education, as it is for the AAUW scholarship? Are there certain values like leadership, service, or resiliency that the scholarship seeks to honor? Be sure to acknowledge the criteria of the scholarship and speak to how you are aligned with these same goals, values, or characteristics.

Part V: Where to begin? Begin with YOU.

Every student who walks onto a college campus for the first time starts at a completely different place compared to other students, even if they are enrolled in the same first set of courses. That's because we're all operating within our own set of inner values, goals, fears, and drives that navigate our path. For example, some students begin college feeling very clear about their ultimate career goal—such as becoming a doctor—but may be unclear about how to get there academically. Other students might enter with a clear passion for a discipline—such as Art—but might not know how to connect their major to a career path. While even more students will enter college knowing only one thing, they want to go to college and earn their degree. All of this is perfectly fine. California Community Colleges (CCCs) offer a multitude of services like Career Centers, Counseling, Transfer Centers, and Workforce Development departments to assist students in exploring their options and identifying the best first steps most suited to them. The following are activities students can utilize to clarify where they are in their pathway and what matters to them most as they explore their options.

Chapter 14: Take a Personal Inventory

What is Pulling You First?

Everyone has to start somewhere. Often something is pulling us *first* toward a direction. It is the thing we consciously or unconsciously prioritize first when sorting through our options. Take a look at the descriptions below and identify which of the following areas best describes where you are and **what you prioritize *first* as you pursue your transfer goals.**

Table 0-1. What's Pulling You First: Self Assessment.

Major First	**This is you if—** You are SO passionate and clear about your major—for example, Engineering or Psychology. You don't care so much where you go so long as you can get into a college with your 1st choice major. You don't mind how long it takes to complete the Transfer coursework, so long as it's in your major. You are willing to take a longer or harder path to study your major.	**Tips to get started—** Utilize the Transfer Major Explorer to find the colleges that offer your major. Next, take time to research each campus and the graduation requirements for your major to compare colleges. Then, start narrowing down to your top two to four campuses to focus on making Transfer applications. Finally, work closely with your Counselor and Admissions rep to plan courses and GPA requirements.
College First	**This is you if—** You are focused on a single college or even a system---like attending a UC. You are flexible on the major if you can attend the College you have in mind. You already imagine yourself at this college, on the campus, and what it will be like. It can be a college that means something special. It can be a college culture that draws you in and feels like home.	**Tips to get started—** Spend time on the individual college website and study the admissions requirements. Narrow down majors that interest you at this college. Next, start talking with the Admissions representatives for this college EARLY. Let them know that their campus is your goal. Ask them for help with your planning process. Finally, work with your Counselor early to ensure you meet the course and GPA requirements.
Career First	**This is you if—** You start with a career in mind, like becoming a nurse or an attorney. You know what you want to do upon graduation and are flexible about how you get there. You are willing to take more courses if needed. You're less particular about the Transfer college or major so long as it leads to your career choice. You have great clarity about your career goal.	**Tips to get started—** Try to arrange an informational interview with someone in this career. That is, ask someone for 30-60 mins of their time for you to interview them about their career and how they got there, and what they would advise you. Also, check with your Career Center about career panels or career-related special events. Finally, work with your Counselor to design a transfer plan best suited to your goal.
Work First	**This is you if—** You see *Transfer* as a long-term goal and want a Certificate or Associate's Degree first to enter the workforce within six months or a year. For example, a student earning an Early Childhood Education certificate may still seek to become a K-12 credentialed teacher but will enter the teaching field first to gain experience as they continue their studies.	**Tips to get started—** Work with your Counselor to learn about local workforce programs available at your college or within your Region. Aim to take General Education courses that will align with your transfer goals in the future to avoid taking more classes than needed. Aim for a manageable course load that allows you to work while going to school. Ask about options for Work Experience. Finally, lean on online/hybrid courses for flexibility.
Options Open	**This is you if—** You're not sure where you want to transfer to, what to major in, or have an ultimate career goal. You're flexible, open, and want to learn more. You're also cautious and do not want to commit too early to any field of study until you feel sure. You mostly know 100% that you want to earn a Bachelor's degree.	**Tips to get started—** Start by taking a Career Guidance course at your College. Check in with your Career Center for assessment options. Meet with your Counselor and Admissions reps. Participate in opportunities to tour 4-year campuses. You are in the learning and exploration phase; that's okay so long as you don't stay passive. Find ways to engage, get more specific about your options

The Major Buckets Challenge

Each of the six areas below represents a *major* bucket of related majors and career pathways that students might gravitate toward. Review the buckets below and circle the ones where you find a major or career that interests you. Cross out those that you have NO interest in or know are just not you.

Table 0-2. Six "Bucket" Areas of Related Majors and Career Pathways: Personal Interest Survey.

Something in Arts	Something in Health	Something in Law
Transfer Major options may include: Animation, Studio Art, Music, Dance, Theater, Graphic Design, Game Design, Photography, Industrial Design, Media Arts, Interior Design, Art Education, Art History, Film Production, Screenwriting, Spatial Art, Creative Writing, Fashion Design, Music Recording, Journalism.	**Transfer Major options may include:** Biology, Chemistry, Health Science, Health Education, Public Health, Health Administration, Kinesiology, Dental Hygiene, Respiratory Therapy, Registered Nurse, Pre-Pharmacology, Pre-Physical Therapy, Nutrition, and Food Science.	**Transfer Major options may include:** Legal Studies, Political Science, Philosophy, Administration of Justice, Communications, English, Sociology, Forensic Science, Criminology, Rhetoric, and Business.
Related Careers may include: Art Teacher or Professor, Animator, Game Designer, Graphic Designer, Actor, Musician, Director, Producer, Web Designer, Sculptor, Screenwriter, Fiction Writer, Fashion Designer, Advertising, Social Media Content Producer, Editor, Music Recording Producer, Radio and Broadcast Producer.	**Related Careers may include:** Doctor, Dentist, Optometrist, Pharmacist, Nurse, Physician's Assistant, Occupational Therapist, Physical Therapist, Physical Education Teacher, Recreational Therapist, Dental Hygienist, Health Care Administrator, Public Health Statistician, Respiratory Therapist, Nutritionist.	**Related Careers may include:** Judge, Local Police Officer, Paralegal, Attorney in Business & Contracts, Attorney in Immigration, Attorney in Education, Attorney in Criminal Justice, Professor, Teacher, Sheriff's Officer, Federal Officer, FBI analyst, Forensic Science

Something in Business	Something in Community	Something in STEM
Transfer major may include: Accounting, Marketing, International Trade, Human Resources, Finance, Entrepreneurship, Real Estate, Hospitality, Management, Operations and Supply Management, Economics, Agribusiness, Business and Computer Information Systems, Business Analytics, Risk Management and Insurance, Technology Operations, Global Supply Chain Management, Public Relations, Communication	**Transfer major may include:** English, Humanities, Foreign Language, Sociology, Psychology, Social Work, History, Liberal Studies, Global Studies, Political Science, Geography, Communication, Journalism, Music, Dance, Art, Ethnic Studies, Child Development, Human Development, Deaf Culture, Urban Studies, Public Administration, Environmental Studies, Urban & Regional Development.	**Transfer major may include:** Chemistry, Biology, Biochemistry, Chemical Engineering, Physics, Civil Engineering, Computer Science, Aviation, Electrical Engineering, Construction Management, Environmental Engineering, Software Engineering, Architecture, Zoology, Animal Science, Earth Science, Geology, Environmental Science, Forestry, Hydrologic Science, Agricultural Science, Bioinformatics, Geographic Information Systems, Meteorology, Applied, Statistics, Mathematics, Actuarial Science, Landscape Architecture, Robotics Engineering, Genetics.
Related Careers may include: Accountant, Investment Fund Manager, Human Resources Manager, Chief Financial Officer, Operations Manager, Actuary, Financial Adviser, Management Analyst, Budget Analyst, Auditor, Underwriter, Real Estate Broker, Data Analyst, Financial Manager, Corporate Lawyer, Non-profit Director, Teacher, Professor.	**Related Careers may include:** Professor, Teacher, Counselor, Social Worker, Preschool Director, Therapist, Non-profit Director, Special Needs Educator, Interpreter, Urban Planner, City Planner, Lawyer, Public Policy Manager, Government Relations, Local Country Affairs, State Political Affairs, Federal Agency Manager.	**Related Careers may include:** Engineer, Computer Scientist, Software Engineer, Research Scientist, Meteorologist, Archeologist, Pilot, Astronaut, Veterinarian, Doctor, Dentist, Pharmacist, Environmental Engineer, Natural Science Manager, Park Naturalist, Quality Control Analyst, Genetic Counselor, Bioengineer, Cybersecurity, Biostatistics Analyst, Telecommunications Engineer, Computer Programming.

 Appendix

A. Sample Educational Plan

This is an example of an Educational Plan for a major in Psychology for a student seeking to transfer to San Jose State University. In this example, the student followed the AA-T in Psychology course sequence, saving the bulk of the major courses for the end.

SJCC Educational Plan

CITY COLLEGE SAN JOSE

Name: _____ ID# _____

Major: Psychology _____ Counselor: _____

Goal: AA-T _____ Transfering Institution: San Jose State University

Semester: Fall	Year: 2022
Course	Units
ENGL 1A	3
MATH 63	3
MUSIC 83	3
COMS 20	3
GEOL 10	3
Total Units:	15

Semester: Spring	Year: 2023
Course	Units
ENGL 1C	3
SPAN 1A	5
ETH 27	3
POLSC 1	3
Total Units:	14

Semester: Fall	Year: 2023
Course	Units
ETH 37A	3
ENVIR 10	4
PSYCH 10	3
PSYCH 92	3
Total Units:	13

In this sequence the student is full-time, taking 13-15 units at one time or 4-5 courses per semester.

Semester: Spring	Year: 2024
Course	Units
PSYCH 22	3
PSYCH 31	3
PSYCH 12	3
SOC 10	3
KINPE 30	1
WORK EXPER	5
Total Units:	18

Semester: < select >	Year: < -- >
Course	Units
Total Units:	0

Semester: < select >	Year: < -- >
Course	Units
Total Units:	0

Also in this example, the student decided on their major early on, avoiding having to take additional classes for their major.

Semester: < select >	Year: < -- >
Course	Units
Total Units:	0

Semester: < select >	Year: < -- >
Course	Units
Total Units:	0

Semester: < select >	Year: < -- >
Course	Units
Total Units:	

GE Pattern:	AA	AS	CSU GE	IGETC	TU:	60
Complete TAA/TAG's fall semester before transfering						

Note that the GE pattern in this example is the CSU GE Pattern, and would not be used for students seeking to apply to a UC.

Comments:

Graduation Requirments: (check when completed)
- [ ] Written
- [ ] Oral
- [ ] Critical Thinking
- [ ] Math
- [ ] Science
- [ ] Science w/lab

Signatures:

Student: _____ Counselor: _____ Date: _____

B. Transfer Fair Questions for Admissions Representatives

Special Thanks to SJCC Counselor M. Daire for providing this resource.

A. Admissions

1. Do I have to finish my associate degree before I can transfer?

2. Do I need to complete all my general education and major requirements completed before applying?

3. If I am an international student, do I need to take the TOEFL? If so, what is the score?

4. Can I use AP/IB credits?

5. Will you look at my high school grades and courses for just college?

6. What are the deadlines for admission? Do you offer alternatives to regular admissions, such as early decision, early action, or rolling admission? How many applications did you receive last year? What percentage were admitted?

7. What academic preparation do you expect for a student to be admitted, and which qualities and experiences are you looking for in a student?

8. What is the average GPA for an admitted transfer student into a _____ major?

9. What kind of student is most successful at your university?

10. Do you have any pointers on writing essays that your school requires with the application?

B. Academics

1. How easy is it to double major? How easy is it to major in one area, such as science, and minor in another, such as business?

2. Is there much informal student-faculty contact outside class, such as students and faculty having lunch or dinner or playing sports together?

3. Does each student have a personally assigned advisor, or is advising conducted by an "advisement center?" Does the student have an opportunity to select or change their advisor?

4. What services are offered to students needing help or tutoring?

C. Setting

1. How is your institution unique? What distinguishes it from most other colleges and universities?

    2. What sort of academic calendar do you use: semesters, trimesters, one course at a time, etc.?

D. Finances
    1. What is the cost of attendance? (Attendance costs include tuition, books, fees, room, board, transportation, etc.).

    2. What percent of students receive merit-based scholarships? How much is offered for the largest merit scholarship? What is the average amount of merit aid given?

    3. What percent of students receive need-based financial aid and grants?

E. Housing
    1. What percent of students stay on campus on weekends?

    2. Describe the variety of housing styles on campus: suites, apartments, etc.

    3. Is housing guaranteed for transfer students?

F. Diversity and internationalism
    1. How ethnically diverse is the campus? What percent of the student body is composed of international students?

    2. What are the opportunities for studying abroad? Does your institution have some unique programs? What percent of your student body studies abroad?

    3. Can financial aid and scholarship monies be used to study abroad? If so, for how many semesters?

G. Service and Internships
    1. What is the availability of campus work opportunities?

    2. What volunteer and community service opportunities are available for students at the college?

    3. What percent of students do internships? How does your college assist students in finding internships?

H. Safety
    1. What campus security measures do you have? For example, is an escort service provided to/from the library for night classes?

    2. Tell me about the crime statistics on your campus – assault, rape, robbery, car theft, etc. What are the most "typical" incidents of crime?

I. Campus Life
    1. What activities on campus are the most popular with students?

2. What transportation means are available? Around campus, to the closest city, airport, etc. Is there a campus bus to town (or the local community) and back?

3. Which religious services, such as a Catholic Newman Center or a Hillel Center, are available on campus? Are religious denominations available on campus for social and counseling purposes?

4. How many and what types of clubs/organizations do you have on your campus?

J. Other

1. What type of support do you offer AB540 students, Veteran students, and students with disabilities?

C. SJCC GPA Calculator

Download Here

Special Thanks to Counselor B. Stewart for providing the GPA Calculator to SJCC

Calculate your Grade Point Average (GPA)

Name: _____ Student ID: _____ Date: _____

Your GPA is calculated based on the following formula:
  Total Grade Points / Units Attempted = GPA

Grade Point Values: A=4pts B=3pts C=2pts D=1pts F=0pts W=0 CR/NC=0

EXAMPLE:

Class	Units	Multiply	Grades	Grade Value		Grade Points
Biology 021	4	x	A	4	=	16
History 017A	3	x	C	2	=	6
Spanish 001A	5	x	B	3	=	15
Totals	12 units attempted					37 total grade points

Placing values into formula above: 37 total grade points / 12 units attempted = 3.08 GPA

- Units awarded for W and for Credit/No Credit (CR/NC) are not calculated in the GPA
- Note: Enter a letter grade, W or CR/NC in the grade column

> Allows students to combine Quarter and Semester units for a true calculation of combined units.

College	Class	Quarter Units	Semester Units	Standard Units	Grade	Grade Value	Grade Points
San Jose City College	ENGL 1A		3	3.00	B	3.0	9.00
De Anza College	POLSC 1	4		2.67	C+	2.3	6.13
				0.00		0.0	0.00
				0.00		0	
				0.00		0	
				0.00		0	
				0.00		0	
				0.00		0	
				0.00		0	
				0.00		0	
				0.00		0	
				0.00		0	
				0.00		0	
				0.00		0	
				0.00		0	
				0.00		0	
				0.00		0	
				0.00		0	
				0.00		0	

> Allows students to combine multiple colleges' coursework for a true cumulative GPA.
>
> May also be used to enter future coursework and projected grades in order to attain GPA goals for transfer.

Total Units: 5.67 Total Grade Points: 15.13

GPA: 2.6706

D. CCC Transfer Resources

ASSIST https://www.assist.org/	Transfer Major Explorer https://www.transferbound.com/
CCC Transfer Counselor Site https://ccctransfer.org/	CCC Toolbox https://ccctransfer.org/ccc-toolbox/
California Virtual Campus (CCC Online Classes) https://cvc.edu/	C-ID Course Search https://c-id.net/courses
List of California Community Colleges https://www.cccco.edu/Students/Find-a-College/College-Alphabetical-Listing	CCC GE, ADT, Catalog, & Transfer Center List https://ccctransfer.org/ge/
CCC Programs & Services https://ccctransfer.org/cccservices/	Online Colleges & Universities https://ccctransfer.org/online/
Associates Degree for Transfer Search https://icangotocollege.com/associate-degree-for-transfer	CCC Salary Surfer https://salarysurfer.cccco.edu/SalarySurfer.aspx
ADT Degrees Offered Fully Online https://cvc.edu/adt/	Certificates of Achievement Offered Fully Online https://cvc.edu/online-certificates-of-achievement/

Made in the USA
Las Vegas, NV
23 September 2023

77969073R00152